Luminos is the Open Access monograph publishing program from UC Press. Luminos provides a framework for preserving and reinvigorating monograph publishing for the future and increases the reach and visibility of important scholarly work. Titles published in the UC Press Luminos model are published with the same high standards for selection, peer review, production, and marketing as those in our traditional program. www.luminosoa.org

D1548339

Of Love and Papers

Of Love and Papers

How Immigration Policy Affects Romance and Family

Laura E. Enriquez

UNIVERSITY OF CALIFORNIA PRESS

University of California Press
Oakland, California

© 2020 by Laura E. Enriquez

Cataloging-in-Publication Data is on file at the Library of Congress.

Suggested citation: Enriquez, L. E. *Of Love and Papers: How Immigration Policy Affects Romance and Family.* Oakland: University of California Press, 2020. DOI: https://doi.org/10.1525/luminos.88

Library of Congress Cataloging-in-Publication Data

Names: Enriquez, Laura E., 1986- author.
Title: Of love and papers : how immigration policy affects romance and
    family / Laura E. Enriquez.
Description: Oakland, California : University of California Press, [2020] |
    Includes bibliographical references and index.
Identifiers: LCCN 2019052048 (print) | LCCN 2019052049 (ebook) |
    ISBN 9780520344358 (paperback) | ISBN 9780520975484 (epub)
Subjects: LCSH: Man-woman relationships—United States—Case studies. |
    Illegal aliens—Family relationships—United States—Case studies. |
    Hispanic Americans—Family relationships—United States—Case studies.
    United States—Emigration and immigration—Government policy.
Classification: LCC HQ801 E57 2020 (print) | LCC HQ801 (ebook) |
    DDC 306.70973—dc23
LC record available at https://lccn.loc.gov/2019052048
LC ebook record available at https://lccn.loc.gov/2019052049

29   28   27   26   25   24   23   22   21   20
10   9   8   7   6   5   4   3   2   1

CONTENTS

TABLES

ACKNOWLEDGMENTS

This book would not have been possible without the people who were willing to share their stories with me. I am grateful that they trusted me with the intimate details of their lives and had faith that I could do justice to their stories. I hope their words resonate with readers and move us to recognize and resist the cascading consequences of exclusionary immigration policy.

I received crucial financial support at various stages. A fellowship from the Social Science Research Council's Dissertation Proposal Development Program allowed me to conduct a pilot study. Led by Katharine Donato and Donna Gabaccia, this interdisciplinary group provided a space to flesh out the project and center the role of gender. Data collection was generously funded by research grants from the National Science Foundation (award no. 1202634), the University of California Institute for Mexico and the United States, and the UCLA Institute for Research on Labor and Employment. Predoctoral and dissertation fellowships from the Ford Foundation and UCLA enabled me to immerse myself in the first wave of the study. The second wave was conducted during my tenure as a UCI Chancellor's ADVANCE Postdoctoral Fellow. Funds from the UCI Libraries and UCI School of Social Sciences aided open-access publication.

Several research assistants helped me complete this project. Tanya Sanabria helped conduct the second wave of interviews. Miguel Carvente, Lizette Ceja, Rosemary Gomez, Carlos Salinas, Daisy Vazquez Vera, and Amy Yu served as interviewers and research assistants. Diego Sepúlveda and Diana Soto-Vazquez provided additional support.

I am fortunate to have been guided by thoughtful and caring mentors. Gilda Ochoa introduced me to research and a way of doing sociology that centers communities. Her early lessons and continued advice over the past 15 years have shaped who I am as a scholar and wound their way into this book. Vilma Ortiz has supported me and my vision since my first day of graduate school, giving me the space to run with my ideas (and helping wrangle them in). Her invaluable advice has seen me through every stage of this project and guided me in carving out a space for myself in academia. Katharine Donato took me under her wing as I began this project and helped shape its direction. Her unwavering support and generosity have been critical to my professional development.

This book has been a long time in the making, and colleagues have supported its development at various stages. At UCLA, Leisy Abrego, Abigail Saguy, and Min Zhou provided critical support as members of my dissertation committee and helped me refine my thinking. William Rosales and Michael Stambolis-Ruhstorfer have supported my work since our first days of graduate school, generously reading drafts and allowing me to bounce ideas off them. Vilma Ortiz established a research group for her graduate students; this group of Latina scholars provided the friendship and critical feedback that allowed me and this project to thrive: Karina Chavarria, Deisy Del Real, Rocio Garcia, Celia Lacayo, Mirian Martinez-Aranda, Erica Morales, Laura Orrico, Casandra Salgado, Ariana Valle, Irene Vega, and Sylvia Zamora. Finally, the women from the SSRC dissertation proposal workshop informed my early thinking, and several have continued their support through the years, including Claudia Lopez, Cheryl Llewellyn, Sarah DeMott, Maria Hwang, and Alison Kolodzy.

My colleagues at UCI have been unwavering supporters. My dean, Bill Maurer, and department chairs, Vicki Ruiz and Louis DeSipio, have ensured that I always have the resources needed to realize my academic visions. Rubén Rumbaut enthusiastically served as my postdoctoral mentor. My department colleagues have generously provided feedback and friendship, making for a joyful work environment, especially Belinda Campos, Anita Casavantes Bradford, Raul Fernandez, Glenda Flores, and Alana LeBrón.

I am thankful to the many colleagues who provided advice at various stages: Amada Armenta, Edelina Burciaga, Jennifer Chacón, Susan Coutin, Jacqueline Dan, Joanna Dreby, Pierrette Hondagneu-Sotelo, Vicki Ruiz, Veronica Terriquez, Kristin Turney, Annie Ro, Zulema Valdez, and Marjorie Zatz. Several colleagues read chapter drafts: Cynthia Feliciano, Cecilia Menjívar, Martha Morales Hernandez, Maria Rendón, Abigail Saguy, and Irene Vega. Katharine Donato, Elizabeth Aranda, and an anonymous reviewer provided incisive comments on the full manuscript. David Axiom, Nicole Balbuena, Elisabet Barrios Mateo, Picha Chainiwatana, Angela Chen, Paola Maravilla Montes, and Guillermo Paez provided insight on the final version.

Finally, I am forever thankful to my family for their endless support. My parents, Evelyn Hill-Enriquez and Luis Enriquez, have long instilled in me the courage and tools to accomplish my goals. My brother, Michael Enriquez, read the entire manuscript and helped refine my argument. My extended family—grandparents, aunts, uncles, cousins, *suegra,* sisters- and brothers-in-law, and nephews—always reminded me of the importance and power of family.

This book is dedicated to my partner, Miguel Carvente, whose love and support enabled me to complete this project. He eagerly joined in the fun, serving as a sounding board, interviewer, transcriber, and reader. We welcomed our daughters, Luna and Maya, along the way, and they have shown me both the joy and pain of parenthood. I am grateful that all three have kept me balanced and focused in my work.

Forming Families in a Context of Illegality

Late on a Friday night in 2010, Daniel Hernandez, Julio Medina, and Mauricio Ortega were sprawled across the floor of an office in downtown Los Angeles. Armed with a collection of markers and poster board, they were making signs for an immigration reform rally the next day. Amid their joking, Daniel recounted his most recent dating fiasco, when he showed up for a date on his bike. Mauricio cut him off saying that his 20-year-old *carcacha* wasn't much better. They chuckled at the reference to the Selena song in which she sings about how her boyfriend's car is so old and broken down that it barely runs—"Un carro viejo que viene pitando / Con llantas de triciclo y el motor al revés."[1] Her friends laugh as they lurch down the street.

Like most young adults in their mid-20s, Daniel was looking for love, but he saw this possibility slipping through his fingers because of his undocumented status. He didn't have a car to pick up his date, and he refused to risk driving without a license. Going out was often beyond his means because he felt stuck working for minimum wage at a fast-food restaurant. When he did go out, he had to show his Mexican passport to buy a beer, revealing his undocumented status to those around him. He feared that yet another girlfriend would think he wasn't good enough.

Sitting in a quiet corner of an East Los Angeles coffee shop, Regina Castro talked about her marriage. She didn't mention driving or money, but her words echoed Daniel's struggles to negotiate his undocumented status. In a whirlwind romance, she and her U.S. citizen husband got engaged after four months and married four months later. Yet her undocumented status led many to doubt their intentions. During her engagement party, a close friend jokingly pleaded, "Cut the bullshit! Just tell us the truth—are you getting married to fix your papers?" Countless moments like this haunted Regina as she sought to assure herself, her partner, friends, family, and eventually immigration officials that she was actually in love with her husband and wasn't using him to legalize her status.

On the other side of town, I met Luis Escobar at a crowded café. Luis avoided dating until he met Camila in college. The citizen daughter of formerly undocumented Mexican immigrants, she understood his situation. They married, hoping to legalize his immigration status, but 11 years later they had yet to file a petition. Meeting with a lawyer soon after their wedding, they learned that Luis faced a risky legalization process that could bar him from the country for 10 years. Uncertain about his future, Luis felt financially unstable as he worked minimum-wage restaurant jobs and supplemented his income teaching Zumba classes. They delayed having children because he feared being separated by deportation. Now raising a toddler, he felt guilty that he could not provide for her in the way he wanted. His voice cracked: "You feel that you're punishing someone that shouldn't be punished. You don't feel that it's society's fault; you feel that it's *your* fault because that's who you are." As we spoke, his wife entered with their daughter. Luis immediately reached to take her, bouncing her on his lap for the rest of our conversation. Their love starkly contrasted with his half-hour reflection on his failings as a father.

* * *

Daniel, Regina, and Luis are 1.5-generation undocumented young adults in their 20s who migrated to the United States as children. Their anxieties may sound familiar to anyone who has dated, married, or become a parent: *Would someone want to date me? How can I be a better partner? Should we get married? Am I doing the best for my children?* Yet their stories reveal that immigration laws and policies are fundamentally (re)shaping Latino immigrant families and individuals' experiences in them.

As 1.5-generation immigrants, they have spent the majority of their lives in the United States. They sat in the same classrooms as their U.S. citizen peers, speaking English and absorbing U.S. culture. As former president Barack Obama contended, "They are Americans in their heart, in their minds, in every single way but one: on paper."[2] But immigration status barriers disrupt their transition into adulthood as they begin to realize the significance of their undocumented status and how it will hinder their ability to complete their education, begin working, and achieve upward mobility.[3]

Although they are not legally barred from marrying or having children, immigration policies crept into the most personal and private corners of their lives.

They created structural barriers in Daniel's everyday life, fueling his dating insecurities. They fostered feelings of exclusion, shading Regina's marriage experiences, Luis's decision to have a child, and their feelings about their ability to be good partners and parents.

In 2012 their lives changed. President Obama announced the Deferred Action for Childhood Arrivals (DACA) program, allowing select 1.5-generation undocumented young adults to apply for two-year, renewable protection from deportation and a work permit.[4] Daniel and Luis both applied for and received DACA; Regina had just become a lawful permanent resident through marriage. They eagerly pursued new opportunities: Regina followed her husband to the East Coast, reenrolled in college, and was preparing to graduate from a prestigious university. Like other DACA recipients, Luis and Daniel reported economic advancement.[5] Luis began a new career as a community organizer, nearly tripling his previous income and receiving benefits for the first time in his life. Daniel chose to work a series of well-paid, part-time jobs in communications. They all began to feel more secure as they settled into their new lives.

Still, the marks of their previous undocumented status remained. The need to maintain a joint household (in case immigration agents investigated their case) influenced Regina's educational and career choices. When she and her husband decided to separate, she worried about how it would look to friends and family. Would they accuse her of using him for papers since she was about to become a citizen?

Daniel was almost 30 and still single. Receiving DACA had reshaped his romantic life by giving him "peace of mind." He had a stable income that he could spend on dates and other nonnecessities. At our second interview, he sported a new $200 bag, a far cry from when we first met and he was wearing faded T-shirts from his high school punk days. He had an official California ID card that easily let him buy a drink. He was finally learning how to drive. All these changes allowed him to date more casually, but his previous experiences with rejection had kept him from committing to a serious relationship for over two years. He felt left behind as his friends hosted baby showers and engagement parties.

Luis, now in his early 30s with two kids, felt as if he had to learn to be legal. Receiving DACA made him "feel like a kid. Like I was a nine-year-old that came into this country again. Where it was like, I don't know anything, I need help." He worked long hours as he struggled to learn the professional skills that his citizen coworkers had been developing for over a decade. His financial stability allowed him to put his older daughter into a better preschool, pay for her ballet classes, cover medical visits, and save up to move out of his in-laws' home. Still, he agonized about legalizing his status and worried about whether policy changes would one day pull the rug out from underneath him and his family.

Theories of immigrant illegality highlight how laws and policies make undocumented immigration status consequential in individuals' everyday lives and for their overall incorporation opportunities.[6] Drawing on two waves of interviews with undocumented and recently legalized 1.5-generation Latina/o young adults and their romantic partners, I explore how immigration policies permanently alter the material, psychological, and social foundations of mixed-status Latino families.[7] I ask, How do immigration policies shape undocumented young adults' dating, marriage, and parenting? How do changes in immigration policy, such as the establishment of DACA, reconfigure illegality and alter its consequences for family formation? What are the implications of these policies for citizen partners and children? I pay attention to the dynamic nature of this process by examining the effects of immigration policies over time as young adults age, relationships progress, and legal barriers change.

I argue that immigration policies cultivate enduring consequences for undocumented young adults and their families. Immigration-related barriers produce long-term consequences for undocumented young adults by continually constraining their family formation, including whom they date, if and how they advance relationships, and how they perform their roles as partners and parents. Although obtaining DACA carries immediate material benefits, negative consequences persist because immigration policies already shaped early circumstances and left emotional scars. These individual enduring consequences transform into lasting multigenerational inequalities as citizen romantic partners and children share in the punishment inflicted by immigration policies.

I elucidate the mechanisms that make immigration policies consequential in everyday life and transform these into enduring inequalities. I point to how the nature of families and family formation prompts persisting consequences, how laws and policies codify structural inequality, and how hegemonic gender norms help turn material constraints into persisting socioemotional barriers. Applying a gender lens adds a critical layer, showing how gendered provider expectations make material barriers particularly salient for men, disproportionally disrupting their participation in the family formation process. Mapping the process and scope of consequences allows us to envision ways to intervene and move toward fuller integration for undocumented immigrants, their families, and communities.

WHY STUDY THE FAMILY FORMATION OF LATINA/O UNDOCUMENTED YOUNG ADULTS?

I turn attention to family formation because families, in their various forms, are key sites of social reproduction in which privilege or inequality can be transmitted from one generation to the next.[8] Familial relationships provide critical social, emotional, and economic support over one's lifetime. Such relationships promote individual well-being and foster the transmission of social, cultural, and economic capital. Thus, everyday family experiences reflect and (re)produce social inequalities.

Members of marginalized families have less access to material, social, and emotional resources, leading individual constraints to ripple through families and persist over generations. Low incomes create financial barriers that limit decisions to cohabitate, marry, or have children, often producing disengagement from family formation or divergence from expected patterns.[9] Economic concerns stress all family members by producing conflict between romantic partners and disrupting caregiving relationships and parenting practices.[10] The resulting family instability—be it through poverty, divorce, parental incarceration, or immigration-related family separation—is associated with poorer economic, educational, social, and health outcomes for children.[11]

Such inequalities are increasingly produced through laws and legal institutions that insert themselves into the lives of marginalized families. Incarceration disproportionately disrupts the family lives of low-income racial minorities, destabilizing familial relationships and harming partners' and children's well-being in the process.[12] The child welfare system relies on normative notions of good parenting, which leaves low-income, racial minority, and immigrant families vulnerable to intervention and surveillance.[13] Detention and deportation undermine immigrant families, increasing their risk of family separation and sometimes termination of parental rights.[14] In all these cases, legal institutions disrupt family processes, increasing the risk of negative long-term consequences for all family members.

I turn attention to Latino immigrant families because they are disproportionately subjected to punitive immigration policies. Estimates suggest that in 2016 there were about 10.7 million undocumented immigrants living in the United States, making up 24 percent of the immigrant population.[15] Although they hail from across the globe, around three-quarters are of Latin American origin.[16] Almost half of Mexican and Central American immigrants are undocumented.[17] A quarter of Latino children have at least one undocumented parent.[18] These statistics reveal that Latino families live in the shadows of immigration policy, but we know little about what this looks like and how it shapes consequential family outcomes. Centering families as a key site of intergenerational mobility, I illuminate how illegality endures to fuel the continued exclusion of Latino families and communities.

ENDURING CONSEQUENCES:
THE NATURE OF FAMILIES

Family formation is driven by a series of choices made at expected times. As undocumented young adults face constrained choices, they make (or avoid making) decisions, which permanently structures their family formation process. Changes to immigration policies or to one's immigration status cannot easily, if at all, undo these past choices. Further, the close social ties and multigenerational nature of families ensure that inequalities bleed into the lives of citizen partners and children, paving the way for enduring consequences.

Constrained Choices

Young adulthood is marked by crucial decision-making and transitions, including those related to college, career, marriage, and childbearing.[19] These life course transitions are produced through a series of choices.[20] Further, the day-to-day realities of family formation require individuals to continually make smaller choices that determine family development: where to go on a date, who will run errands, or whether to enroll a child in an after-school activity. Illegality constrains these choices so that the imprint of undocumented status remains, even as undocumented young adults transition into more secure immigration statuses.

Previous work suggests that moving from an undocumented to a more secure immigration status improves incorporation. Immigrants who legalized their status via the 1986 Immigration Reform and Control Act experienced improved long-term social, political, and economic integration.[21] Those who obtain temporary protected status (TPS) have better economic outcomes than they did when undocumented.[22] DACA recipients experience improved educational, economic, social, and well-being outcomes after obtaining work permits and protection from deportation.[23]

Yet choices made while undocumented continue to affect one's life after transitioning into a more secure status. Cecilia Menjívar and Sarah Lakhani find that undocumented immigrants undergo intimate transformations as they make themselves look like desirable candidates for legalization; for example, they choose to marry instead of cohabitate, or they become active community members through volunteer work. These prelegalization choices transform them as people: "They learn certain values, norms, and new ways to think about themselves that persist after legalization."[24] Likewise, I suggest that relationships are profoundly shaped by the sociolegal context in which they are formed and progress. Outcomes may improve, but the consequences of undocumented status, particularly if prolonged, remain because of previously constrained choices.

The timing of sociolegal changes, and whether they align with the timing of expected family formation transitions, determines the extent to which undocumented young adults see enduring consequences. This follows the logic of life course scholars who argue that the timing of life course transitions has long-term consequences because they affect subsequent transitions.[25] In this case, undocumented young adults could not simply pause a relationship while waiting for inclusive immigration policies to allow them to date, marry, and parent in the ways they desired. As time passed, natural progression required them to make choices about if and how to advance their relationships. Structural barriers shaped the foundation of the relationship, dictated how it would blossom and grow, and influenced their feelings about the relationship and their role in it. It determined if and when they would have children. As children aged, parents could not provide certain opportunities when needed or desired.

Undocumented young adults and their relationships suffered when their constrained choices prevented them from transitioning to and participating in marriage or parenthood in line with their own, their partners', and others' expectations. These choices and memories remained with them, even as they transitioned into a more secure immigration status. When expected relationship transitions coincided with receiving DACA, relationships thrived. But for some it felt too late; their families had already been intimately shaped by immigration policies.

Multigenerational Punishment

Family members are inherently (inter)dependent on one another, linking their stress, misfortune, opportunities, and upward mobility. This fosters shared experiences of illegality within mixed-status families as social ties and daily interactions lead citizens to witness and share in the punishments produced by immigration policies and adopt corresponding risk-management strategies. I refer to this as *multigenerational punishment,* wherein the sanctions intended for a specific population spill over to harm individuals who are not targeted by the law.[26] This concept highlights the structural nature of this phenomenon—rather than attributing these spillover effects to chance—and emphasizes the widespread effects of the law. In this case, enduring consequences emerge as immigration policies embed themselves in citizen family members' everyday experiences, limiting their opportunities for upward mobility and imposing inequality over generations.

Previous research has established that illegality limits citizen children's lifelong outcomes. Undocumented parents' economic hardship, psychological distress, and limited access to suitable childcare lead to delays in children's early cognitive development.[27] In the wake of a parent's deportation, children experience short- and long-term economic instability and psychological distress.[28] As children age, parental undocumented status contributes to lower academic performance and to a higher likelihood of behavioral problems, adjustment disorders, and anxiety disorders.[29] Even in adulthood, those with undocumented parents have worse educational and economic outcomes than the children of legalized or U.S.-born parents.[30]

Additionally, immigration policies shape family relationships and dynamics. Deportation fears can weaken parent-child bonds, straining parents as they focus on alleviating these fears rather than nurturing children's development.[31] Economic barriers can also undermine relationships and create family instability when parents work long hours that prevent them from spending time with their children.[32] Further, in a reversal of family roles, citizen children help their parents navigate illegality and may try to manage their parents' feelings and actions.[33]

Sibling relationships can be strained as citizen children are granted opportunities that undocumented ones are not.[34] Romantic partnerships can also suffer as economic instability, deportation, and legalization processes expose citizen partners to inequalities.[35]

I pay attention to the experiences of citizen partners—a group that has been overlooked by scholars—and move beyond establishing negative outcomes for family members to examine how these emerge. My approach views familial relationships as interrelated and multidirectional; it is not just undocumented family members creating barriers for citizens but also citizens helping undocumented individuals navigate barriers and potentially mediating negative outcomes. Ultimately, I explore the long and complex process through which illegality shapes not only structural barriers but also relationship dynamics and decision-making.

To understand the full circumstances, I trace how the citizen partners and children of undocumented young adults experience illegality. They adopt a de facto undocumented status as they share in the limitations raised by their undocumented partner's or parent's status: fearing deportation, sharing the same low socioeconomic status, and self-regulating their movement and social participation. Many adopt strategies to mediate these shared consequences by helping their undocumented partners and parents navigate immigration-related barriers. These shared consequences and experiences ensure that illegality limits the incorporation and upward mobility of later-generation citizen family members.

SHARING STRUCTURAL INEQUALITY: CONTEXT OF ILLEGALITY AND SHIFTING IMMIGRATION POLICIES

The nature of families paves the way for consequences to endure over time and into future generations, but it is the structural character of illegality that produces these consequences in the first place. Illegality has been created and sustained by embedding inequalities into laws and policies that make immigration status consequential in everyday life. Scholars use the concept of immigrant illegality to theorize this process. I develop the concept of *context of illegality* to embed U.S. citizens' multigenerational punishment into this framework.

Conceptualizing Context of Illegality

Scholars refer to immigrant illegality to theorize the sociopolitical condition of undocumented immigrants as well as those who have other insecure immigration statuses. This work focuses on immigration laws and policies to show how illegality is produced and how immigration status functions as a source of social stratification.[36] Structural inequality is produced by immigration law, immigration enforcement and deportation practices, employment policies, and rules dictating access to social services; these restrict undocumented immigrants' everyday activities, shape decision-making, and limit upward mobility. In making these connections, many scholars have offered additional concepts to capture how the law functions in everyday life. For example, Susan Coutin coins the term *legal nonexistence* to conceptualize how undocumented immigrants are "physically present but legally absent" because they do not have permission to be in the country.[37] Cecilia Menjívar advances the concept of *liminal legality*, the "gray area" between documented and undocumented statuses that enables vulnerability and uncertainty.[38] These and other related concepts maintain theoretical focus on the immigrant and the role of the law in their everyday lives and incorporation trajectories.

Immigrant illegality has also been used to discuss the spillover effects of immigration-related laws and policies on U.S. citizen family members.[39] This extension beyond immigrants' sociopolitical condition to the sociolegal context makes it difficult to theorize how enduring consequences emerge in individual lives and proliferate over generations. Thus, I use *immigrant illegality* to refer only to the sociopolitical condition of immigrants caught in insecure legal statuses; it is a legally constructed state of being. I offer *context of illegality* to conceptualize the sociolegal context created by laws and policies that produce (il)legal statuses. Clearly devoting attention to the larger social context provides theoretical leverage to understand how inequality is shared within immigrant families and communities.

Previous research has established the power of sociolegal context in determining immigrant incorporation outcomes. Segmented assimilation theory implicates governmental policy as one of three factors that shape immigrants' *context of reception* and determine the diverging incorporation patterns of immigrant groups over generations.[40] Elizabeth Aranda and colleagues focus on the *legal context of reception* to highlight the increasingly insecure and exclusionary nature of contemporary immigration policy and how this reduces immigrants' ability to perceive and achieve material advancement.[41] Further, Tanya Golash-Boza and Zulema Valdez refer to *nested contexts of reception* to capture how undocumented immigrant incorporation varies in light of state and local policies.[42] Following this logic, I focus on the sociolegal context to identify how the enduring effects of illegality are established at the family level.

I define *context of illegality* as the social context that is constructed by immigration-related laws and policies and occupied by all members of mixed-status families and communities, regardless of immigration status. It is a marginalizing social world that produces substantial individual, familial, and social inequalities. Like *context of reception,* it embeds the structural nature of inequality into theory, attributing individual and shared consequences to immigration policies rather than chance. *Multigenerational punishment* is a key mechanism through which the context of illegality produces enduring inequalities. Thus, the context of illegality provides a theoretical foundation from which we can imagine immigrant illegality as a deeper source of intergenerational inequality.

Constructing the Context of Illegality

Illegality is constructed by a broad set of immigration-related policies, including immigration laws that determine who can legally enter and remain in the United States, immigration policies that determine how agencies handle immigrants, and other laws and policies that determine if undocumented immigrants are granted various rights and privileges. Interviews revealed four specific policy areas: (1) employment authorization or lack thereof, (2) deportation threats and immigration enforcement policies, (3) access to state-issued driver's licenses and identification cards, and (4) limited pathways to legalization. Although not a formal legal status, DACA altered the nature of illegality by shifting these barriers to foster recipients' tenuous legal inclusion.[43] I outline these four aspects of illegality, how they shifted with DACA, and their consequences for undocumented young adults and their families.

Economic (Im)mobility and Employment Authorization. The most salient aspect of illegality for participants was their inability to access a valid Social Security number. Immigration policies have made this increasingly consequential over the past three decades with the implementation of employer sanctions for hiring undocumented workers and the establishment of the E-Verify program to enable employers to quickly verify employment authorization.[44] These legal barriers exclude undocumented immigrants from employment opportunities, ensuring that they earn less and face restricted pathways to socioeconomic mobility.[45]

Without employment authorization, undocumented immigrants often use invalid Social Security numbers to complete hiring paperwork, are paid under the table, or are self-employed. This restricts employment options and increases their concentration in low-wage work. In 2012, about 62 percent of undocumented immigrants held service, construction, and production jobs, twice the share of U.S.-born workers in these occupations.[46] Further, undocumented status increases the risk of low earnings and labor violations, including a higher likelihood of earning below minimum wage and experiencing wage theft.[47] One study found a 17 percent wage gap between undocumented and documented Mexican immigrant men and a 9 percent gap between undocumented and documented Mexican immigrant women; controlling for human capital and occupation reduces, but does not eliminate, these significant differences.[48] Employment barriers subsequently limit their ability to move out of impoverished areas that further stymie upward mobility.[49]

Reflecting these larger patterns, the undocumented young adults I interviewed reported economic immobility. Without employment authorization, about one-fifth struggled with unemployment or the instability of self-employment or short-term work. Another fifth worked in service and production jobs common among undocumented immigrants: factory and warehouse workers, janitorial and maintenance staff, and nannies. Almost a quarter worked in restaurants, often in fast food, where many became low-level managers. Slightly more than a quarter used their educational credentials and social networks to obtain self-described "better" jobs as administrative assistants, educational service providers (e.g., tutors), and salespeople. A few, mostly college graduates, obtained professional employment, often in the nonprofit sector.[50] In all, they averaged an annual income of $15,936, ranging from $1,500 to $50,400. On average they earned $8.90 an hour, slightly more than California minimum wage at the time. But their income paled in comparison to the $40,000 median earnings of full-time young adult workers aged 25–34 in 2016. It was also substantially less than the $25,400 median earnings of young adults who did not complete high school.[51] Many also reported economic stagnation; they had been in the same job and had earned about the same for years. Their undocumented status ensured that standard approaches to pursuing economic mobility—promotions, additional training, or higher education—were unlikely to pay off. Their ability to achieve socioeconomic mobility depended on immigration policy changes that would provide employment authorization.

Economic instability had substantial consequences for romantic and family lives. Many men spoke about how their low incomes made it difficult to afford dating and feel like a desirable partner. They struggled to develop stable partnerships, transition into marriage, and have children because they feared being unable to provide for the family. When they did form families, economic instability manifested at the family level and was shared by citizen partners and children. Partners felt pressure to use their own citizenship privilege to close their family's financial gaps, sometimes leading to conflict. Parents struggled to meet children's basic needs and provide opportunities that would pave the way to a better life for the next generation.

DACA reshaped this aspect of illegality by providing access to a work permit. Most suggested that obtaining a work permit was the most significant impact of DACA.[52] Indeed, the average income of the employed DACA recipients I interviewed increased by almost $500 a month to $21,900 annually. Of the 72 recipients, about a fifth experienced upward mobility as they moved into professional employment, and 7 percent elected to forgo employment to pursue educational opportunities. About a third saw moderate changes, staying mostly within the service sector, but 19 percent moved to less labor-intensive jobs, and 13 percent moved out of recurrent unemployment. Almost two-fifths saw little change; 14 percent of participants worked in the same job, and 24 percent in a similar job.

In most cases, DACA fostered economic flexibility. This translated into more stable romantic and family lives as recipients felt it was easier to go out on dates, make family formation decisions, and provide opportunities for children. But those without a college education and extensive social networks struggled to turn their employment authorization into substantial upward mobility.[53] Many felt that the impact on their family formation was minimal. Some had previously established strategies to manage their low incomes and move forward with their romantic lives, while others had made choices that had already precipitated consequences that they could not undo.

Fear and the Deportation Regime.   A less salient but highly significant aspect of illegality was undocumented immigrants' deportability. Historically, immigration enforcement occurred primarily along the U.S.-Mexico border.[54] Increasingly punitive internal immigration enforcement policies have, however, built up a deportation regime that fosters a state of hypervigilance and fear in everyday life. Emerging in the late 1990s, 287(g) agreements multiplied throughout the 2000s to deputize local police officers to enforce immigration law by detaining immigrants for immigration officials. Other programs, such as Secure Communities, conducted immigration status checks in jails and prisons to identify individuals with deportation orders. These enforcement practices filled minor police interactions with deportation risk, and deportations rose to unprecedented levels, totaling 4.2 million from 1997 to 2012, more than double the 1.9 million deportations conducted before 1997.[55] Hoping to avoid these risks, undocumented immigrants may withdraw from society, stay close to home, and avoid driving without a license; such behaviors negatively affect their educational, economic, social, and health outcomes.[56]

The threat of consequential interactions with immigration enforcement varies by how much police cooperate with immigration officials. Some state laws increase police encounters' significance; most infamously, Arizona's SB 1070 requires police officers to determine the immigration status of *anyone* whom they have lawfully stopped, detained, or arrested.[57] By contrast, California state laws seek to lessen the threat of deportability; the 2014 TRUST Act, for example, limits the scope of who can be detained by police for immigration officials, reducing risks for noncriminal undocumented immigrants.[58]

The undocumented young adults I interviewed had unique understandings of their deportability. Their fears were situationally triggered by seeing police, interacting with immigration and law enforcement officials, and hearing about raids, detentions, and deportations. Many believed they occupied protective locations that shielded them from these interactions. In addition to living in progressive California, they blended in with their U.S.-born peers, and spent most of their time in spaces where immigration officials would likely not enter.[59] Yet they recognized that Latino men's hypercriminalization and raced-gendered policing procedures increased this group's risk of interacting with police officers, developing criminal records, and being transferred to immigration custody.[60]

Undocumented young adults, their romantic partners, and citizen children were often concerned about how deportation separates families. Unaccustomed to this threat, many citizen partners initially feared their partner's deportation. Like their undocumented partners, however, they became accustomed to this threat and tailored activities to minimize this risk. Fears reemerged in parenthood as they recognized equally unbearable options for managing deportation—family separation or family relocation outside the United States. Both options carry severe material, social, and emotional consequences.[61] Intent on avoiding these risks, undocumented young adults and their citizen family members avoided unnecessary travel, limiting partners' opportunities to build intimacy and parents' ability to foster their children's social and cultural capital.

DACA established a new protective location by "deferring action" on a recipient's deportation. This, coupled with their ability to receive a driver's license, substantially reduced the threat of sudden, groundless removal. As a result, DACA recipients and their families felt more secure and became more comfortable expanding the family's horizons beyond their immediate neighborhood.

Spatial and Social (Im)mobility: State-Issued Driver's Licenses and ID Cards. Although not an immigration policy, driver's license laws and related law-enforcement practices construct illegality within social interactions. Like most states, California denied undocumented immigrants access to state-issued driver's licenses and identification cards during my first wave of interviews. As a result, many drove without a license. While this increased their risk of deportation, most participants were preoccupied with the material costs of driving without a license. In 2013 the fine for driving without a license in California was $402, and counties had the discretion to increase this fee. Cars were regularly impounded for 30 days, racking up thousands of dollars in fees.[62] Participants feared being caught by sobriety checkpoints, which are routinely used to detect unlicensed and undocumented drivers.

Avoiding or minimizing driving without a license raised problems when dating, particularly for men who were expected to drive. The resulting negotiations often presented citizen partners with their first opportunity to help by taking on the role of licensed driver. As this responsibility grew, some couples reported that it stressed their relationship by burdening citizens and exacerbating undocumented partners' feelings of dependence. Children also faced consequences—being stranded on the side of the road when cars were towed and learning to keep an eye out for police.

The ubiquity of a state-issued license or ID also created challenges when individuals could not present this form of identification. About 95 percent of eligible adults held a California ID or driver's license in 2013.[63] Not having one could make it difficult (sometimes impossible) to open a bank account or credit card, obtain government records, access health care, purchase controlled over-the-counter medications, obtain a library card, apply for apartments, and identify one's self to police or other government agents.[64]

For undocumented young adults, this constraint posed a barrier to social participation. Being unable to apply for driver's license in their late teens was a key moment when they began to realize that their undocumented status would limit their opportunities.[65] Feelings of difference extended into their transition to adulthood as those in their 20s and 30s were required to show proof of age to enter bars or clubs or to purchase alcohol. In most cases, they resorted to using identification issued by their country of origin's consulate—foreign passports or *matrícula consular* identification cards. While these forms of identification sometimes work, those presenting them risk being denied access or subjected to questioning that forces them to reveal their undocumented status. Fearing embarrassment and rejection, many avoided places where they had to show identification. This infused stress into their dating lives, especially for women who often had to negotiate this concern if their date planned something that required an ID.

DACA's provision of a valid Social Security number allowed recipients to obtain state-issued driver's licenses and identification cards.[66] Further, in January 2015, California implemented Assembly Bill 60, allowing undocumented immigrants to access California driver's licenses.[67] This change facilitated spatial mobility and social participation, making dating and everyday family life easier.

Limited Legalization Opportunities: Marriage and the 10-Year Bar. Ultimately, immigration law produces illegality by regulating undocumented immigrants' ability to adjust their status, or "legalize." The U.S. immigration system rests on principles of family reunification according to which lawful permanent residents and U.S. citizens can petition for their family members' permanent residency.[68] Although many family petition categories exist, the most straightforward is that of U.S. citizens who petition for immediate family members—spouses, parents, and unmarried children under 21—as these are not subject to annual visa limits. When I was conducting interviews, these petitions were processed in about six months and, when approved, resulted in immediate permanent residency.[69] All other types of family visas have wait times of one or two decades.[70]

Legalization pathways became more complicated in 1996, when the Illegal Immigration Reform and Immigrant Responsibility Act established reentry bars to punish undocumented immigrants who had "entered without inspection." Immigrants who entered the United States on a valid visa or who had preexisting petitions filed for them before 2001 can adjust their immigration status while remaining in the United States.[71] Many, however, do not meet these requirements and must return to their country of origin to process their application. Leaving to do so triggers a 10-year bar on their reentry if they have been in the United States for over a year as an adult, even if their application for permanent residency is approved.[72] While they can petition to lift this bar citing "extreme hardship" for their citizen petitioner, this is a high and ill-defined standard that is subject to immigration officials' discretion. With no guarantee that this reprieve will be granted, they risk being unable to reenter the United States, which discourages many from applying.[73]

The undocumented young adults I interviewed had limited opportunities for family-based visa petitions. Almost all had undocumented parents.[74] Forty-four were parents of citizen children but would have to wait years until their child turned 21 and became eligible to file a petition for them. Extended family petitions were an option, and a handful of participants reported having petitions filed for them, usually by an aunt or uncle after arriving to the United States; they were still awaiting adjudication on these cases or had "aged out."[75] Thus, a petition filed by a U.S. citizen spouse appeared most viable, yet most of the 126 undocumented participants faced the 10-year bar. Only 18 reported entering on a valid visa, and 17 others reported a preexisting legalization petition that may exempt them from the bar.[76]

Despite legal realities that dramatically limited this option, many undocumented young adults reported being urged to pursue legalization through marriage to a U.S. citizen. They were unceremoniously proposed to by friends and partners, or encouraged by friends and family to quickly move their romantic relationships to marriage. Many invested energy to assure their romantic partners that their relationships were built on love, not a desire for papers. It shaped their relationship progression, some of them electing to delay marriage to allay suspicion and others fast-forwarding their relationships to marriage. Although citizen partners longed to provide this form of security, many couples found this to be a long and risky process. Those who could pursue it found that it restructured the very foundation of their relationship.

Although DACA did not provide a pathway to legalization, it created an opportunity that could facilitate legalization. DACA recipients could apply for advanced parole, which provides permission to travel outside the United States for educational, employment, or humanitarian reasons. Subsequently, they reentered with inspection, enabling them to adjust their status without the threat of the 10-year bar.[77] Some DACA recipients took advantage of this opportunity and became permanent residents through marriage.

These four legal barriers structure the context of illegality and jointly limit how undocumented young adults and their citizen family members socially engage in the world around them. In the following chapters, I explore each barrier as it becomes relevant throughout the family formation process and trace how its role shifts as relationships progress and policies change.

HIGHLIGHTING GENDER AND THE ROLE OF HEGEMONIC CULTURAL IDEALS

Applying a gender lens further elucidates how illegality is made consequential within mixed-status families. Previous research reveals the critical role of gender in shaping a wide variety of migration outcomes: individual and household migration decisions, migration journeys, settlement experiences, legalization patterns, initial and long-term labor market outcomes, family formation and maintenance, transnational activities, and return migration patterns.[78] Within the context of the family, hegemonic cultural ideals—particularly gendered roles and expectations—influence when, where, and how undocumented immigrants experience and negotiate illegality.[79] They turn material constraints into socioemotional barriers to family formation.

Cultural expectations (re)produce contemporary inequality. Cecilia Ridgeway traces how cultural stereotypes about men and women enable gender inequality to persist.[80] They make gender consequential by assigning intrinsic characteristics and prescribing standards of behavior based on the idea that men and women are unequal. Acting on these beliefs reinforces their persistence and maintains unequal access to resources and power. Although individuals and subgroups may hold alternative gender beliefs, certain stereotypes become hegemonic, predominating over others so that they must be either adopted or negotiated. Often these hegemonic ideals are grounded in white, middle-class, heterosexual experiences because this group has the power to shape cultural images; theirs become the "default rules of the gender game" as they are "inscribed in the media, government policy, [and] normative images of the family."[81]

Gendered stereotypes and other hegemonic cultural understandings enable gender and immigration status to mutually construct experiences of illegality. Undocumented young adults acculturate to gendered expectations that are based in U.S. middle-class realities; women are expected to be dependent and nurturing caregivers and men economic providers. These ideals inform the roles men and women expect and are expected to take on as they date, marry, and become parents.[82] Although gendered expectations are in flux, people encounter and must grapple with hegemonic ideals as they participate in family formation and assess their self-worth.[83] Cultural ideals about romantic love, lavish weddings, the American dream, and intensive parenting function similarly and intersect with gendered expectations to influence men and women's approaches to family formation.

Undocumented young adults had to find ways to align their material constraints with gendered expectations; otherwise they developed socioemotional barriers that prevented full participation in family formation processes. In some cases, participants took risks to meet gender expectations; other couples renegotiated expectations to align them with their constraints. Although some women hoped to avoid dependent gender roles, accepting them insulated many from the material and socioemotional barriers that limited men's family formation. Ultimately, gendered provider expectations constructed diverging experiences of illegality, disproportionally disrupting men's participation in the family formation process.

Throughout, I highlight variation in experiences of illegality, paying particular attention to gender. This approach departs from previous research that argues that undocumented status is a master status that eclipses all other social characteristics in its effect on individuals' lives.[84] Instead, I adopt an intersectional approach that envisions social locations as rooted in interlocking systems of oppression, in which marginalization is produced at the intersection of multiple structural inequalities. This moves away from the idea that one social location can supersede another to highlight how individuals simultaneously occupy multiple social locations that work together to determine how they experience the world.[85] Within this framework, I focus on gender to highlight how it intersects with immigration status to fundamentally shape experiences of illegality. This approach complements recent efforts to explore undocumented immigrants' diverse experiences along the lines of immigrant generation, gender, race/ethnicity, class, and sexual orientation.[86]

DATA AND METHODS

Following the changing context of illegality, this project evolved into a longitudinal study of the family formation experiences of undocumented young adults. I conducted 286 in-depth interviews with 196 young adults in Southern California: 126 were initially undocumented, 31 had recently legalized their status, and 39 were their romantic partners. I interviewed about half the undocumented young adults and about two-thirds of the legalized participants twice, once in 2011–12 and once in 2014–15. This allowed me to reach saturation across multiple comparison groups and subpopulations at two significant time points.

Initially interested in incorporation patterns, I interviewed 125 young adults from November 2011 to August 2012: 95 were undocumented, and 30 had recently legalized. These interviews broadly covered how immigration status affected their participation in school, work, civic life, and family formation. As I finished these interviews, President Obama announced the DACA program, dramatically shifting the consequences of illegality. I also had new questions given how deeply immigration policies were influencing romantic relationships.

I conducted a second wave of interviews from July 2014 to August 2015. I and a research assistant reinterviewed 90 original study participants: 69 from the undocumented sample to assess the impact of DACA and 21 from the recently legalized sample to see how their integration was progressing. Both groups were asked more detailed questions about their family formation experiences. For those 35 whom I was unable to reinterview, I found others to take their place: 31 who would have been undocumented in 2011 and one who legalized their status just before 2011. We also interviewed 39 of their current romantic partners to understand how they were experiencing immigration policies.

I used snowball sampling, initiating recruitment with 12 participants who had varying levels of education and separate social networks. I drew these initial participants from my social networks built through four years of personal involvement and previous research with college- and community-based undocumented youth organizations. I selected undocumented participants along two lines of comparison—gender and education level—as these composed key lines of difference within undocumented young adults' experiences of illegality. In the first wave, I aimed for equal numbers of men and women from six education levels that ranged from not having completed high school to having a bachelor's degree. I maintained gender and educational diversity in the second wave.

We sat in coffee shops, restaurants, parks, and homes talking at length about their relationships. I asked broad questions that traced their overall romantic trajectories from dating to marriage to parenting. They described their romantic lives: how they felt about their current relationship status, their partners and why they chose them, past heartbreak and relationship problems, and dreams for the future. We covered key turning points—why relationships ended, if and how dating relationships turned into permanent partnerships, decisions to marry or not, whether they would have children and when. We talked about how their immigration status affected their partners and children. Our conversations were punctuated with laughter and tears as we wound through the pain and promise of romance.

Participants embraced the opportunity to talk. I asked questions and listened as they wound their way through self-discovery. I followed as they moved off topic, trusting that this was part of their process and could reveal something new. I encouraged them to ask me questions, and I often found myself recounting my own experiences, explaining immigration law, and describing preliminary findings as participants sought insight into their relationships.

All undocumented and recently legalized participants were Latina/o, 1.5-generation young adults who had spent the majority of their lives living in the United States. All but six migrated from Mexico. The majority arrived as young children, but there was variation: 38 percent arrived before age six, 40 percent arrived between ages six and 10, and 22 percent arrived between ages 11 and 16. Almost all immediately settled in Southern California. All were undocumented when they were growing up and transitioned into young adulthood. By the second wave of interviews, participants spanned the spectrum of (il)legality; a portion remained undocumented, most had received DACA, some had adjusted their immigration status, and a few had become naturalized citizens. Additional demographic data is presented in table 1.1.

Almost all participants wanted to build a family. Of the undocumented participants, about two-fifths were single or casually dating, about one-quarter were in exclusive dating relationships, and one-third were in committed partnerships, including cohabitation and marriage. Of those in a relationship, almost two-thirds were partnered with a U.S. citizen or permanent resident, and one-third were with undocumented individuals. Of the recently legalized participants, 22 had adjusted their status through marriage to a U.S. citizen; of these, 16 were still married to the same partner and the remaining six had legalized through strategic marriages. The nine who had legalized through long-pending natal-family petitions were mostly single or dating. Around four out of every five participants were partnered with a Latina/o. Slightly more than a third were parents.

TABLE 1.1 Demographic characteristics of interview participants

	Undocumented young adults $(n = 126)^\dagger$	Recently legalized young adults $(n = 31)^{\dagger\dagger}$	Romantic partners $(n = 39)$
Immigration status in 2011–2012			
Undocumented	125	—	—
Work permit, pending LPR application	1	—	—
Lawful permanent resident	—	29	—
Naturalized citizen	—	2	—
Immigration status in 2014–2015			
Undocumented	20	—	4
Work permit, pending LPR application	2	—	0
DACA recipient	72	—	1
U visa	3	—	0
Lawful permanent resident	3	18	0
Naturalized citizen	0	4	6
U.S.-born citizen	—	—	28
Age at most recent interview			
Mean age	27.17	28.44	29.03
20–24	37	3	6
25–29	58	19	16
30–34	24	9	9
35–39	3	0	3
40+	—	—	1
Not reported	4	0	4
Gender			
Women	66	17	19
Men	60	14	20
Education level[†††]			
High school, incomplete	12	3	4
High school diploma or GED, in progress	4	0	0
High school diploma or GED	26	0	4
Two-year college, incomplete	15	3	3
Two-year college, trade certificate	2	0	0
Two-year college, associate's degree	5	1	2
Two-year college in progress	23	1	4
Bachelor's degree, incomplete	1	2	3
Bachelor's degree, in progress	20	2	4
Bachelor's degree or higher	18	19	13
Not reported	0	0	2
Annual individual income in 2011–2012			
Mean annual individual income of employed participants	15,931	32,435	—
Median annual individual income of employed participants	14,400	27,600	—
$0	11	3	—
$1–$5,000	3	1	—

(contd.)

TABLE 1.1 *(continued)*

	Undocumented young adults $(n = 126)^\dagger$	Recently legalized young adults $(n = 31)^{\dagger\dagger}$	Romantic partners $(n = 39)$
$5,001–$10,000	11	0	—
$10,001–$15,000	27	3	—
$15,001–$20,000	12	1	—
$20,001–25,000	9	4	—
$25,001–$30,000	3	4	—
$30,001–$40,000	1	2	—
$40,001 or more	2	5	—
Not reported	16	7	—
Annual individual income in 2014–2015			
Mean annual individual income of employed participants	21,942	34,598	28,059
Median annual individual income of employed participants	19,200	34,080	24,600
$0	8	1	5
$1–$5,000	6	0	0
$5,001–$10,000	7	1	5
$10,001–$15,000	13	1	3
$15,001–$20,000	19	1	2
$20,001–25,000	11	2	4
$25,001–$30,000	9	1	4
$30,001–$40,000	11	4	3
$40,001 or more	8	6	7
Not reported	8	5	6
Relationship status at most recent interview			
Single, never married	36	4	—
Single, previously married	11	2	—
Casually dating	5	2	0
Committed dating relationship	33	6	13
Cohabitating	11	1	3
Married-like relationship	10	0	3
Married	20	16	20
Parental status at most recent interview			
No children	82	20	23
Parent	44	11	16

†Sample size varied by wave. Overall, $n = 126$. When reported by time period, $n = 95$ in 2011–12 (wave 1) and $n = 100$ in 2014–15 (wave 2).

††Sample size varied by wave. Overall, $n = 31$. When reported by time period, $n = 30$ in 2011–12 (wave 1) and $n = 22$ in 2014–15 (wave 2).

†††Reported based on 2011–12 attainment level for undocumented and recently legalized samples and 2014–15 attainment level for romantic partners.

Of the 39 romantic partners, most were U.S. citizens, usually second-generation children of immigrants. All but three were Latina/o, with equal numbers of men and women and a range of education levels. Of the 28 partnered with the undocumented sample, their relationship status ranged: 12 were in committed dating relationships, three cohabiting, three in marriage-like relationships, and 10 married. One-third were parents. Of the 11 partnered with the recently legalized participants, 10 were married to the spouse they petitioned for, and one was the partner of a participant who had legalized through marriage to someone else; almost two-thirds were parents.

Most of my participants were heterosexual, but I spoke to 15 who identified as lesbian, gay, bisexual, or queer (LGBQ). I include LGBQ participants' experiences throughout and, where salient, speak to how same-sex couples experience and negotiate immigration laws differently from straight couples.

Additional details about project design, recruitment, interview content, analysis, and positionality are available in appendix A. Participant demographics are summarized in appendix B.

ORGANIZATION OF THE BOOK

Of Love and Papers tracks the traditional course of family formation, moving from dating to marriage to parenting. I trace the everyday consequences of immigration policies to show how they shape intimate relationship decisions and family dynamics. In most chapters, I focus first on the barriers raised by undocumented status and then show how receiving DACA created immediate material benefits but did not fully reverse the effects of beginning relationships in a context of illegality. I bring in the perspectives of citizen family members throughout to show how they also experience illegality. In all, I show how immigration laws and policies cultivate enduring consequences that fundamentally (re)structure Latino immigrant families and individuals' experiences in them.

Chapter 2 establishes how the prospect of legalization through a U.S. citizen spouse shapes undocumented young adults' approaches to romantic partnerships. I trace the enduring consequences of this complicated legal reality: developing preferences for citizen partners, the emotional toll of prematurely ending relationships with undocumented partners, and the social costs of being judged for their partner choices.

Chapter 3 focuses on how illegality structures the development of undocumented young adults' romantic relationships. I show how gendered expectations and immigration status intersect to limit their ability to feel like a desirable partner, go on dates, and advance relationships. Incongruent gendered expectations make it particularly difficult for undocumented young men. Although obtaining DACA facilitated participation, most had already found ways to manage their status while dating, limiting substantial impacts.

Chapter 4 explores how mixed-status couples jointly negotiate illegality in committed romantic partnerships. I focus on citizen partners to show how they come to understand their partner's undocumented status, realize that they will share in the consequences, and commit themselves to mediating these to the best of their ability. This can take a toll on relationships as it restructures relationship dynamics—infusing stress and guilt into relationships—and in some cases, laying the foundation for conflict. DACA provides important relief to both partners, but its temporary nature transforms some of their fears into new ones.

Chapter 5 examines the experiences of 22 mixed-status couples who married and successfully legalized the undocumented partner's status. I show how participating in this legalization pathway has enduring consequences as couples have to construct and perform their relationship in specific ways. This legal process opens up opportunities to pursue upward mobility but simultaneously produces new emotional and material consequences that persist even after the undocumented partner has become a lawful permanent resident.

Chapter 6 turns to parents to show how immigration policies shape parenthood. I identify how immigration policies create family-level economic instability that prevents undocumented young adults from meeting their own and others' parenting ideals. The disconnect between their material resources and gendered cultural ideals disrupts childbearing and parenting experiences. Receiving DACA increased parents' sense of financial security and flexibility, but some negative feelings endured, particularly when parents struggled to leverage DACA to pursue upward mobility.

Chapter 7 focuses on citizen children to show how multigenerational punishment emerges, places them in a de facto undocumented status, and limits their opportunities for upward mobility. I describe how children witness parental barriers, internalize differences between themselves and their peers who have citizen parents, and have limited access to opportunities for upward mobility. These effects crystalize as children age; as a result, DACA came too late to undo the limitations that some experienced.

I conclude by situating my findings in a broader legal context. I reflect on how immigration laws and policies are responsible for deepening, transforming, and alleviating the consequences of illegality for undocumented young adults and their families. Such policies will have sweeping implications for immigrant and racial/ethnic communities far into the future.

"It's Because He Wants Papers"

Choosing a Romantic Partner

With [my ex-girlfriend, who was a citizen], it was her mom thinking that I'm just trying to get her pregnant or married for papers. . . . With [my current girlfriend, who is undocumented], her dad is like . . . "You should just marry somebody who has a good job and papers and [can] fix your status."

—DANIEL HERNANDEZ

Sitting at a sidewalk table outside a coffee shop, Daniel and I rehashed his dating experiences. He recalled how his ex-girlfriend's mom warned her, "He doesn't have papers, so that means he only wants you for one thing." She invoked a common belief that undocumented immigrants marry citizens only to gain legal status. Daniel's words became heated as he recounted these conversations from two years before: "I was fucking annoyed. . . . You seriously think that?" He laughed at the impossibility that "I can get you pregnant . . . force you to settle down with me. Like it was a Jedi mind trick," brainwashing his partner into a relationship. We chuckled, but he was exasperated that people assumed his immigration status drove his romantic choices.

Similar comments had haunted Daniel since he was a teenager. His family members pleaded that he "shoulda just married some white girl. Fix your shit and you would have your own house and business right now." His girlfriend at the time of our first interview was also undocumented and receiving similar comments from her family: her dad was unhappy with their relationship because it cut off her chances for legalization.

It is true that marriage to a U.S. citizen opens up a *potential* pathway to lawful permanent residency. U.S. immigration policy prioritizes family ties, allowing citizens and permanent residents to petition for immediate and extended family members' entry into the United States, or adjust their status if already present. These laws favor U.S. citizens' spousal petitions by immediately providing permanent residency to these approved applications; most other family petitions have extensive backlogs because there are annual limits on the number of visas issued by country of origin.[1] Yet this seemingly straightforward path through marriage is complicated for more than half of undocumented immigrants, who face a 10-year bar on their admission because they entered the United States without inspection. Scholars Ruth Gomberg-Muñoz and Jane Lilly López document how this policy disproportionately affects low-income, Latino undocumented immigrants, particularly those of Mexican origin, and dissuades their legalization.[2] Indeed, most of the undocumented young adults I interviewed entered without inspection and had slim chances of legalizing through marriage. Despite this, immigration policies loomed large, placing a unique strain on their romantic relationships.

Previous work by Cecilia Menjívar and Sarah Lakhani suggests that immigrants experience "transformative effects of the law" as they pursue legalization because the specific contours of immigration law influence intimate life decisions, including those about marriage and family. They contend that those who undergo the most arduous and lengthy pathways to legalization experience the most enduring transformations as they strive to look deserving of relief. Alternatively, those who have no pathway to legalization are assumed to not transform their lives because there is no reason to.[3] However, immigration law is complicated, and many undocumented young adults do not fully grasp their legalization options, especially given that they are frequently framed as deserving relief and as the focus of proposed immigration policy. As a result, undocumented young adults straddle hope and hopelessness, creating tensions in how they understand the law and complicating its potential to inspire transformative effects. I extend focus to those who are not in the midst of legalization processes to explore these tensions. I show how the power of the law extends outside formal legal contexts and into social interactions in which immigration law is commonly invoked and navigated.

In a world where romantic images drive dating and marriage, immigration law pushes undocumented young adults to think in terms of papers. I detail the mythic messages they receive about legalization through marriage and the legal realities that hinder many from pursuing this option. Most highlight legal realities and romantic narratives as they attempt to deprioritize immigration status when selecting a partner. Yet immigration law still determines how undocumented young adults approach and experience relationships. Some develop preferences for citizen partners, and others struggle with the emotional toll of not pursuing relationships with those who share their undocumented status. Couples must manage comments about their partner's immigration status, regardless of what it is. Navigating the myths and realities of legalization policies permanently shapes undocumented young adults' romantic and personal relationships.

"THINK ABOUT YOUR FUTURE": MARRIAGE MYTHS
AND MESSAGES

Undocumented young adults face two myths about legalization through marriage to a U.S. citizen: (1) it is easy to legalize one's immigration status through marriage, and (2) legalization prospects are the only reason for an undocumented immigrant to pursue a romantic relationship. The first marriage myth circulates messages that this legalization pathway is a viable reality and feeds the second myth's message that undocumented immigrants make purely rational romantic decisions. Together, they promote a pervasive message: undocumented young adults should consider their immigration status and legalization desires when choosing romantic partners.

It's Easy to Legalize Your Status through Marriage:
The First Marriage Myth

The first marriage myth—that it is easy to legalize one's immigration status through marriage—stems predominantly from uninformed messages that legalization through marriage is a quick, accessible legal reality for all. Julián Salinas recalled, "My aunt is very . . . outspoken. . . . She would tell me, 'Mijo [son], don't date Mexicans; they are illegals. Go get yourself a güera [white girl]. Get your papers like that." He snapped his fingers—fast. These messages often rest on references to others who successfully legalized through marriage. Gloria Telles shared, "My mom's just been like, 'You should get married. You're 21. Your sister did it when she was 19 . . . and she's a [permanent] resident now.'" Seeing family, friends, or coworkers successfully legalize through marriage, many assume that it must be easy. Legal realities are, however, obscured by the fact that many couples elect not to apply when they have risky cases and because unsuccessful cases are not discussed.[4]

Media representations powerfully fuel stereotypical images of undocumented immigrants.[5] An increasingly common one is that of undocumented immigrants legalizing through marriage. This trope is so well recognized that over the past two decades, it has been a comedic plot point in a variety of prime-time TV shows, including *Friends, Will & Grace, Parks and Recreation, How I Met Your Mother,* and *Superstore.*[6] It is even featured in shows like *Melissa & Joey,* which target preteen and young adult audiences.[7] It forms the story line of several mainstream movies, including *Green Card* and *The Proposal.*[8]

Released around the time of my first interviews, *The Proposal* features Sandra Bullock as a Canadian business executive who forces her assistant to marry her when her employment visa expires. The two attempt to portray a legitimate marriage while an immigration official investigates them. Their antics lead them to fall in love, and he ends up proposing: "Marry me—because I'd like to date you." Their coworkers swoon at his romantic speech. The two kiss as the camera pans to their interview with the foiled immigration agent and the film ends.

Raul Robles shared how this particular movie shaped the messages he receives about legalizing through marriage: "My friend is like, 'You should marry me. We should get married.' I was like, 'I don't know what you're talking about. It's not like those movies that they show you, that you just get married.' I blame *The Proposal* for that. It's not like you're just gonna get your papers right away. It gets more complex." When talking about going to see the movie, Teri Balboa's friend asked, "Why are you watching that? Are you considering [it]?" These media portrayals circulate strong messages that prompt undocumented immigrants and citizens to view marriage as a quick and straightforward legalization pathway.

These narratives elicit direct messages that undocumented young adults should view romantic partners primarily through the legalization options they provide. Sol Montes recounted explicit messages from her mom: "You need to date and marry someone that's a citizen. That's your only way out." Others, like Ana Aguirre's father, condemned budding relationships: "Don't date somebody who doesn't have papers. Think about your future. . . . While it's nice and dandy [now], you're going to feel frustrated later on in your life." These portrayed marriage as a deromanticized business transaction. Celia Alvarez recalled, "I would date guys and [my relatives] would ask me, 'Oh, is he from here? Oh, you should marry him.' My aunt would tell me, 'I'll pay him $1,000, and then you just get divorced [if the relationship doesn't work out].'" Suggesting that the citizens she had just begun dating were candidates for immediate marriage, Celia's family often decoupled marriage and romance.

Some undocumented young adults internalize these messages, subsequently circulating them among other undocumented young adults. Leo Campos recounted a conversation when he advised his undocumented friend to stop dating his undocumented girlfriend:

> I told him, "Look, I'm not trying to be messed up. It looks like you really like each other, but you should really find somebody who has papers." And he goes, "Yeah I think you're right." . . . It was already in his head. I didn't put anything in there. . . . You have to move forward, not two steps back. Getting with someone who's undocumented just like you is two steps back! The boat's sinking, what do we do? Add more weight? Add another hole in there? Sink faster?

Leo's conversation offered a grim assessment. Others reported less direct comments, often jokes that nonetheless weighed on their minds. Manuel Serrano quoted a friend's joke: "Before I ask the girl what's her name, I should ask her if she's legal." Hearing recurring comments like these, undocumented young adults internalize marriage myths, drawing on them as they make romantic decisions and reinforcing them in their peers.

Legalization Is the Only *Reason You're Together:*
The Second Marriage Myth

The fact that marriage is a pathway to legalization, paired with the myth that it is an easy process, fuels a second marriage myth: legalization prospects are the only reason an undocumented immigrant pursues a romantic relationship. These messages surface early in relationships, often from citizen partners' family and friends. Enrique Escobar recalled comments that he and his citizen girlfriend heard when they began dating four years before: "[My girlfriend] told me that one of her friends told her, 'You know, he's only gonna marry you for your papers.'" Messages like these implied that undocumented partners were luring citizens into fake relationships. Such warnings were common, and many reacted like Enrique—trying to laugh it off and hoping that their partner would not think that it was true. Alexa Ibal, a citizen partner of another participant, recounted similar reactions from her parents: "I knew they would think that he was dating me just for papers. They didn't tell me anything. We don't talk about it. . . . But I feel like my mom would probably be like, 'Pues es porque él quiere papeles. [Well, it's because he wants papers].' Like in a joking way, but still sometimes a hint of truth." Even when these messages are not voiced, undocumented young adults and citizen partners sense them in others' thoughts.

This myth also affects how friends and family understand a couple's relationship. Antonio Mendez, who was living with his citizen girlfriend, explained, "That's something that people always ask: . . . 'Are you guys for real, or is it just for papers and everything?' But, I mean, right now we've [been] together five years, so it's like, how can someone be with someone else for papers if we've been together for this long?" These questions bewildered Antonio and others in long-term relationships because the length of their relationship—especially in the absence of marriage—should have suggested that they were a legitimate couple.

When mixed-status relationships become more serious, friends and family members revive this myth as they pressure the couple to pursue a petition. Mario Barillas and I were sitting side by side on some steps when I asked him if anyone had suggested he marry his citizen girlfriend. He quickly twisted toward me and interrupted: "My family. Mostly my oldest brother. He's like, '¿Cuándo se casan? [When will you marry?]' And I'm like, 'Whatever. Jerk.' And I know he's saying it for that reason. Because he told me once, 'Hey, you guys should marry so you can get your papers.' And I felt kind of offended when he said that." Mario immediately connected his brother's questions to the second myth: "It makes me think that he thinks that I'm with her just because of that [legalization]." Anger tinged Mario's memories of these conversations.

Bombarded by these myths, some undocumented young adults do begin to consider making marriage decisions based on legalization desires. When I first interviewed Felipe Moreno, he was a senior in college struggling to pay for his final few courses. Desperate and concerned about how he would get a job after graduation, he was trying to identify a friend whom he could ask to marry him:

> We have to legalize ourselves whichever way [we can]. . . . I've texted girls, I've asked them a key question so I can know which ones [might be willing to marry me]. I ask them, "Where do you see yourself five years from now?" So that way I can have an idea. If she says, "Nothing, just going to school," then you're good. Maybe I can ask her 'cause she ain't doing nothing. . . . Maybe she can take a couple of years [and be married].

Having faith in the myth of easy legalization through marriage, Felipe accepted the idea that some people marry "just for papers" and began to think strategically.

"IT'S NOT LIKE THAT": MATCHING MARRIAGE MYTHS WITH REALITY

Besieged by marriage myths, undocumented young adults searched for ways to reject insinuations that they were using their partners "for papers." Many developed counternarratives highlighting legal realities and romantic notions to deny that their undocumented status was playing a role in their relationships. They employed these to reject assumptions that they wanted to pursue legalization through marriage, convince romantic partners that their relationship was real, and assure themselves that they were not compromising their romantic and moral selves.

Highlighting Legal Realities: Complications to Legalizing through Marriage

Those pushing marriage myths rarely understood immigration law's complexities. Legal realities guarantee that legalization through marriage is a slow process and not available to all undocumented immigrants. Of note are variations in the riskiness of the process because of the 10-year bar and the long duration of the process, brought about by requirements related to the two-year conditional residency. Undocumented young adults who knew about these aspects of immigration law used them to counterbalance the first set of myths and reject the idea that they would pursue a relationship solely for legalization purposes.

"They Still Kick You Out for a Good While": The 10-Year Bar.   The specifics of one's immigration history, including mode of entry and previous legalization petitions, determine the riskiness of legalizing through marriage. Forty-two percent of undocumented immigrants entered the United States "with inspection," meaning they were formally admitted and then overstayed a visa.[9] They face a relatively straightforward legalization process: a petition filed by a U.S. citizen spouse allows them to adjust their immigration status while remaining in the country, and this

usually takes less than a year. A special provision of immigration code allows the same for those who have pending legalization petitions filed before 2001, regardless of their mode of entry.[10] The remaining half, those who entered without inspection and do not have a pending petition, undergo a very different process. They are required to return to their country of origin to process their application at a U.S. consulate. If they have been in the United States for over a year, leaving the country to do so triggers a 10-year bar on their reentry.[11] They can petition to remove the bar by demonstrating that their absence would create "extreme hardship" for their citizen spouse, but, as I will show in chapter 5, this is a tall order. With no guarantee that this reprieve will be granted, they risk living apart from their family or forcing them to relocate outside the United States.[12] These obstacles make the legalization process incredibly risky for many.

Many participants did not know much about the 10-year bar when I mentioned it. Felipe Moreno, the one considering strategically marrying a friend, was taken aback. He claimed that the process would take only about six months to a year, which he had learned from a citizen friend who had petitioned for her husband. I shared that the process depends on how someone entered the country and that some people have to leave and could then be barred. He was adamant that I was wrong: "For marriage? No!" As I detailed the legal realities, he became puzzled. "I've never heard of this," he said. "No way. Why did he get to stay?" I pointed out a small detail he hadn't considered—his friend's husband had overstayed a tourist visa. Recognizing that this would not apply to his case, he referenced his earlier plans, "So I've been living a lie." He continued to ask more questions about the laws, shaking his head in disbelief, and commenting, "I didn't know this" and "There's always gotta be some bull." Without these legal details, undocumented young adults had little reason to challenge marriage myths.

Yet a number of participants knew about the bar, using it to spin a counternarrative that it was better to remain undocumented than risk a 10-year separation. Cruz Vargas shared his vague understanding: "I heard it's still like . . . you still gotta pay a lot of money, and then they still kick you out for a good while, you know?" He paused, looking to see if I knew what he was talking about. I added simply, "Ten years," and he continued, "Yeah, 10. Yeah. So I'm like, Why am I gonna go out if I'm already here?" Though he did not know all the details of the process, Cruz knew enough. He felt it was safer to remain undocumented.

But this caused conflict with his citizen girlfriend, who brought up the possibility of legalizing him "all the time." He recounted how these conversations usually went: "She'll see something on TV. She'll [be] like, 'See!' . . . I'll tell her it's not that I don't want to do it, but it's not that easy." Like Cruz, many struggled to explain legal complexities to others who had latched onto the marriage myths. As with Cruz and his girlfriend, who seemed to suggest that he was too lazy to start the process, conflict can emerge between those who offer legally based counternarratives and those who subscribe to the marriage myths.

"You're in the Pedo for Three Years at Least": Time Commitment.   Intent on decreasing the emergence of fraudulent or strategic marriages, the legalization process includes provisions that dictate how long a couple must remain married.[13] If a couple has been married for two or more years when their application is approved, the undocumented spouse is granted a 10-year lawful permanent residency. If they married less than two years earlier, they are granted a two-year *conditional* residency, dependent on the continuation of the marriage. Before its expiration, the couple must jointly submit a petition for permanent residency, including additional documentation of their relationship.[14] The undocumented partner can apply to transition from conditional to permanent resident on their own only if there were extenuating circumstances, such as domestic abuse; this also requires documentation and depends on the reviewing agent's discretion.[15] Thus, couples must commit to at least two years together, three if they want their citizen partner to sponsor an accelerated citizenship application rather than waiting five years to apply on their own.[16] Counter to the myth of a fast process, this legal reality requires petitioning couples to commit multiple years to marriage as they gather application materials and meet legal requirements.

Many interviewees used the extensive time commitment to create a counternarrative that it would be tough to sustain a relationship purely for legalization purposes. Paco Barrera had considered the possibility of marrying for papers: "It might have crossed my mind at some point. It will be cool, easy, just do it. Just do it. [But] you're in the pedo for three years at least." Aptly summarizing how easy it is to be swayed by messages, he joked that he would be trapped in a *pedo*—literally a fart or, in this context, a mess if he initiated a strategic relationship for legalization purposes. Similarly, Claudia Arellano stressed the need for a strong and committed relationship to weather this lengthy process:

> It's not easy, and it's not even guaranteed [to be approved]. So if I'm gonna go through something like that, it's gonna be with someone that is gonna be there with me through it. 24/7. No matter what. . . . A lot of people offer their help, but I don't think they really know what it entails or they really know what they're gonna have to go through.

She contended that such commitment can be found only in a long-term romantic partner, because "even if it's a friend that really cares about me, it's not gonna be the same." Indeed, Jesus Perez shared that he had moved in with a friend so that they could strategically marry and file a petition. In the midst of building evidence to establish their partnership—opening joint accounts and taking pictures together—"it fell apart." The time and effort were already more than his friend could handle, an indicator that she would not last the required two to three years.

The time commitment also meant that pursuing a relationship solely for legalization purposes would endanger future romances. Edith Sandoval spoke to this: "I would be giving up on finding someone. I mean, who's gonna say, 'OK, I'll be with you [in a relationship, but go] marry that guy?' I don't think so." Similarly, Zen Cruz suggested that quickly pushing an emerging relationship to marriage would present difficulties if they broke up: "Either they're stuck with me—if I can somehow talk them into sticking around with me—or the whole thing's [legalization petition] gonna get dissolved. I'm probably just gonna waste their time and my time." Both frame marriage to anyone besides their true love as creating irreversible consequences for future relationships.

Centering Romance: Love as a Necessary Requirement

Regardless of the extent that they understood legal realities, almost all participants cited love as a necessary requirement for marriage and concluded that they would not marry someone simply to legalize their immigration status. Though we might expect this romantic narrative to be gendered, men and women equally adopted similar romantic counternarratives. Take Norma Mercado and Joaquin Salas:

> *Norma:* My whole thing was that I wasn't ever going to marry somebody for the interest of my papers. . . . So I thought whoever it was, papers or not, that I just needed to fall in love.
>
> *Joaquin:* I would never get married to be able to legalize myself or benefit from that. I think that the only way I would get married is if I loved someone.

As early as the 17th century, marriage began to transition from a political and economic tool to a search for love and companionship. Though class status complicated the spread of this cultural revolution, love-filled marriages became the predominant relationship norm. In contemporary U.S. society, cultural ideals about marriage are heavily influenced by media images of romantic love and intimacy.[17] Undocumented young adults internalized these dominant romantic notions growing up in the United States, and draw on them to resist pressures that they should think strategically about marriage.

Relatedly, some participants viewed marriage as a sacred event, not to be tainted by immigration considerations. Lupe Gonzalez remembered joking with a friend who was going through an expedited legalization process through her husband, an enlisted Marine: "I was like, 'Hey, hey, does he have a Marine friend?'" She continued, "It just crossed my mind, but it just went right out [*laughs*]. I consider marriage something sacred, so I wouldn't mess around with it like that." She explained, "It's something that you can only do once. . . . You can't just hit replay, you know? Try it with a new one." Reflecting on her parents' 40-year marriage and the seriousness of divorce, Lupe rejected the possibility of marrying for papers. Although Lupe's counternarrative about marriage's sacred nature is likely connected to her deep involvement in the Catholic Church, others, like Jaime Rios, also used these narratives: "I'm not a very religious person, but I still think marriage is an important thing. It's not something you can take lightly. That's why I don't want it." Transcending religiosity, participants saw marriage as an important and serious commitment that cannot be undone. Though divorce is an option, it is an expensive, emotionally draining, stigmatized, and legally dense process that further shapes one's romantic life.

Reinforcing narratives about romance and love, participants portrayed loveless marriages as immoral. Victoria Sandoval noted that she would not marry someone simply to fix her immigration status: "What if you don't *love* that person? What if you *like* that person? I don't know. I don't think it's right. I don't think it's right to take advantage of somebody else." Such narratives of "taking advantage" or "using someone" moralized the importance of romantic love in marriage. Gloria Telles's mom told her, "You're just so young and dumb. . . . You can do love later. Just do it [legalize through marriage] now." Moral narratives helped Gloria reject this message because it was not simply about *wanting* the luxury of love; it was immoral to marry without love.

Although undocumented young adults were adamant about not "using" a partner for papers, romantic narratives helped justify the possibility that they would legalize within a loving marriage. Responding to her mom's messages, Gloria believed love and legalization could coincide:

> [Legalization's] not the first reason why I want to do it [get married]. . . . I like marriage. I like the idea of two people coming together and creating a life. . . . So I want to find somebody that I can get married to. And if papers come, then that's a plus. I'm not gonna be like, "No, let's not do the process."

Continuing to prioritize romantic love while recognizing this legalization pathway, Gloria and others suggest that falling in love with and marrying a citizen is a "plus" or "bonus." As Yahir Villa suggested, this is ideal because one can "get romance *and* documentation." These narratives reinforced the idea that their search for legal status should not compromise their romantic or moral selves.

"IT'LL BE PROBABLY ON THE LIST": EDUCATIONAL DIFFERENCES IN COMPLYING WITH MARRIAGE MYTHS

Legal and romantic counternarratives seek to dispel the mythic messages directed at undocumented young adults. Yet marriage myths still shape their partner preferences and shade how others view their relationships with citizens. Notably, pursuing higher education makes it more likely that an undocumented young adult partners with a citizen by increasing their sense of exclusion—making the marriage myths more appealing—and fostering exposure to citizen-dominated dating markets.

Reacting to Exclusion: Preferencing Citizens

When I asked participants what they look for in a partner, almost all talked about personality, physical appearance, and romantic chemistry. Reflecting previous research, many stated a preference for and/or were dating other Latinas/os who shared their cultural background and would fit into their Spanish-speaking families.[18] Those with higher education often desired a similarly educated partner, reflecting patterns in the general population.[19] Marriage myths, however, added a unique consideration by forcing many to weigh immigration status. Those who felt highly excluded from U.S. society were most susceptible to the myths and more likely to develop explicit preferences for citizen partners to keep their legalization options open.

Some undocumented young adults successfully resist marriage myths, while others restrict themselves to citizen partners. Carolina Sandoval and Abel León exemplify these two diverging viewpoints:

> *Carolina:* [Immigration status] doesn't have to do with being in a relationship with somebody. If you like the person, you wanna be with the person, that has nothing to do with it.
>
> *Abel:* One of my friends . . . called me [and] said, "Hey [Abel], I have two girls [who want to go out], can you help me with one of these girls?" I'm like, "Sure, but are they AB 540 [undocumented]?"[20] He's like, "Yeah, man." I'm like, "No . . . I don't even want to waste my time. I don't want to waste my money. I don't even want to try. I don't care if they're cute. . . . I'm sorry, dude, call somebody else. I don't go out with AB 540 girls."

Marriage myths forced both Carolina and Abel to negotiate the fact that a citizen partner opens up a potential (albeit complicated) pathway to legalization. Carolina refused to let this dictate her choices and had been with her husband, also an undocumented young adult, for 10 years. Internalizing marriage myths, Abel limited his dating pool to citizens to ensure that he would fall in love with someone who could adjust his immigration status.

Although illegality raises the same structural barriers for all undocumented young adults, those who *understand* their immigration status as a severe source of exclusion tend to develop citizen preferences. Abel's successful pursuit of a bachelor's degree at a California State University campus was filled with many legal barriers. Initially, he believed his immigration status barred him from attending college. College application deadlines had passed when he learned about Assembly Bill 540, which allows Californian undocumented youth to pay more affordable in-state tuition rates. A high school teacher managed to get him enrolled. Still, he battled to balance full-time enrollment with full-time employment, which was necessary due to undocumented students' ineligibility for financial aid at the time. Since graduating, he had struggled to use his degree to pursue his desired career in politics. Thus, Abel thought about his immigration status "all the time" and felt it was an unrelenting barrier. These exclusionary experiences led Abel to believe that legalization would transform his life:

> *Abel:* I feel like I can't do anything. I do a lot of stuff. But still, it's hard. I feel like I'm waiting for somebody else to make it happen.

> [For lawmakers to say,] "OK, let's give them the opportunity. . . ."
> I feel that someone is holding me back.
>
> *Laura:* Do you think you'll eventually gain legal status? How important
> is that to you?
>
> *Abel:* It's like a dream come true! It is.

To Abel, legalization through marriage appeared to be his only hope for upward mobility, leading him to only date citizens.

It is important to recognize that Abel's explicit preferences are unique; many participants resisted expressing such unequivocal citizen preferences because of competing narratives of romantic love. Reflecting on the hypothetical question of whether she would date someone who was undocumented, Juana Covarrubias, then a community college student preparing to transfer to a top University of California campus, quickly acknowledged how this would limit her: "Of course, sometimes you think it's not gonna get me anywhere. We're still gonna be stuck in a hole." She reasoned, "But, I mean, if it's love, then, of course, I wouldn't mind [their undocumented status]. Um, like, again, it's just papers, right? And although it would limit me—because, again, I want to achieve big things—at the same time if it's true love, then, of course, I wouldn't mind." Trying to convince herself, she repeated, "If it's love, then, of course, I wouldn't mind." Attempting to merge their exclusionary realities with romantic narratives, Juana and others tried to leave space for both. Yet many left only hypothetical room to date an undocumented person and had not done so.

On the other hand, Carolina was able to deprioritize marriage myth messages when she first met her husband because, at the time, she understood her immigration status barriers as less significant. They met in high school when she was 15 and he was 16. They moved in together a year later and had their first child a year after that. Carolina recalled that she knew about her undocumented status, but "at that time I thought it was just paper and numbers. It didn't really mean anything. . . . I didn't really get the point of how it was going to affect me until I started trying to look for jobs and stuff." Like others who partnered in high school, Carolina and her husband were not fully attuned to the barriers raised by undocumented status. Indeed, previous research shows that the real and perceived significance of immigration status is relatively low during high school and increases over the life course.[21] By establishing their relationship before their immigration status became a source of explicit exclusion, Carolina and her husband could reject marriage myth messages.

Carolina has since faced staunch immigration status barriers. Soon after graduating high school, she visited a for-profit cosmetology school and left in tears after the admissions counselor told her she needed a Social Security number and then ignored her. Abandoning her dream, Carolina worked a series of "boring" jobs in customer service, at times not being paid and experiencing intermittent unemployment. Despite this, she deprioritized the significance of legalizing her status: "I'm living my life. Like, I do want it [legalization] to happen. It would be so cool, but I don't [wait], I'm just living my life." Less convinced that she needed to legalize her status, both when she was in high school and 10 years later when we spoke, Carolina justified ignoring messages to not date undocumented immigrants.

Abel's and Carolina's stories represent larger trends among undocumented young adults: when they perceive strong barriers based on immigration status, they often keep legalization options open by developing preferences for citizen partners. This was more likely among participants, like Abel, who pursued higher education; they tended to face explicit and overwhelming immigration status barriers as they pursued upward mobility. They recognized that legalization would strongly improve their chances of using their higher education to transition into the middle class. Alternatively, those who did not pursue college were more likely to believe that they could negotiate their immigration-status barriers as needed.

In a few cases, highly excluded, college-educated participants intentionally selected undocumented partners. At the time of her first interview, Iliana Guzman was dating another undocumented college student. She explained this choice:

> Let's say something happens and I'm venting and I'm crying and I'm telling my partner about it. He understands what I'm going through and what I would need. My [citizen] partner before, I feel like I would have to tell them what I would need. . . . You know how sometimes you feel crazy because you feel like you're the only person that's feeling . . .? Like when someone makes a stupid comment and no one says anything. . . . You look for that reassurance. . . . I feel like that's what's afforded to me quicker when I share those things with him.

Such stark social exclusion was more likely in higher education settings where undocumented students often felt they were the only ones. They longed to feel seen and understood. Iliana reasoned that her socioemotional well-being was more important than keeping legalization options open. She did not feel trapped in the same way Abel did, anticipating that her higher education and self-advocacy would allow her to find alternative ways to advance herself, even if she remained undocumented.

Several participants who had not pursued a bachelor's degree asserted that undocumented partners would provide stronger avenues to upward mobility, despite cutting off legalization opportunities. Nancy Ortega and Erick Godinez explained how their undocumented partners compared to previous citizen partners:

> *Nancy:* I knew his immigration status was the same as mine, but
>   I guess because he has a lot of willpower and he's not afraid

to work for what he has. . . . [Other guys I dated], they just assumed that because they were U.S. citizens, life would be easy on them, and it's not how it is.

Erick: People who were born here, it's like they want more [from you]. . . . And people who don't have papers, they are tough . . . flexible. . . . [My citizen ex-girlfriend], she wanted me to provide everything, and I tried my best. I gave her a [rented] house. I gave her all the necessary [things]. But she found someone else that is supposedly better and she left. . . . [My current undocumented girlfriend], she comes from a noble family, like "If we have it, we have it. And if we don't, we wait." So she's not a material person. If she could get it for cheap somewhere else, we go [there].

Both invoke gendered expectations of men as economic providers to explain how citizen partners may not be strategic choices for jointly pursuing mobility. Nancy hinted at the reality that second-generation Latino men face structural barriers to upward mobility, particularly if they did not pursue higher education. In this stratified social context, citizen Latino men may stagnate, leaving undocumented men to be perceived as more hard-working and thus better partners. On the other hand, undocumented men like Erick believed that undocumented women were more willing to renegotiate their gendered provider expectations. Both saw a shared immigrant work ethic as a more reliable pathway to upward mobility than legalization through a citizen partner.

Notably, DACA relieved some of the stress put on partner choice. Marina Balderas reflected on her decision to date another DACA recipient:

Sometimes we joke around like, "Oh, I can't marry you because you're undocumented so it's going to make me extra undocumented." But no. I mean, we don't really—now that we have DACA . . . we don't really see it like ohhhh [negative]. It's more like now we're in it together.

With DACA providing for their economic and social inclusion and the California DREAM Act facilitating their education by enabling access to financial aid, Marina and her boyfriend no longer saw their immigration status as a severe source of exclusion. Both pursuing higher education, they anticipated being able to achieve upward mobility, allowing them to uncouple their romantic choices from legalization desires.

Dating Markets: Availability of Citizens

Even when undocumented immigrants do not expressly prefer citizens, their partner selection is still interpreted through marriage myth assumptions. This is particularly consequential for undocumented young adults who partnered with citizens because of their social networks' composition. Most participants reported meeting partners in high school or college and at work. Some met through community organizations, church, friends, and family, or in clubs and bars. These spaces comprised a mixed-status dating market, but some had more citizens than others. Often, pursuing higher education increased spatial and social mobility, which increased access to citizen-dominated dating markets and increased the chances of unintentionally partnering with a citizen.

Undocumented Latinas/os/xs in Southern California disproportionately live in less desirable neighborhoods and experience residential segregation.[22] Most participants reported growing up and currently living in mixed-status Latino areas. They had both citizen and undocumented peers during their K–12 education, and many reported early romantic relationships with both undocumented and documented people.

But those who experienced spatial and social mobility also gained access to citizen-dominated dating markets. During his first interview, Daniel Hernandez explained that he dated only citizens during six years of community college because "I wasn't hanging out with other undocumented people. . . . It's all citizens, just like, that's what's there." Like others who pursued higher education, Daniel found himself surrounded by citizens who make up the vast majority of students. Only when he became active in an immigrant rights organization did he develop undocumented social networks and begin dating an undocumented woman.

Similarly, Lili Moreno, who had completed her bachelor's degree, compared how her spatial mobility differed from her undocumented cousin who grew up in the same neighborhood:

> She didn't go to school [college]. . . . Her job is very different from what I do. It doesn't pay as much. So she's always more in [the city] where we're from. Because I went off to school and because of the type of work that I do [as a community organizer], I'm always out and about meeting new people and connecting with people and stuff like that. It's more like she's stuck and I have more opportunities [to meet citizens].

As Lili's contends, those who pursue higher education or employment in sectors dominated by citizens expand their dating market. Thus, those who do not have specific preferences for citizen partners may still find themselves primarily dating citizens by virtue of who surrounds them.

The undocumented young adults who spent most of their time in citizen-dominated spaces avoided pressures to reject undocumented partners. Romantic ideals kept many participants from stating strong preferences for citizen partners, speaking instead of a partner's citizenship status as an added benefit. Lupe Gonzalez noted, "I think about their schooling. And then maybe status. . . . It'll be probably on the list [of dating criteria], but it wouldn't be a priority. If it comes down to it, it was not gonna matter his status if we fall in love. But I would rather him be born here, you know, have a cool status." Although Lupe admitted a preference for a citizen partner, she was open to the possibility that she might fall in love with an undocumented partner. Yet she was never faced with this choice because she mostly encountered citizen peers in college. Her dating market spared her from having to act on marriage myth messages and choose between legalization and love. Still, she appeared to prefer citizens, exposing her to potential suspicion when she began dating her citizen partner.

"I STILL CAN'T GET OVER IT": THE CONSEQUENCES OF PUTTING MARRIAGE MYTHS INTO PRACTICE

Marriage myths continue to shape romantic relationships as they progress. Those who cling to the myths must put their citizen partner preferences into practice by ending relationships with undocumented partners. Those partnered with a citizen may feel pressure to advance the relationship. Most encounter judgment for their partner choices, regardless of their partner's citizenship status, as others assume that romantic relationships only serve legalization purposes. Negotiating these marriage myth messages has enduring emotional and social consequences.

Rejecting Undocumented Partners: Emotional Consequences

Marriage myth messages encourage undocumented young adults to reject undocumented partners, creating emotional baggage that haunts future relationships. Juan Valle declared no preference for a citizen partner and spoke briefly about his slight preference for an undocumented partner, because "we can relate more, and the life experience is a little bit more similar." In his first interview, he noted that his three most recent romantic interests had been undocumented men. Their shared undocumented status had, however, prevented him and a potential partner from pursuing a relationship:

> Juan: I was talking to somebody from campus. And I think he had other objectives in his life. He wanted someone that had better opportunities or, you know—
>
> Laura: Like upward mobility or—
>
> Juan: Um, just someone that had status in this country—someone that could provide. I was like, "That probably won't be me." [Laughs.] Just because of my status. So that just ended.

At the time, being gay would have prevented Juan and his prospective partner from legalizing their statuses through marriage because the federal government did not recognize same-sex marriage and prevented same-sex spouses from filing immigration petitions.[23] Despite this, the strength of the marriage myths led Juan's prospective partner to internalize messages to not date other undocumented immigrants. Further, they both recognized that their undocumented statuses would make it hard to work together to achieve upward mobility. Indeed, Juan spoke at length about how his immigration status made it difficult to find a well-paying job, repeatedly preventing him from being able to afford transferring to a four-year university. These experiences permanently shaded Juan's approach to relationships and forced him to seriously reevaluate whether he was willing to date other undocumented men.

These same issues reemerged in Juan's most recent relationship with another undocumented man. They came to a mutual decision to break up because of the potential long-term consequences of remaining together: "This year I was dating an individual who is undocumented as well, but I was very hesitant about it." He paused, wiping away the tear rolling down his cheek: "I think he was my ideal guy, and I had put up this wall between us 'cause I didn't wanna let him in." Collecting himself, he clarified: "We both knew that we were undocumented. We just understood that it probably wouldn't work out." Juan was clearly heartbroken; he chided himself later in the interview, laughing: "The last guy I was crying about . . . it's been like five months now. I still can't get over it." Despite seeing the decision as a necessary sacrifice, there were still deep emotional costs.

Similarly, Sarai Bedolla spoke about the enduring consequences of being dumped because of shared undocumented status:

> A lot of it was because of the fact that I was undocumented and his parents had a strong influence on him. . . . He ended it because he was like, "I'd rather end it now after three months than later down the road end it because we're not going to be able to fix our status." And at one point he told me, "I'm going to get married to someone with documents. And if you still want to be together, I can marry you after that." And then I was like, "No! Go to hell!"

Given the resistance to explicit partner preferences, it was often after relationships were established that one or both undocumented partners gave in to pointed marriage myth messages. Sarai explained that this experience made her feel like her undocumented status marked her as an undesirable partner: "Because he broke up with me for these reasons [of immigration status], it was kind of like a stab." Though she eventually got over the heartbreak, she feared that her undocumented status might hurt her future relationships.

These breakups can haunt people long after ending a relationship. When we began talking about the role of immigration status when dating, Antonio Mendez's first comment was about when he was in 10th grade and decided not to date a girl who was also undocumented: "That's how I dealt with my [undocumented] reality then at the time. I was like, 'This cannot go anywhere.'" He remembered the desperation he felt in high school: "I didn't want to affect her situation ... and her possibilities of fixing her status and mine either." A decade later, he vividly recalled the difficulty of this decision and still tells others about it. Other undocumented people often get mad, telling him that love should conquer all. Confronting romantic narratives, he is chastised for a choice he made as a 15-year-old boy trying to understand what it means to be undocumented. Notably, Antonio's early enforcement of citizen preferences was burned into his memory and continued to haunt him even though he was happily living with his partner of five years.

Embracing Citizen Partners: Relationship Consequences

Alternatively, marriage myth messages can push undocumented young adults to embrace citizen partners, putting undue pressure on the progress of their relationships. Luis Escobar explained how his undocumented status changed his relationship's trajectory by spurring him to marry his partner after a year of dating: "I told her my reality. I actually told her, 'You know what, I think I'm actually gonna go back to Mexico. This is it. I can't do this anymore.' And she was like, 'Let's get married now and try to do this.' I'm like, OK. So we got married." They abandoned their plans to delay marriage until completing college.

A few felt that immigration laws may also push them to marry when they did not want to. Pablo Ortiz had been with his citizen girlfriend for two years, and they had a daughter together. He explained,

> I'm not a big believer of marriage. Maybe 'cause it hasn't happened in my family. . . .
> That's the reason I thought that it wasn't important, that it's not necessary. . . . Now
> in the present, that's when I have heard a lot more people tell me, "Oh, don't be a
> pendejo. Don't be a dumb ass. You should get married and get your documents." . . .
> So maybe for reasons of frustration lately, I have thought about it . . . to secure our
> baby's future. . . . Getting married so we could adjust my documents.

Despite being a college graduate, Pablo struggled to provide for his family because he could not find a well-paying job. This—and his fear of being separated from his daughter through deportation—motivated his consideration of marriage. Similarly, Alexa Ibal, the citizen partner of an undocumented participant, noted that the only reason they would marry was "so he would get papers." They were already living together, and in other circumstances they would simply continue to cohabitate because she didn't agree with "the whole institution of marriage. I don't want to get married through the church." People like Pablo and Alexa are pushed by immigration realities to consider marriage, a social institution that they would otherwise choose not to participate in.

Still others reported that their immigration status created pressure to maintain relationships, even if they were not ideal. Lili Moreno spoke about her recent decision to end a five-year relationship. Her partner was about to acquire citizenship and could have petitioned to adjust her status.

I was hoping that things would work out with this person and that we would marry. But they're not. It was difficult because I was thinking how I'm losing an opportunity to get married with someone and legalize my status. When I was trying to decide to break up with him or not, this issue came up. If I want to get married and fix my papers, I'm gonna have to start over again and to get to that comfort level where you're sure you want to get married to this person. I had to let that go for the sake of my well-being.

Though all individuals, regardless of legal status, struggle with ending long-term relationships, marriage myths give undocumented young adults an extra factor to weigh when making these decisions. In Lili's case, legal myths and realities fueled a desire to legalize her status through her soon-to-be-citizen partner. Without these expectations, she would have had an easier time ending her relationship when she realized it was unhealthy.

Managing Judgment of Partner Choices: Social Consequences

Marriage myths and realities also shape others' opinions about partner choices and relationships. Having dated both undocumented and citizen individuals, Daniela Sanchez expressed a common theme: "If you're dating somebody that has papers, they think, 'Oh, you're dating him because he has papers.' If you're dating somebody that doesn't have papers, they're like, 'Are you stupid? What's wrong? Go and date somebody that does have papers!'" These messages pass judgment on all partner choices, creating a frustrating, lose-lose situation for undocumented young adults. Such judgmental messages negatively impacted undocumented young adults' relationships with their family, friends, and romantic partners.

Undocumented young adults who partner with undocumented immigrants are judged for cutting themselves off from a potential legalization pathway. Carolina Sandoval discussed her mom's early interactions with the man who is now Carolina's husband:

My mom made a dinner because I had a boyfriend, so she wanted to meet him. . . . And that was her first question, [Do you have papers?]. And I was . . . thinking like, Oh my God! . . . I was serving his plate, and I looked at him, and then he's like, "Oh no, I don't have papers." And then after she's like, "Hmmm [disapproving]." . . . [He asked me after], "Why did your mom tell me that? And I was like, "Well, because she says that I should marry somebody that has papers."

This conversation foreshadowed persistent tension. Carolina explained that her mom used to tell her, "You need to marry somebody that has papers in order for you to have papers. So she doesn't like my husband because of that." She laughed dismissively, and perhaps nervously, when I asked if her mom still does not like her husband: "She's not mean-mean to him, but we know she doesn't like him."

[Laughs.] . . . She's always said negative things about him, but I tell her [to] see the positive. . . . Because she always says that we didn't turn out to be what she wanted us to be." She believed that her mom's only dream for her was to marry a citizen. Many participants who partnered with another undocumented immigrant reported similar disapproval. In some cases tensions eased, but these early exchanges often soured relationships with families and friends.

Alternatively, undocumented young adults who partner with citizens often face strong suspicion that they pursued the relationship only for legalization purposes. Aida Mendoza recounted a particularly stark example in which her mom overheard her husband's family members talking at the Laundromat just weeks before their wedding: "My mom overheard her [my sister-in-law] say that her parents said, 'Oh, I'm gonna make sure that he doesn't fix papers for that hoe.'" Aida's frustration erupted as she recalled her conversation with her husband afterward: "I was so upset! . . . [My legalization] would've been a benefit . . . for your family because I'm not that type of person. I would've helped your family. . . . Your parents are older than mine. I know that one day you're gonna have to take care of them. . . . But now they're assed out!" Though they had planned to file her petition after the wedding, she refused to do anything to confirm their suspicions and instead "wasted all the money" they had saved for legal fees. Four years had passed, but the heat of her words suggested that her relationship with her in-laws still suffered. She also seemed to hold this decision against her husband, since she remembers that, at his parents' urging, he had refused to apply for her legalization when she heard about a time-sensitive legal loophole that would have allowed her to get her papers "in months." Though it seems unlikely that her application would have proceeded so smoothly, her belief that they prevented her legalization permanently warped these relationships.

While most mixed-status couples did not face such strong suspicion, many reported that their relationships were assumed to be fake or strategic, especially when they seemed to be marrying too early. Regina Castro, a permanent resident who legalized her status through her citizen husband, explained that they married out of love after dating for less than a year. She stressed that she had believed that she faced the 10-year bar until after they were married. Despite this, her friends questioned their relationship. Regina remembered a conversation at her bridal shower: "A friend of mine said, 'Cut the bullshit! Just tell us the truth. Are you getting married to fix your papers?' She was disinvited from my wedding that night! I was like, 'You are not coming because you are not my friend.' By that point, I was tired of it." Engaged and newlywed couples, like Regina and her husband, often had to prove that they loved each other. In addition to being emotionally exhausting, such suspicions can crack the foundations of trust with friends and family. Many of Regina's friendships suffered as people raised similar suspicions; her friendship circle shrank to the few people she felt were genuinely happy for her and supported her relationship.

Suspicions about a mixed-status relationship's veracity can also shape expressions of love in romantic relationships. Many undocumented partners attempted to assure their citizen partners that they were together for love, not papers. Lena Gomez remembered,

> Once it gets more serious, [you think], "Are they gonna think you're trying to marry them because of the papers?" . . . And even if they don't, will their family think that? How much can their family influence them into thinking that's why you're getting married? Do you put it off to prove that that's not why you're getting married? And if you decided to marry out of love, it's just such an awful experience to have to prove that you love him. No one else has to do that.

Aware of circulating marriage myth messages, many undocumented young adults tried to figure out if their partners were concerned and strained to prove that their love was real.

Some undocumented partners also sought to delay marriage to prove this was not their motive. Alma Molina vividly remembered what her boyfriend told her six months into their relationship: "My mom thinks you're with me because you want to fix your status." Over their eight-year relationship, this had been at the forefront of her decision to avoid marriage: "There's been days where I'm like, 'Ugh, I just want to get married and become a resident.' But there's days that I'm like, 'I don't want him to feel like I'm just using him.'" While intended to strengthen their romantic relationships, their concerns and actions highlight how marriage myths shape expressions of love.

Citizen partners also receive myth-based messages that encourage them to legalize their partner and pass judgment if they have not petitioned for them. Arianna Guerrero, a citizen who has been with her boyfriend for four years, shared that others pressure her: "Oh, you guys should get married so he can start the process." Rudy Beltran, a citizen, noted that the pressure increased after he married his wife. Asked whether anyone ever asks why she is still undocumented, he responded, "Yeah, my dad. He said, 'Dummy, so what do you mean she has no papers? You guys are married. ¡Ya arréglale! [Fix it for her already!]'" Encouraged by the myth that legalization through marriage is easy, family and friends often placed the responsibility for legalization in the citizen partner's hands. Thus, partners can feel guilty when marriage does not lead to legalization because of the realities hidden behind the myths.

CONCLUSION

As undocumented young adults enter adulthood, they realize the full extent to which their undocumented status contributes to their exclusion from U.S. society.[24] This is around the same time that that they begin seriously dating and are told that a citizen romantic partner opens a pathway to legalization. Daniela

Sanchez explained this connection: "Sometimes it's like you feel like you're sick and somebody has the antidote." The metaphor of citizen spouse as antidote captures how outsiders assume that undocumented young adults would make purely logical choices in pursuit of a life-altering opportunity for legalization. But these widely circulated marriage myths ignore legal realities that over half of undocumented immigrants are unable to securely legalize their status through a citizen spouse. Further, as scholar Kara Cebulko notes, these strategic assumptions overlook internalized U.S.-based norms, including those about marriage timing and romantic love. Indeed, she finds that resistance to legalization through marriage persists among undocumented young adults who have entered with inspection and have relatively straightforward pathways to permanent residency.[25]

Despite their resistance to legalizing through marriage, immigration law intimately shapes undocumented young adults' early romantic choices. This occurs outside formal legal contexts and even when legalization options are murky at best. Enduring consequences ensue as they develop partner preferences and make decisions about pursuing romantic relationships. Even when they refuse to let their immigration status dictate with whom they will partner, marriage myths inch into their relationships as they attempt to prove that their relationships are for love, not papers. Slowly but surely, laws inform if and how undocumented young adults proclaim romantic love. These intimate transformations continue to emerge as family formation progresses, leading to additional enduring consequences.

3

"You Feel a Little Bit Less"

Gendered Illegality and Desirability When Dating

You feel like you're missing something, maybe not physically [unattractive], but unattractive as a person, I guess. . . . Just because of the [undocumented] situation that you're in, [it] makes you feel a little bit less.

—ENRIQUE ESCOBAR

Sitting in the same coffee shop where I interviewed him two years before, Enrique struggled to articulate why he felt like an undesirable partner. Initially, he replied, "My legal situation—I don't know." Laughing uncomfortably, he eventually concluded that his undocumented status made him "feel a little bit less." He had been with his partner, a second-generation citizen Latina, for almost four years. She had never said anything to make him feel "less," but he still internalized negative feelings about his undocumented status.

In his previous interview, Enrique shared that his undocumented status and economic struggles complicated the development of their relationship. Despite earning a mechanic's certificate at a local community college, he was repeatedly turned down for jobs because he lacked a valid Social Security number. Instead, he worked as a manager of a small tire shop, earning $1,800 a month. He remembered that the friend who introduced him to his partner dismissively said, "She is not going to like you because of your job. You *only* work at [a tire shop]. . . . You don't earn that much." On an early date he was pulled over by police and forced to reveal that he did not have a driver's license and was undocumented.

As their relationship progressed, they figured out ways to handle the barriers his undocumented status raised—she would drive, they would stay in if money was tight, they didn't travel outside Los Angeles. But concerns around his undocumented status haunted their relationship: "People think that I don't deserve her just because [of] my situation. . . . They say I won't be able to provide for her as other people can."

Receiving DACA a year before his second interview changed Enrique's feelings: "I guess it gives me some type of confidence. It gives me that boost." He had quickly capitalized on his newfound employment authorization and got a job at a national shipping chain, almost doubling his salary to $3,500 a month. Finally feeling economically stable, he proposed to his girlfriend. He credited this decision to receiving DACA: "I felt more [like] I would be able to take care of a family. Like being able to have more doors open to where I could get a better job and stuff like that. It made me feel more comfortable with making those types of decisions."

Like Enrique, most undocumented young adults negotiate multiple immigration status barriers as they date and make decisions about their relationships. Simultaneously, they face hegemonic gendered dating norms according to which men are expected to be providers and women dependent participants. Previous research by Joanna Dreby and Leah Schmalzbauer has established that dependent gender roles intersect with illegality's constraints to heighten first-generation undocumented women's dependence on their husbands, making them vulnerable to unequal relationship dynamics and even abuse.[1] I expand on this to trace how gendered illegality emerges early in relationships and evolves as they progress. Doing so reveals how gendered expectations also disrupt undocumented young men's family formation.

I focus here on how immigration status and gender jointly shape feelings about desirability, determine early dating activities, and can impede relationship advancement. Much of this revolves around the financial constraints produced by illegality and the nuance involved in negotiating the economic nature of men's provider expectations. These factors disproportionately disrupted men's dating experiences, increasing their risk of disengaging from family formation. In many cases, enduring consequences emerged as illegality pushed many men to stop dating, delay marriage, and/or feel inadequate. Receiving DACA eased dating, but few experienced the dramatic relationship impacts Enrique did, often because they had found ways to negotiate barriers or because the policy's timing did not align with their relationship trajectories. Overall, I demonstrate how enduring consequences emerge over the course of a relationship as couples attempt to align material barriers and gender ideologies to successfully establish, build, and solidify their romantic relationships.

FEELING UNDESIRABLE: GENDERED EXPECTATIONS

Most undocumented young adults and their citizen partners disregarded undocumented status and relied on romantic notions to explain their attraction to each other. They spoke primarily about personality, and to some extent physical characteristics, as markers of desirability. Many cited qualities like being "caring," "supportive," and "respectful." Like marriage myth counternarratives, this romantic framing de-emphasized the role of undocumented status. Yet immigration-related barriers reshaped undocumented men's ability to meet gendered expectations and present themselves as desirable partners.

Many undocumented young men recognized that structural barriers, particularly economic ones, could make them appear undesirable. Rafael Montelongo remembered how he avoided revealing his status to his citizen girlfriend for four months: "I was really scared, and I was thinking in my head, She might not want you just 'cause you don't have papers. She probably thinks you have no future with her. She would have to work a lot more than if she went with another person. She would have to sacrifice more of her time." Rafael's fiancée, Jimena Santiago, confirmed that these thoughts ran through her head: "I felt . . . like, I don't know if I wanna stay with this person. It's gonna be hard, and I'm not ready for hard. . . . But then as I . . . kept on dating him, I was like, Well, that doesn't really matter. . . . He's really what I was looking for." Drawing on romantic narratives and confident in her own ability to achieve upward mobility, Jimena set aside Rafael's limitations.

Most undocumented young adults and their partners professed egalitarian ideals while holding traditional gendered expectations. Explaining this discrepancy, scholar Kathleen Gerson finds that young men and women aspire to flexible and egalitarian partnerships, but structural barriers prompt diverging practices. While women fear dependence and thus develop self-reliant strategies, men develop a neotraditional stance: they continue to imagine themselves as the breadwinner. They welcome their partner's economic contributions but prioritize their own work and expect their partner to handle housework and childcare.[2] These discrepancies emerge early in relationships as young men and women maintain traditionally gendered dating scripts: men take an active role as they initiate and plan for the date, often pick up the woman, and pay for all or most of the date. Women are dependent participants at all stages as they are expected to react to men's advances.[3] A recent survey of 17,607 unmarried heterosexuals found that women pay for some of the date, but not as much as men; 39 percent of women wished men would reject their offers to pay, and 44 percent were bothered when men expected them to help pay.[4] These traditional gendered expectations are most salient at relationship turning points such as initial dates, becoming exclusive, and proposing marriage.[5]

Material barriers constrain men's ability to perceive themselves and be perceived as desirable partners if they cannot perform these expected gender roles.[6] Cultural norms are key modes of reproducing exclusion by fostering negative social judgment and internalized feelings of inadequacy.[7] In this case, they help turn the material constraints associated with illegality into socioemotional barriers to family formation. Gendered norms thus set the stage for undocumented young men and women to experience illegality differently as they build romantic relationships.

GENDERED BARRIERS: NEGOTIATING IMMIGRATION
STATUS WHEN DATING

Undocumented status may not be inherently undesirable, but it does create conditions that prevent positive self-presentation in relationships. Limited incomes and an inability to access a state-issued ID or driver's license constrain undocumented young adults' ability to participate in expected dating activities. These barriers emerge in gendered ways: women's gender expectations insulate them from having to negotiate most immigration status barriers, while men's expectations limit their ability to accommodate immigration-related constraints early in a relationship.

"I'm Broke": The Persistent Weight of Gendered Provider Expectations on Men

Low-income men of color often struggle to meet provider expectations and participate in family formation. Economic constraints, particularly unstable employment and unreliable earnings, undergird men's limited marriageability. Race compounds these concerns as men of color have declining job prospects and skyrocketing criminalization and incarceration rates.[8] Undocumented status further exacerbates these challenges by prohibiting access to formal employment, limiting them to low-income jobs with little opportunity for upward mobility despite education and training. They are effectively dependent on immigration policy changes to enable their economic mobility.

Although not representative, about three-quarters of the undocumented sample reported holding minimum-wage, service-sector jobs in restaurants, stores, and offices. Employed participants earned an average annual income of $15,936 and said they had little financial flexibility; this is consistent with working a little less than 40 hours a week and earning $8 an hour, then California's minimum wage.[9] Women, on average, earned about $1,000 less a year than men because they worked about five hours less a week and often held jobs that paid less than men with equivalent levels of education. Higher levels of education translated into modestly higher pay (see table 3.1). Despite earning more, men were much more likely to cite their limited income as a dating constraint.

"Maybe He Can't Provide": Feeling Undesirable.   Most undocumented men were concerned that their financial situations would signal their undesirability. Ivan Cardenas explained, "I have that fear that maybe she'll think less of me or in her head she'll think, Well, maybe he can't provide what I want in the long run." Working as a gardener severely limited his income to around $1,000 a month and kept him living with his parents. He feared that he would never be able to provide for a family, keeping him from becoming more serious with the woman he had been seeing for almost a year.

TABLE 3.1 Employed participants' average annual income, weekly hours worked, and hourly pay by gender and education level (2011–2012)

	Mean annual income ($)	Mean weekly hours worked	Mean estimated hourly wage ($)
All participants (n = 68)	15,936	36	8.90
By gender			
Men (n = 36)	16,467	38	8.51
Women (n = 32)	15,319	33	9.35
By education level			
High school diploma or less (n = 23)	15,188	41	7.39
Some college education (n = 10)	18,267	40	9.26
Currently enrolled (n = 23)	13,161	29	9.02
Bachelor's degree or higher (n = 12)	20,940	37	11.29
By gender and education level			
Men with a high school diploma or less (n = 12)	16,450	42	7.66
Women with a high school diploma or less (n = 11)	13,811	40	7.09
Men with some college education (n = 6)	17,600	42	8.38
Women with some college education (n = 4)	19,600	37	10.59
Men currently enrolled (n = 13)	15,738	32	9.55
Women currently enrolled (n = 10)	9,810	24	8.33
Men with a bachelor's degree or higher (n = 5)	17,040	41	7.98
Women with a bachelor's degree or higher (n = 7)	23,726	33	13.66

Note: Hours worked are reported only for participants who reported income. Hourly wage was estimated by dividing the annual income by 52 weeks and the number of hours worked per week. The sample size for income and hours worked per week is 67; one woman with some college education reported only an hourly wage.

Men also worried about how their lifestyle signaled economic instability. Josue Contreras-Ruiz, divorced and in his mid-20s, posited, "Living with my parents doesn't make me stable. So again they're look for a stable guy." Aaron Ortiz, married and in his early 30s, commented, "Confidence and cleanliness. Clean shoes is what kind of gets a girl. . . . If a guy has dirty shoes, it's like, no." I glanced at his gleaming white Nikes; they not only signaled economic stability—his ability to afford new ones—but also distanced him from his muddy work boots. His self-presentation became a way to reframe his desirability.

Alternatively, women did not believe that their income, job, or living situation contributed to their desirability. Claudia Arellano, a single college graduate making $1,600 a month as a waitress, explained, "[I'm doing] the online [dating] thing. . . . If a guy puts online [on his profile] like they work at a restaurant, it's like, Ahhh [warning sign]. But if a girl puts it, the guy doesn't even care. It's like, Oh, whatever, she's cute. . . . So I kind of feel like I can get away [with that] . . . a little bit more." Women did not mention their living situation, and only a few connected their limited income with an inability to conform to hegemonic beauty standards. For example, Juana Covarrubias, a single community college student who worked a few hours a week as a private tutor, noted that being unable "to buy whatever you want, like a new pair of shoes or certain clothes that you need, does affect how you see yourself. . . . You just have to wait for so long to get what you want."

Once in relationships, women continued to feel unhindered by their economic situations. Karen Rodriguez, who worked at a fast-food restaurant making $1,200 a month, explained that it was never an issue in her six-year relationship with a citizen because "he was the one that was going to provide." Dependent expectations ensured that most of the undocumented women I spoke to did not believe that their economic status impeded their desirability or long-term relationship viability.

"I Like to Pay": Pressure to Provide.   Men strove to perform their provider role early in relationships. "I gotta pay," Omar Valenzuela stated bluntly. "It's just that traditional mentality. It's up to the man to pay and the woman shouldn't pay. I think out of all times we went out, she paid once. 'Cause she didn't let me pay; she pulled her card quick." Male citizen partners, like Lucas Maldonado, professed these same expectations: "I'm very old fashioned, and I like to pay."

These convictions persist regardless of women's actual expectations. Most men strove to meet unquestioned provider expectations, attempting to lower costs instead of asking their partner to help. Many opted for conventional activities—dinner, drinks, or movies—but selected cheaper venues or went out less frequently. Ivan Cardenas shared, "If I get my paycheck and I already paid my bills and all I have left is $50, I'd rather tell her, 'Let's go out next week when I have more money.' Or I say, 'I can't go out. I'm busy.' Sometimes it's a bad feeling when you go out and you can't really buy everything you want."

Alternatively, some men identified unconventional dating activities that were free or low cost. Abel León elaborated, "You have to always think out of the box. . . . I was dating this young lady, and we went hiking. There's a waterfall in [the foothills] . . . so we went, and it was pretty good. In my backpack, I had a little bit of wine. . . . She was like, 'Wow, that's pretty cool!' [She] was very impressed. And I didn't spend a lot of money." Paco Barrera described taking dates to a local café that hosted free poetry events. This not only allowed him to sidestep his financial limitations, but it also made women "think you're all cultured and this cool guy." These alternative activities were particularly beneficial early on in relationships because they allowed men to portray themselves positively without breaking the bank.

Finally, some men strove to simply spend time together at no cost. Alejandro Torres, who had been dating his girlfriend for two years, explained, "When I don't have money, I just let her know: 'You know what, I don't have money right now.' . . . And we just stay home, watch a movie . . . or, I have guinea pigs. Sometimes we just play with them." He believed his partner was fine with this: "She's told me, 'OK, I understand because you're paying your school.'" When partners have already established interest, desirability becomes less tied to going out.[10] Such renegotiations allowed men to continue to spend time with their partners and advance their relationship without incurring significant costs.

Although the undocumented women I interviewed had lower or comparable incomes to the men, none discussed limited funds as a barrier to dating or developed parallel negotiation strategies. For some, like Patricia Santamaria, women's dependent positions erased financial concerns: "I'm a girl. I have no problem with a guy paying for everything. I would make him pay for everything." Others, like Lili Moreno, expressed more egalitarian gender roles: "In terms of who pays, we're pretty equal. Usually it's a trade, if someone pays one day, the other person pays the other day." Although egalitarianism increases the prospect that women's low income could limit dating, this did not occur, in part because their financial burden was halved. They also selectively adhered to their own egalitarian expectations—paying only when they could or covering the cheaper portion of the date—as men did not expect them to pay. Ultimately, women's dependent gender role created slight spaces of agency when dating in uncertain financial situations.

"You Wanna Have Your Own Place": Barriers to Building Intimacy.   As couples sought to solidify their relationships, earlier financial barriers transformed and new ones emerged. Many single or dating participants were living with their parents and siblings. This economic management strategy hampered their ability to build intimacy. Siblings Felipe and Lili Moreno separately explained that they both lived at home because they could not afford to live on their own and wanted to help their undocumented parents. Their three-bedroom house was cramped; Felipe and his two brothers shared a room while Lili slept in the living room since her bedroom had been rented out for extra income. Felipe felt this was "rough" on his sex life: "I can't take girls in there. Obviously, my girlfriend's been in my house. But in the six months, we've only had sex once." Many couples reported having sex less frequently than desired because they had to wait until their families were out.

Lili delved into how her lack of privacy limited intimacy with the man she was seeing: "Everything takes practice in terms of learning about each other; not only what will please us physically, but our emotions. Having that space to even have intimate conversations . . . to create a safe space for each other is important." Lili disentangled the physical and emotional role of sex in romantic relationships, noting how her living situation disrupted both. Research shows that both are important as sexual satisfaction significantly predicts emotional intimacy and mediates couples' assessment of relationship satisfaction.[11]

Most women did not believe this was an insurmountable barrier; several men, however, explained that being unable to provide an intimate space could highlight their inability to meet provider expectations. Although his previous girlfriend had her own apartment, Zen Cruz did not feel comfortable there: "As long as her roommate was home, we weren't gonna [have sex]. They each had their own room, but the walls are paper thin, and you don't wanna bring that ruckus to somebody else's house." These are concerns that any person may have, but Zen tied it to larger issues of desirability and financial stability: "It's a little emasculating. You wanna have your own place." Similarly, Chris Moreno, Felipe and Lili's brother, commented, "You don't want to be 28 and still living with your parents. How are you going to become a man and do your own thing?"

A common management strategy included finding spaces outside their homes, such as traveling or getting a hotel room locally. Chris joked, "That's why God invented hotels!" when asked if sharing a room with his two brothers limited his sex life. Indeed, Lili noted that she and her new boyfriend have "done a lot of getaways" so that they could have privacy. Receiving DACA and having a stable, salaried job ensured that she had the money and flexibility to do this. Low incomes, however, often limited this option. Josue Contreras-Ruiz reflected, "I do remember one time I hooked up with this girl. . . . I took her out, went to dinner, then went to a hotel. . . . [I spent] my lunch money for the week [on the room]. . . . So I had to resort to [eating] Cup O'Noodles and stuff like that."

Travel also represented an opportunity to build nonsexual intimacy. Diego Ibáñez detailed, "One of the things [I want] is to be with a partner that 10 years from now, you can say, 'Hey, remember when we were doing this? Remember when we were changing our tire for the first time?'" By providing an opportunity to spend quality time with a romantic partner, travel—even to nearby destinations—symbolized an opportunity to build memories and evaluate the relationship's viability: "You get a better idea of who your partner is and if you really want to be with your partner." Yet this opportunity is limited for undocumented young adults who cannot travel internationally and feel deportation risks when traveling domestically. Additionally, Diego pointed to the high expense, and Julio Medina invoked many undocumented immigrants' limited job flexibility: "I couldn't take a day off in order to go somewhere because that meant not getting paid that day." Julio joked that he barely had time to do our interview because of his long hours as a community organizer. While undocumented young women faced these same barriers, none mentioned them as relationship obstacles.

Driver's Licenses and ID Cards: Gendered Barriers to Going Out

At the time of my initial interviews, California, like most states, did not allow undocumented immigrants to obtain an identification card or driver's license—documents held by approximately 95 percent of the eligible population.[12] Most participants were driving unlicensed and using alternative forms of identification—*matrículas consulares* (identification cards issued by the consulate) or passports from their country of origin. This restricted dating activities as undocumented young adults tried to limit their driving and risked rejection when pursuing activities that required proof of age. These barriers emerged in gendered ways and were more likely to harm undocumented men's relationships.

"I Try to Avoid Driving": Men's Struggle without a Driver's License.   Both undocumented and citizen men and women ascribed to traditional dating norms for men. Gilbert Morales shared, "I don't like that [my dates would pick me up] because I feel like I should be the one. . . . My mom always taught me not to . . . [have] the lady doing everything." Many accepted this norm. Lili Moreno remembered that men automatically drove. "When I didn't have a car," she said, "I think the guys were the ones who supported me. Picking me up, taking me places and stuff like that." In most cases, women appreciated this dating script because it allowed them to avoid the risks of unlicensed driving without having to reveal their immigration status.

Faced with their own and their partner's gendered expectations, most undocumented men privately accommodated this barrier by driving without a license, subjecting themselves to financially and physically risky situations. Omar Valenzuela recounted,

> [My girlfriend's] like, "I don't know where you're taking me, so you drive." It's kind of like the man's role. . . . It does come up [that it's risky]. Especially after . . . I got pulled over. . . . That's why I try to avoid driving. But then when you're with somebody [and] crazy about them, a fear of status, everything, goes out the window.

Performing his role, Omar was pulled over and given a $1,000 ticket for driving without a license. This could have been even more expensive if his car had been towed and subject to thousands of dollars in impound fees.[13] These tickets and fines are deep economic risks for undocumented young adults. Further, potential collaboration between local police and immigration agents raises the threat of deportation in these instances.[14] Even though Omar had a citizen girlfriend who was licensed and knew about his immigration status, unquestioned gender roles led him and many undocumented men to risk driving without a license.

Some undocumented men attempted to avoid these risks by asking their citizen partners to drive. Zen Cruz, a single man in his late 20s, explained that he asked his dates to pick him up, but "I try to do the most for them too. I fill up their [gas] tank. I pay when we go eat. . . . Let's get drinks; I'll pay for the drinks. Let's go to the movies; I'll pay for the movies. . . . So I kinda make up for that." These strategies do not appear to disrupt desirability when men still perform some traditional gender roles and citizen women partners can frame driving as doing their share. They can, however, generate conflict in some mixed-status relationships when women resist renegotiating gender roles. Cruz Vargas described his citizen girlfriend's reaction: "I don't wanna feel like this [insecure and unsafe] every day.

[I tell her,] 'You can drive. You can actually legally drive. So why don't you just drive.' She's like, 'Oh. Well, I'm tired. I don't wanna drive.' So I'll drive." Though she would sometimes drive, Cruz was frequently unable to avoid risk-taking.

A few undocumented men refused to take these risks and found that this made them look undesirable, especially when their partner was not licensed or did not have a car. Erick Godinez explained, "[Girls,] they ask me, 'Why don't you get a car?' They know I could get a car, but I don't want to do it because I don't want to risk it. . . . They get tired of going in a taxi or a bus." The normalization of unlicensed driving made it difficult for him to convincingly avoid driving; he believed his choice pushed several women to break up with him. Thus, gendered expectations force undocumented men to choose between the risk of driving without a license or sacrificing a potential relationship, especially in sprawling urban spaces like Southern California or rural areas where driving is necessary.[15] Living in cities with normalized use of public transportation might increase undocumented young adults' flexibility to (re)negotiate these expectations.

Depending on a partner for rides can insulate undocumented young adults from deportation risks, but it may create other risky situations. Although no women spoke about this, Alonso Guerra, a single gay man, explained,

> When I was living with my family, my sex life was mostly anybody who was willing to pick me up and take me to their place. . . . It also gave them the wheel in the relationship, or the encounter. Where I couldn't really displease them because then I'd be stranded somewhere. . . . It just gave them the power, and that's always very dangerous or unpleasant at times.

No other participants spoke about experiencing coercion related to their inability to drive. But women's higher likelihood of being in a dependent situation increases the possibility that they may encounter such risks.

"Are They Going to Take My Passport?": Women's Struggle without a State-Issued ID.   Not having state-issued identification, either in the form of a driver's license or a California ID card, limited undocumented young adults' participation in age-restricted activities, such as entering clubs and bars, or purchasing alcohol. Alma Molina recounted a recent experience when out with her boyfriend:

> We went to a Buffalo Wild Wings, and they didn't accept my passport [to order] a drink. And we just got up and left. . . . I was like, How is it possible that I go through TSA [airport security] and they have no questions, and you can't even give me a drink because you think my ID is fake?

Such denials were common for those who used *matrículas,* but foreign passports were usually accepted because of the stringent security measures used to prevent counterfeiting. While Alma tried to brush this off as "not a big deal," it clearly disrupted their date and determined their future activity choices.

Men face less risk of being denied access; their active dating scripts enable them to select activities and establishments, allowing them to somewhat manage their lack of state-issued ID. Cruz Vargas detailed how he navigated this: "I'm very good with words, so I'd just work my way around it. . . . Let's say some girl wanted to go somewhere. I'll just be like, 'I heard the place is wack. . . . I know a better place.' . . . And then I'll just convince them . . . [to go where] I know I can go." Cruz, like most men, embraced his gendered role as courter, and used this as a source of agency to privately manage his lack of a California ID.

Alternatively, women's dependent gender roles disempowered them by fostering situations in which they risked being denied access or outed as undocumented. Julieta Castillo described her anxieties when preparing for a date:

> Are they [venue staff] going to take my passport? Are they going to give me crap about it? . . . [Will they] go through it and see if there is a visa or not? Sometimes they'll be assholes. . . . And then there's times they'll be nice and . . . it will be fine. But it's an anxiety. . . . The embarrassment it's going to cost because they are going to put you on blast. Or how are you going to explain, "Oh wait, I can't go in." [Or being asked,] "Why don't you have a California ID?" So I hate it! I hate it!

Like Julieta, most women reported anxiety about being unable to participate in the activity their partner planned. Even when a non-California ID was accepted, it raised questions that required them to either reveal their undocumented status or lie. Neither is preferable when trying to develop a relationship.

Often, women developed strategies to avoid rejection. Julieta recalled, "If I didn't know the place or if I heard of other people that they can't get in, then I would just avoid it." Tanya Diaz explained, "Sometimes I'd be like, 'Oh, I'll meet you there.' 'Cause I didn't want to go there and have to show my ID [in front of my date]." Other women suggested alternative activities. Unlike men who could simply plan activities that avoided risk of rejection, women had to negotiate their lack of a state-issued ID in public, and this was not guaranteed to work.

Despite their anxieties, none of the women I interviewed reported being rejected by a partner when they were denied entrance or made to reveal their undocumented status. Mercedes Valdez recounted when her ID was rejected on her first date with a citizen man:

> We wanted to go out to a bar . . . and it was a cool place he had been to, and he wanted to show me the place. But I got denied because of my matrícula. . . . And I was like, "Welcome to my world." . . . I think it showed a lot about him too, though, [that] even though I got denied, he was like, "Well, let's go somewhere else." . . . I think that's what made me get more attracted to him.

Though embarrassed, Mercedes found that his supportive reaction strengthened her attraction. Indeed, Dante Chavez, a citizen partner, recalled a similar incident in which his undocumented partner was carded. When asked how he felt about her ID being rejected, he was adamant—"I don't care." Although women are denied entrance and feel stigmatized, most of their partners do not see this as a testament to their undesirability. Ultimately, not having an ID was significantly less consequential when establishing a relationship, especially when compared to the fallout of men's unmet driving expectations.

STRIKING EVEN: RENEGOTIATING GENDER EXPECTATIONS IN LIGHT OF IMMIGRATION STATUS

Despite early potential pitfalls, most undocumented participants had been able to establish a committed romantic relationship, at the time of their interview or in the past. Doing so required that the couple continually accommodate the tension between gender expectations and illegality. For some men, this meant simply performing provider roles, regardless of the risk. But most men and women relied on romantic notions that partners should support each other, which included helping manage immigration-related constraints. Alma Molina, who has been dating her boyfriend for eight years, and Zen Cruz, who was single but dated frequently, explained:

> Alma: I think if the person really wants to date you . . . if that person really cares about you, they're gonna be willing to drive for you, or pay for you, or whatever.
>
> Zen: I'm thinking—if they really like me for me, they wouldn't have a problem driving in the first place anyway.

In many cases, partners helped—paying for dates, driving, making concessions about activities. This happened relatively seamlessly in relationships between undocumented women and citizen men as immigration status did not disrupt the performance of gendered expectations in these cases. Yet relationships between undocumented men and citizen women or between two undocumented partners required the active accommodation of immigration status limitations, since both had to align dating roles with gender ideologies. If these could not be reconciled, conflict emerged.

Mixed-status couples accommodated reversed gender roles, minimizing potential conflict by developing *strategic gender egalitarianism*. They adapted their dating scripts to fit the limitations posed by undocumented status, giving the illusion of an egalitarian relationship without changing underlying gender ideologies.[16] In most instances, this negotiation happened smoothly when citizen women, like Jimena Santiago, recognized it as the rational option: "If we get pulled over, I'm gonna feel bad because I have a license and I'm not the one driving." Like other citizen women, she imagined this renegotiation as doing her share: "When we would go out, I would usually drive and he would pay. Or sometimes if he would drive, I would pay. So we always had it kind of even." Their arrangement was purely strategic, as she explained: "Before [DACA], I would help him more because I knew that he was limited." His receiving DACA enabled them to revert to more traditional roles: "Now [with DACA] it's more that he pays most of the time 'cause he's able to afford it more. . . . Now it's more on him." Those couples who seek to be strategic about the benefits and drawbacks of their various immigration statuses often developed more egalitarian practices to manage illegality; however, underlying gender norms remained as men anticipated and desired to return to their provider role when their legal and/or financial situations changed.

Couples composed of two undocumented partners similarly practiced strategic gender egalitarianism to manage their shared limitations. Marina Balderas shared how she and her boyfriend Omar Valenzuela, both DACA recipients, shifted to more egalitarian dating practices: "At the beginning, he would pay for mostly everything, but then when I started working at the hospital [as a nursing assistant] . . . his job was really slow. So then I started paying for a lot of stuff. So we would kind of do it together. . . . If he has it, he pays, and if I have it, I pay." This shift required their open negotiation of traditional gender norms:

> He was like, "I feel like I'm always paying. . . . I don't feel support when I don't have a job." . . . And for me, I was like, A guy's supposed to pay. [But] he's . . . like, "I see you like my partner. I don't see you like my girlfriend." . . . So it did change. I was like, Oh, damn. And then I started paying for a lot of stuff. And then now he tells me, "I feel like you're always paying." I'm like, Oh my god.

Omar reflected on their current arrangement:

> It's tricky because in our culture, it's like, if you can't provide, you're not a man, you know? Right now, I'm kinda struggling with that because before when we were busy at work, it was like every weekend we would go out, like restaurants, movies, anywhere. . . . It was never like, Oh, I didn't have money this weekend. And, like, this whole month, it's been like that. It kinda sucks 'cause it's out of my control, but she's working, so she pays.

He framed this arrangement as temporary and anticipated making up for it when his new job at an upscale restaurant would start to give him more hours: "[Then] it's whatever she wants, new watch, new bag, new whatever, no problem." Marina and Omar's case suggests that strategic gender egalitarianism may be effective in avoiding external and internal conflict over an inability to perform traditional roles. It enables undocumented men to draw on egalitarian notions to see themselves as progressive partners, rather than as undesirable men who cannot fully provide.

Many undocumented men struggled to accept strategic renegotiations because it made them feel dependent. David Soto passionately recounted a fight he had with an ex-boyfriend:

> We got in a fight at Taco Bell, and I was like, "No! I will buy my own Taco Bell!" . . . But he was like, "Don't worry about it. You only have $20. Save your money. I will pay for it." But he was [always] paying for everything, [and] I was like, "No! No, I can pay for it! I have money!" And that was me, the undocumented David, saying, I can provide for myself.

David recognized that paying for tacos was his partner's way of sympathizing. Still, he struggled to accept his help after years of feeling infantilized and dependent because of his undocumented status. Iliana Guzman recognized that negotiating gender roles may be logical, but it is often hard for men to accept. She recounted how her ex-partner, who was also undocumented, struggled with the logic that Iliana should drive because she held a valid out-of-state driver's license. They argued regularly because she believed he was trying to assert his independence by driving.

In a few cases, undocumented women struggled to accept help because it required them to renegotiate their own gender ideologies, which prioritized independence. Research suggests that most young women fear being dependent on their partner.[17] These aspirations made it difficult for them to allow a citizen partner to help. While this did not have significant consequences for their early relationships, it could infuse stress into a relationship, as I show in the next chapter.

Citizen women also grappled with renegotiating gender ideologies, especially when they felt it extended past egalitarianism to place disproportional responsibility on them. Isabel Montoya, the citizen wife of an undocumented man pursuing legalization, remembered how she began to pay after they finished high school: "I was able to get my first job, and he really couldn't. So that's when I started having to be the one to pay for everything." She was the first to buy a car, leading her to "always be the one driving." She admitted, "There would be some times where I would get really angry about it. Like, I knew I shouldn't, but it would get frustrating." She would fantasize that "it'd be nice to be driven around once in a while" or wonder what it would be like if "my boyfriend had money to take me out when I'm broke." In part, Isabel's willingness to revise dating scripts stemmed from her desire to develop a more egalitarian relationship, but her frustration emerged from consistently doing most of the work.

Women who found themselves doing a disproportionate amount of relationship work were faced with a critical question: Do I stay or do I go? Isabel poured a lot of energy into helping mediate her partner's undocumented status. Had this ever made her think she should not be with him? She admitted, "Honestly, yes. That did cross my mind." She ultimately decided to stay and framed the relationship as egalitarian because she expected that he would resume his provider role as soon as they legalized his status. Her actions reflect those Joanna Dreby documents among first-generation, mixed-status couples; she finds that many citizen women accept the extra responsibilities of mediating illegality for undocumented men. This creates a triple burden because they also continue to do gendered household labor to protect their partner's masculinity.[18]

Some citizens, however, chose to break up with their undocumented partner when they decided that taking on these roles was incompatible with their expectations. Daniel Hernandez described how he understood his ex-girlfriend's decision:

> She finished school, even grad school too. . . . [She] had her stuff together. And I was still in [community college] . . . working part-time [at a fast-food restaurant],

going to school full-time. The whole me-not-being-independent thing just started becoming too much for her. 'Cause she's the one driving everywhere, and I didn't even know how to drive. . . . [She's] like, "I'm investing more time in this than you are and sometimes more money." 'Cause I'd be like, "Hey, I don't have money right now." . . . I think she realized that she might end up having to support me in some way while I finish school. . . . So she's like, "No, it's over."

Focusing on all the relationship work she did, Daniel's partner was unable to reconcile their relationship with her own expectations. Seeing no end in sight, she marked Daniel as undesirable and broke up with him.

ENDURING CONSEQUENCES: MEN'S DISRUPTED FAMILY FORMATION

Despite strategic renegotiations, exclusionary dating experiences often piled up as relationships progressed. Scholar Kathleen Gerson finds that low-income men of color are the most likely to opt out of family formation, staying single because of their economic uncertainty.[19] Indeed, financial concerns and men's inability to meet economic-provider expectations undergird men and women's desires to put off marriage.[20] Undocumented status further confounds these challenges by making economic mobility unlikely. Thus, some undocumented young men stopped dating when they repeatedly came up against barriers related to their immigration status, resulting in their rejection. Others successfully negotiated illegality in early relationships but then delayed marriage or struggled to feel like good husbands because of heightened provider expectations.

"I've Been through Hell": Giving Up on Love

Some men reported that they avoided dating after repeated rejection for immigration-related issues. After being dumped, Daniel avoided dating for over two years. Jesus Perez suggested that this avoidance can be unintentional, emerging when men do not have the financial stability to consistently pay for dates: "It makes me afraid. . . . Let's say my [hypothetical] partner wants to go out, and she asks me to go out. I don't want to say, 'I don't have any money.' [It] makes me embarrassed, I guess. I want to be the one in power." Jesus noted that he had not been on a date in two years as he waited to be able to meet his own, and his potential partner's, financial expectations. He suggested that this was unique to undocumented young adults because citizen men can "use their credit cards" to make ends meet. Still others, like Abel León, elected to date casually and not "take it so seriously . . . [because] I don't feel confident enough. Especially because of money." As undocumented men date, smaller incidents and negative feelings accumulate to discourage their serious pursuit of long-term partnerships. This is consistent with other research findings that men's sense of prestige, self-worth, and romantic desirability is tied to their earnings and work.[21]

Undocumented status compounds these concerns when it presents seemingly insurmountable barriers that lead some men to internalize their undesirability after repeated rejection. This was particularly common when they were unable to meet their own and their partner's gendered expectations. Leo Campos explained that he frequently felt "less than" when dating:

> *Leo:* Usually they drove. But then, I didn't feel like . . . I don't know if that's the machismo part of me—I would be like, "No, no, I'll meet you there." I'll freaking take the bus, I'll walk, because I didn't feel comfortable.
>
> *Laura:* Having them pick you up?
>
> *Leo:* Yeah, I just didn't. It was like, even though I'm not a machismo-type guy, I just felt like that's something that the guy's supposed to do. . . . I would never let them pay. I'm not the type that will let the girl pay. I'm paying for everything. . . .
>
> *Laura:* So you would meet them there and then—
>
> *Leo:* No, most of the time I'd just break down. "OK, pick me up." . . . But then I'd be sitting in the car all depressed, and they'd be like, "Why do you not want to come out with me?"

Although women were willing to help out by driving or paying their share, Leo was unwilling to renegotiate his expectations to match his limited employment at a fast-food restaurant and fear of driving without a license. Further, recognizing his future inability to provide, he rationalized that he was inherently undesirable: "I don't want to hold her back. So I rather be by myself. If I'm gonna have this crappy life, then I rather just be doing it myself going through it and not bring somebody else down with me."

Leo eventually stopped dating after he was repeatedly broken up with because of his immigration status. Unlike most participants who perked up with interest when I moved interviews toward discussions of dating, Leo simply replied, "nonexistent."

> I don't call them dates because the minute we went out . . . the minute they found out my situation, it's like, "Oh, I never liked you." So if they never liked me, then it wasn't a date. . . . Even though we might have made out, but apparently you don't like me. Apparently you never liked me, my mistake. . . . [I've stopped dating] because it wasn't just one or two girls. . . . If I would count between the time I was 18 to like now [that I'm 27], like 20 to 25 girls have rejected me like that.

Recounting a few dates in detail, Leo clarified that he and his prospective partners struggled to accept how his status would limit both dating activities and their potential future. He blamed his prospective partners, but these negative experiences were likely exacerbated by his own resistance to renegotiating gender roles.

Internalizing this repeated rejection, Leo was one of the few respondents who believed that he would never establish a permanent partnership:

> I'm less and less open to it [a relationship] because I've been through hell and back, so I don't want to go through it. I don't want to emotionally invest in someone and have it be the same outcome that I've known for years. It's kind of hard. If you keep touching the stove and you keep getting burned, eventually you'll be like, "Hey, I'm not gonna do that again."

Indeed, two years later, at his second interview, he still had not dated anyone. He had even rejected a few women. He worried that "since my life is kind of in limbo," even after receiving DACA, that he didn't want to put himself in a provider position.

Leo's experiences are not representative, though. Many men renegotiated their gender expectations and found women who supported this. However, his story demonstrates the cumulative effect that gendered expectations and immigration status barriers can have on relationships. Repeated or extremely painful rejections can have long-term consequences as undocumented young adults internalize these experiences and abandon attempts to build permanent, loving relationships.

"It Kind of Holds You Back": Feeling Unprepared and Avoiding Marriage

Many men successfully dated only to find that gendered expectations reemerged as a problem when they considered marriage. Joaquin Salas, who was single and almost 30, explained,

> You tend to think a little bit about what you have to offer to that person. And obviously that becomes a little worrying in your mind when you're not here legally. It kind of holds you back a little from actually getting married or something. You think that . . . you're not a legal person and you won't be able to offer good things to that other person, like stability or a house.

Although many men negotiated financial barriers effectively while dating, their established strategies—canceling a date or finding a cheaper option—do not transfer to fulfilling breadwinner expectations. Although most women expected and desired to work, men did not consider this when weighing whether they could sustain a family after marriage.

Women, though, insisted that their financial situations would not affect their marriage decisions. Most women held gendered expectations that they would be financially (inter)dependent on their husbands, either contributing to the household income or being stay-at-home wives and mothers. Yet, Tanya Diaz was one of the few who believed that her immigration status and its financial limitations could cause marital tensions: "I'm going to be a financial struggle to them if my car gets taken away." Earning $1,200 a month as an office assistant, she worried that she couldn't "contribute as much." Despite this, she had not considered delaying marriage, in part because her dependent role did not require her to alleviate the financial burdens her status might place on her partner.

Rafael Montelongo provided a clear example of how immigration status, particularly economic barriers, affect marriage decisions. In our first interview, he shared that he avoids talking with his citizen girlfriend about marriage. He noted that this is mostly because she has high expectations: "She wants me to take her from her dad['s house] to [our] house. I don't even have a house! She wants me to buy all the furniture and all that stuff. In my head, I'm just seeing that as pretty much impossible right now. I can barely afford to live by myself [in a rented room] and pay for school." Rafael's two part-time jobs at fast-food restaurants did not allow him to meet her or his own provider expectations on the $1,200 he earned a month. "In the future, if I have a job as an engineer, maybe. But I don't know, that's in the future."

Postponing this decision was straining their three-and-a-half-year relationship. "She gets impatient," he noted, when he tried to talk to her about the pressure he felt:

> *Rafael:* She says dumb stuff, like "I should look for another boyfriend." I'm like, "Fine, you should." But we go back, just little fights here and there.
>
> *Laura:* Do you ever think that maybe she will go find somebody else?
>
> *Rafael:* Like, in my head, I don't mind. Just 'cause if it makes you happy, why not. But I think if I wait too much [longer], I think she will [leave].

He got her to agree to put off marriage discussions until they finished college the next year. He worried, "Even by then, I don't think I'm gonna have enough money to even get married." In many cases, immigration status barriers and gendered expectations led undocumented men to delay marriage. This endangered their long-term romantic relationships.

"I Haven't Felt like a 100 Percent Husband": Struggling to Meet Provider Expectations

Some undocumented men had married despite their status. Buffered by romantic feelings that it was "time" to marry, they set aside their fears that they could not meet the intensified provider expectations that awaited them as husbands. Tomás Fernandez proposed to his wife in their early 20s after they had been friends for a year and dated for another year. He proposed because he felt it was "the right time." He remembered that they had "the same goals" and wanted to "start striving and working together to reach those goals together." Yet he did not feel as if he were ready to become a husband: "Not a hundred percent ready" because of "the economics part. There's going to be things you're not going to be able to provide. But at the same time, you know that if you keep working hard, that it is going to happen." Specifically, he felt "stuck" in his job as a low-level manager at a fast-food restaurant and worried that he was not making enough to build a stable home.

Despite trying to ignore it, Tomás's low socioeconomic status plagued their relationship. He reflected on the issues that led to their separation after six years: "Some of the things she would say was the economics. That she wouldn't see any movement. She would see we were stuck in the same place. And she would give up.... I used to work crappy hours. And I wouldn't make enough." In these cases, husbands' intensified provider expectations did not prevent marriage, but they did feed conflict.

Like Tomás, Aaron Ortiz did not let his inability to provide discourage his decision to marry. Though he saw no threat of separation, his low income made him doubt his performance as a husband:

> *Aaron:* There's some things that I'm missing. . . . I haven't felt like
> a 100 percent husband because there's certain things I can't
> provide yet.
> *Interviewer:* Like what?
> *Aaron:* Like a home. Like fun stuff.

Unable to obtain DACA, Aaron continued to work as a landscaper earning $2,600 a month. He wrestled with the idea that he, his wife, and their daughter continued to share a bedroom in a house they shared with family members. He also aspired to buy an RV so that they could go camping together and have other family adventures. "There's a lot of things," he lamented, "that I'm missing to become that person."

"IT'S EASIER": DACA FACILITATES MEN'S RELATIONSHIP TRANSITIONS

DACA transformed illegality as recipients obtained work permits and benefits like state-issued driver's licenses and ID cards. David Soto explained how this removed barriers to family formation:

> I can talk about where I work. I can pay for dinner. I can buy a drink without having to worry about taking out my matrícula. . . . I can drive. I can drop [them] off. . . . The biggest shift is I don't have to immediately divulge that I am undocumented. Because when I am paying for that bill or when I am taking out my California ID or when I am picking you up, none of that [undocumented status] is going to be obvious to you.

The employed DACA recipients I interviewed reported substantial changes in their economic situations, as their average income increased by almost $500 a month, reaching $21,900 annually. This is because they averaged working three hours more a week and earning $2.78 more an hour. The wage gap between men and women increased as men saw greater changes, earning on average $6,442 more a year than women because they worked an average of nine hours more a week and often held

TABLE 3.2 Employed DACA recipients' average annual income, weekly hours worked, and hourly pay by gender and education level (2014–2015)

	Mean annual income ($)		Mean weekly hours worked		Mean estimated hourly wage ($)	
	With DACA	Amount changed compared to 2011–2012 data	With DACA	Amount changed compared to 2011–2012 data	With DACA	Amount changed compared to 2011–2012 data
All participants (n = 59)	21,900	5,964	39	3	11.68	2.78
By gender						
Men (n = 33)	24,739	8,272	43	5	12.31	3.80
Women (n = 26)	18,297	2,978	34	1	10.93	1.58
By education level						
High school diploma or less (n = 11)	22,233	7,045	45	4	10.36	2.97
Some college education (n = 20)	22,037	3,770	39	–1	12.40	3.14
Currently enrolled (n = 13)	16,187	3,026	35	6	9.02	0
Bachelor's degree or higher (n = 15)	26,427	5,487	38	1	13.91	2.62
By gender and education level						
Men with a high school diploma or less (n = 6)	25,800	9,350	51	9	11.60	3.94
Women with a high school diploma or less (n = 5)	17,952	4,141	38	–2	9.12	2.03
Men with some college education (n = 12)	25,900	8,300	42	0	12.66	4.28
Women with some college education (n = 8)	16,241	–3,359	32	0	11.98	1.39
Men currently enrolled (n = 6)	18,600	2,862	45	13	9.25	–0.30
Women currently enrolled (n = 7)	14,119	4,309	29	5	8.87	0.54
Men with a bachelor's degree or higher (n = 9)	26,578	9,538	39	–2	14.00	6.12
Women with a bachelor's degree or higher (n = 6)	26,200	2,474	37	4	13.78	0.12

Note: For 2014–15 data, hours worked are reported only for participants who reported income. Hourly wage was estimated by dividing the annual income by 52 weeks and the number of hours worked per week. The sample size for hours worked per week is 49; one or two people within seven of the gender and educational-level categories did not report hours worked. The sample size for average hourly wage is 50; one woman with some college education reported an hourly wage in addition to her income. Amount increased was calculated based on data reported in table 3.1.

jobs that paid more than women with equivalent levels of education. Higher levels of education translated into higher pay with relatively similar improvements in hourly wage, with the exception of those in college who continued to earn around minimum wage (see table 3.2). Out of every five DACA recipients, approximately two reported working in the same or a similar type of job, one moved to a self-described "better" job usually within the service sector, one entered professional employment, and one forwent employment to pursue educational opportunities. About three-quarters obtained a driver's license, and all the others had a California ID card or were in the process of applying for a license. Although DACA lessened illegality's everyday consequences, its impact on family formation varied based on where participants were in their relationships and the extent to which gendered illegality had already determined their relationship trajectories.

Men were most likely to experience markedly transformed relationship trajectories if they received DACA at a critical transition point in their relationship, allowing them to meet gendered expectations. As Rafael described earlier, pressure to marry could endanger long-term romantic relationships when men sought to delay marriage until they could meet provider expectations. In Rafael's case, I left our first interview suspecting that his relationship was doomed. Two years later, he happily shared that their wedding was a month away.

Rafael was granted DACA about a year after our first interview. While finishing up his bachelor's degree, he found stable employment as an engineer making $3,200 a month, almost triple what he had made working in fast food. Soon after this, he proposed. His fiancée reflected, "I'm literally thankful because of the DACA, or else he wouldn't have a job right now. We wouldn't be able to get married. That would have delayed a lot of things. 'Cause we wanted to get married since a long time ago. But we were like, We don't have the money for that. You don't have a job and [are] not stable." Rafael also suggested that DACA made him feel confident advancing their relationship: "With DACA . . . I am going to be able to provide income that is sufficient enough for both of us, and her not [to] work." He looked forward to becoming the breadwinner when she returned to school for her master's degree.

Rafael and Enrique (in the introduction of this chapter) were the only two participants who reported that DACA dramatically shifted their ability to transition into marriage. It brought financial stability that allowed them to continue the family formation process because they could meet their own and their partner's expectations. If it had not been implemented when it was, their relationships would likely have floundered.

A few single undocumented men experienced substantial changes in their family formation trajectories because DACA inspired significant life changes that helped combat their underlying feelings of undesirability. Felipe Moreno reported persistent singlehood and long-term unemployment in his first interview. After obtaining DACA protections, he used his work permit to find employment as a car salesman earning approximately $3,000 a month, obtain a driver's license, and purchase a car. Receiving DACA changed how he felt about himself as a potential romantic partner:

> Back in the day [before DACA], [I felt] a little bit [bad]. Like, I'm not going to be able to do this or that. Or I'm not going to be able to have a better-paying job. But now [with DACA], I think it's more understandable. . . . [A girl] wouldn't trip out so hard. If I just tell her I have nothing, [she'd say,] "Oh shit, nah, I can't do that." [But] now I can work, I can drive. . . . A partner would be more like, OK, [that's] not too bad.

Felipe and a few of the other men who had internalized their undesirability found that DACA improved their ability to date. Indeed, Felipe felt that potential partners would no longer see his status as "an uphill battle." These types of transformational impacts were most common among those who struggled significantly to meet gendered expectations and thus had avoided dating. Their newfound stability made them feel like more desirable partners, and DACA emerged early enough in their romantic lives that they had not yet given up on finding a partner.

Unlike Felipe, most single undocumented young men or those in emerging relationships felt that DACA did not necessarily redirect their family formation trajectories. They had already found ways to negotiate illegality when dating so that DACA mostly expanded potential dating activities and fostered more enjoyable experiences. Obtaining a work permit allowed Alonso Guerra to move from being an unemployed college graduate to having two part-time jobs. This improved his romantic relationship: "I had a lot more income. . . . We didn't have to go eat dollar tacos every time [we went out]. We could go to different places. We could go to museums. We could go do a lot more fun things." DACA's employment authorization created financial flexibility that allowed many men to afford higher-quality dates. Cameron Peña further explained that his newly issued driver's license opened some new doors and made dating smoother, but it did not necessarily transform what he could do because most bars accepted foreign passports. Josue Contreras-Ruiz spoke about having "more freedom" and feeling comfortable driving his girlfriend over 50 miles to visit her family: "Before, I wouldn't drive that much because I didn't have a license. The less you drive, the less you are likely to get pulled over." Francisco Garza reflected on how his sex life suffered before DACA because he worked as a manager at a pizza place where he was on his feet, rushing against the clock to fill orders:

> I would just be working, working. [I'd] just want to go home and pass out and knock out. And even when I was with my girlfriend in college, there was times when she wanted to have sex and I'm too tired. . . . [I'd go to clubs and] my friend would say, "Those are two hot girls. Let's go talk to them." So I'd be like, "All right, let's go." I wasn't so excited about going. . . . My legs were hurting, I didn't shower. I was like, Ugh.

Obtaining a work permit through DACA allowed him to start an office job that left him with more energy: "I have more time. I'm not stressed. . . . I have more energy. I perform pretty good [sexually]." In all these examples, DACA made dating easier but did not transform relationship trajectories because these men had already established ways to negotiate illegality.

In some cases, DACA's impact on relationships was minimal because economic benefits did not materialize. A few of the men who received DACA experienced only small changes to their employment opportunities and so still faced financial barriers. In other cases, newfound employment opportunities simultaneously translated into new responsibilities and commitments that could detract from relationship building. Before DACA, Zen Cruz had started a fledgling computer repair and web design business, and with it he accepted part-time office employment making $1,800 a month. He explained how DACA shifted his dating: "I kinda put that in the background. So I'm more interested in trying to make the best of it . . . trying to use my work permit, work as much as possible, save as much as possible, and try not to get into too much debt." In these cases, undocumented young adults struggled to balance pursuing newly available education and employment opportunities with their romantic relationships.

No women reported that receiving DACA transformed their relationship trajectories or dating participation, likely because their dependent gendered roles often insulated them from facing related barriers. They largely categorized DACA's impact as making dating easier. Sarai Bedolla remarked that having a driver's license reduced the risk of stigmatization: "You don't have to pull out your one-foot [long] passport out of your pocket. . . . You realize how much easier it makes your life." These changes were emotionally significant because they felt more normal and did not have to think about their immigration status when going out; they did not, however, have material consequences for women's ability to date or advance relationships.

Notably, many of the men who had already established committed relationships or married found that DACA's changes came too late. Immigration status barriers had already shaped their relationship experiences and choices. DACA only had the power to prevent damage before it occurred. Timing was key.

CONCLUSION

Undocumented young adults' dating experiences mirror those of their low-income, racial-minority peers who also face material constraints. Their immigration status, however, uniquely governs the production of these barriers and ensures that economic mobility is not forthcoming without legal intervention. Most can manage these barriers and establish romantic relationships. Still, illegality and hegemonic gendered expectations collide, turning material constraints into socioemotional barriers by making them feel undesirable and forcing them to alter their dating activities and relationship decisions to match their material realities. This has fewer lasting consequences for undocumented women than men, as these barriers align with gendered expectations. Barriers accumulate for undocumented men as they make concessions to meet, reimagine, or renegotiate such expectations. In many cases, enduring consequences emerge over time as men experienced repeated rejection, delayed marriage, or were haunted by their inability to perform provider roles.

I shed new light on marginalized men's family formation process by showing that men can potentially manage their economic constraints by renegotiating gendered expectations with their partners. Indeed, committed citizen partners helped mediate barriers and adjusted their expectations accordingly. These relationships, however, remain on rocky ground, since renegotiating gender ideology is a difficult and ongoing task for both partners. These early experiences alerted couples to the potential struggles they will face if they commit to building a family together—economic instability, spatial immobility, and complicated power dynamics. I turn to these negotiations in the next chapter.

"It Affects Us, Our Future"

Negotiating Illegality as a Mixed-Status Couple

[Immigration policy] does affect us in the sense [that it affects] his own opportunities and his limitations on how much he can and can't do to, not just provide for the relationship, but just provide for himself . . . his own goals. How fast can he get there or how much access he has to the things he needs to get there.

—XOCHITL LAZO

Reflecting on her two-and-a-half-year relationship, Xochitl conceded that her partner Chuy Soto's undocumented status affected her. It didn't worry her when they began dating, but she "knew there was going to be struggles if in the future we stayed together and we pursued something more serious." Sitting in Chuy's rented storefront on a busy boulevard, she recounted how he had closed down his shop because of financial difficulties. She suffered when this also forced them to move out of their shared apartment and back in with their respective parents. Before he obtained a driver's license, she drove, "making sure our lights were on and things were safe" to avoid the police. She speculated about the possibility of legalizing his status through marriage and resented that the law could take control of their relationship in this way. Although Chuy had received DACA by the time we spoke, Xochitl feared that he could lose the employment authorization and deportation protection it provided.

Nonetheless, they had built a strong relationship and were committed to working together in pursuit of upward mobility. They had serious conversations about how Chuy's undocumented status might disrupt their ability to achieve their goals together:

> I went back to school, so we were making that decision about can I go back to school? Should I go back to school? Should he go back to school before me? At the same time? So certain things like that. And ultimately because it's all a trickle effect on what our security is at our jobs, our incomes and all that.

Xochitl acknowledged that she harbored fears about how it could affect them in the future, "just thinking all the what-ifs." The more she shared, the clearer it became that immigration policies governed their relationship—and her life.

Xochitl's experiences mirror what Jane Lilly López finds in mixed-status marriages: U.S. citizens "come to live the life of an undocumented immigrant."[1] As citizen partners commit to mixed-status relationships, they become increasingly subject to the consequences of living in a context of illegality. Indeed, Xochitl asserted, "it affects us, our future," referring both to their future as a couple and to citizen partners' own futures. Immigration policies inflict shared consequences, affecting family-level outcomes and altering relationship dynamics.

This chapter explores the experiences of citizen partners of undocumented young adults to examine how illegality is experienced by someone who loves— and is building a life with—an undocumented immigrant. I find that citizens commit themselves to mediating illegality to establish stable, upwardly mobile partnerships. This infuses stress and guilt into relationships and, sometimes, lays the groundwork for unequal power dynamics. Importantly, DACA provided relief to both partners. Yet negative consequences endured because immigration policies had already introduced inequality into mixed-status relationships and citizen partners' life chances.

"I DON'T KNOW WHAT'S GONNA HAPPEN TO US": TIED FUTURES AND SHARED CONSEQUENCES

Marriage is an important social contract that centers economic well-being as both a precursor and desired outcome.[2] Like any committed couple, mixed-status partners saw themselves as working together to establish upward mobility and achieve the American dream. A pervasive cultural narrative, the American dream "is the promise that the country holds out to the rising generation and to immigrants that hard work and fair play will, almost certainly, lead to success."[3] It is particularly palpable in immigrant-origin families who aspire to economic markers of full integration in hopes of achieving social acceptance; yet it is often an impossible goal for most who face structural barriers to upward mobility.[4] Despite this, undocumented young adults and their citizen partners held fast to this omnipresent ideology of upward mobility. As romantic relationships progressed, however, citizen partners began to see that immigration policies endangered the possibility of realizing these shared goals as deportation risks and limited economic mobility threatened the family.

Deportation Threats

Most partners initially stressed fears that their family would be separated through deportation. Xochitl confided, "I don't think I've ever told him, but I do get scared.

Like, what if he does get deported. . . . That's always in the back of my mind." These fears were magnified when children entered the picture. Alexa Ibal explained,

> You always see those things on Facebook or in the news, "Oh, sign this petition to help this father of four not get deported." . . . It's stuff that's always kind of sub-consciously in my mind. . . . And there was times that I thought I could've been pregnant. . . . So that started popping up in my head: "He doesn't even have papers. What am I gonna do if he gets deported? I'm gonna be here by myself. Oh my god!"

Like Xochitl and Alexa, most citizen partners feared their partner's sudden deportation. They dreaded the possibility of separation but also rejected the possibility of relocating outside the United States.

Citizen partners who had less exposure to deportation threats were more likely to develop intense, everyday fears. Alexa, who had been dating her partner for nine months, explained, "I always think about it [deportation]. Whenever he's driving. Or whenever I know he's going to get here in an hour and he takes like two and a half. I'm like, Oh my god, what happened? . . . I've never had to deal with these kind of worries, and now I do." These fears often instigated conflict with her boyfriend, who perceived it as "nagging." He felt like, "I've been 'doing me' for some time now. Get off my back." Most undocumented young adults did not often think about their deportability; it had been part of their lives for so long that they knew how to manage risks and often thought about it only when triggered by things like police presence or media coverage. But citizen partners often did not understand deportation risks or processes, leaving their imaginations to run wild with fears of an ever-present threat to their relationship. Alexa noted, however, "Give me like a year, and then I'll get used to it." Indeed, many long-term partners did not report such intense fears of deportation.

Partners believed that deportation posed a threat to the family's long-term stability, no matter if they reunited outside the United States or remained separated. Max Aguilar, who had been married to his undocumented wife for five years, recalled that he had told her, "Screw it, we'll go to Mexico. We'll live together in Mexico." But after he secured a job in a county agency making $3,500 a month and buying a house, he felt that "so much stuff is holding us here now. It's like we have a lot to lose, we have a lot to lose, especially me, especially her." They found it hard to imagine abandoning their piece of the American dream. Similarly, Ariana Guerrero feared how her fiancé Enrique Escobar's deportation could affect her upward mobility:

> If he ever were to get deported, I don't know if I would leave to be with him 'cause I worked so hard here. I mean, I speak Spanish, but not to the level where I can get a career. . . . I have a lot of family in Mexico, so it wouldn't be so bad if I went to Mexico. But I know what I'll be able to do there is not the same [as what] I'll be able to do here [in the United States].

Ariana had invested in her education and was on the verge of earning a master's degree to become a school counselor. Like her, most couples avoided considering deportation scenarios because they recognized that family unity may come at the cost of their own and their family's chances for upward mobility.

Limited Economic Mobility

Undocumented partners' employment barriers infused couples' lives with economic instability. Simon Mendoza explained that his undocumented wife of six years "was limited with anything. I guess everything. . . . She couldn't have the same lifestyle most people have. She couldn't even get a job at McDonald's. That's like, Whoa!" His wife had struggled with persistent unemployment, and he felt that this had made it "really difficult for us to give our child a much better life. If she had her status, it [would be] a little bit better, would make the job a lot easier for both of us." Their combined income of $2,500 a month was enough to pay the bills, but little was left over to buy things or pay for activities for their son.

Similarly, Jimena Santiago perceived her fiancé's previous employment at a fast-food restaurant as the epitome of how his undocumented status might threaten them: "I'm afraid that if something, a law changes, and he loses the privilege [to work] that he has right now. I don't know what's gonna happen to us. That's gonna bring our financial life to a downfall. It scares me." DACA had transformed her fiancé's employability, allowing him to use his college degree to work as an engineer and make $3,200 a month, almost triple his previous earnings. Jimena's comment highlights the unique nature of these concerns as low-income citizen couples are not dependent on policy changes to enable potential mobility. Marginalized citizens may experience persistent structural barriers, but they are not as legally impermeable as those faced by undocumented young adults.

Immigration-related issues also added costs to couples' strained finances. For example, Dan and Ana Aguirre worked, respectively, as a plumber and a part-time office assistant; their shared income was between $3,000 and $4,000 a month. Although he had relatively well-paid and stable employment, Dan shared his frustrations: "We were kind of F-ed. She got pulled over once [without a license], and you know what it cost us? We were a newlywed couple. Fortunately, the cop was Latino, so he understood the situation . . . let her off [without towing the car]. But I think it's like a $700 ticket." Ana also worried about the cost of immigration-related paperwork. She was agonizing over their ability to afford around $5,000 to submit her application for permanent residency. If they could not, they would have to pay $495 to renew her DACA and continue saving. These costs, as well as more universal costs like repairing aging cars, added up.

Undocumented status also prevented wealth accumulation, such as purchasing a home, which is an essential mode of ensuring generational mobility. Undocumented immigrants' low income and lack of a Social Security number make it difficult to purchase a home, although many still aspire to homeown-ership.[5] Anthony Gutierrez spoke about how his wife's undocumented status created barriers:

> We plan on buying a home eventually someday. And the thing is, a lot of this was going to affect us . . . getting an apartment, getting a car, anything like that. . . . They wanted to see her credit on there as well. And because she didn't have any, that obvi-ously was an issue. So putting her on any contracts, that was a no. And of course, that limited us as well.

Because of this, Max Aguilar and Celia Alvarez were the only couple who had purchased a home. She remembered the irony: "They wanted proof that I was undocumented to make sure I didn't have any debt. They thought I was lying that I was [undocumented]. I was like, Oh, God. I'm always fearing that they will find out, and now I'm dying to prove that I am." After struggling to come up with ways to document her undocumented status, they were finally approved for a loan based *only* on Max's income. They both felt that this restricted them to a lower-quality house in a less desirable neighborhood.

"I WANT HER, I WANT *US* TO BE OK": CITIZEN PARTNERS MEDIATING ILLEGALITY

Citizen partners had to engage with immigration policies as they tried to mini-mize shared consequences and negotiate their diverging social positions. Antonio Mendez lived with his partner of seven years. He pointed to how she drew on her privileged position as a citizen to ensure their joint stability:

> She would be the resource. She would be the one that—I'll be like, "Hey, can you drive?" . . . when we're going into risky areas. We were using her credit card to make purchases for home . . . things that we needed, for necessities because you're the one that can get higher credit, lower interest because you have that option.

These actions build on citizen partners' attempts to help their undocumented partner negotiate barriers when they were dating by driving or paying for dates. In committed partnerships, however, these obligations multiply as citizen partners must continually mediate illegality.

Most citizen partners recognize that they will function as their family's pri-mary avenue to upward mobility as long as the undocumented partner cannot pursue legal employment. Xochitl tried not to think about their respective immi-gration statuses but admitted,

> Income-wise, I have been able to find work more easily or more permanently than him. So I see how that itself, without me wanting to, it becomes the advantage. . . . If worst comes to worst and he was ever to lose a job because of his status or whatnot, well then I come into play. . . . My income can be more of a security net.

She is adamant that she does not think of herself as "the one that's going to save us." Rather, she recognizes that her U.S. citizenship opens up opportunities for stable employment.

Citizens also committed themselves to driving to diminish the deportation and financial risks associated with unlicensed driving. Angel Padilla and Amelia Prado gave examples:

> *Angel:* I hate it when he drives to school. I hate it when he drives to work. On my days off, I'll take him . . . and I'll pick him up. Because I'd rather not deal with that. . . . Being undocumented is enough. But all the fees and [car] impoundment of having an unlicensed driver, it's not worth [it]. Especially if I have my license. It'd be really stupid for him to drive.

> *Amelia:* If she wants to go grocery shopping, she can go ahead. I don't doubt she would have done it even without a license, but most likely she wouldn't or I would probably be the one telling her, "I'll just go, I'll drive."

Taking on these responsibilities requires citizen partners to commit time and resources and can make couples renegotiate household chores. Often they take on these responsibilities without prompting, since they learned earlier in the relationship that driving is a way that they can help.

In the end, there is little that citizen partners can actually do in the face of staunch structural barriers, so they offer emotional support. Emma Gray Delgado, Antonio's fiancé, explained that she could "help out a little bit financially. . . . But he's still going to have that burden on him that he can't do what he would like to do, just because of his status." She recalled watching Antonio come home after long days attending classes and working. She saw the toll his status took as he struggled to pay his full tuition with small scholarships and his meager wages as a waiter: "I felt bad. I couldn't help. I just listened if he wanted to talk. . . . If he didn't want to talk, I would try to have that safe space for him." Antonio remembered a few times of extreme stress: "We both had moments of crying and stuff like that because I had to expose myself through these threats. And that our being together might be in jeopardy, that we might have been separated." Emma's support and encouragement helped him manage his fears and stress but could not fix underlying problems.

Providing emotional support left many citizen partners feeling helpless in light of immigration policies. Natalie Sieu cried as they recalled witnessing their undocumented partner endure a medical emergency:

She was on the floor crying because she had a gall bladder attack, and I can't take her to the hospital, I can't take her to the doctor. . . . It's frustrating. . . . Here you are lying on a floor crying, and I can't take care of you. She is like, "Give me the pills!" And it's the pills that she kept from her last ER visit, and they are old. . . . Stress affects it [the attacks]. . . . Just a lot of things in her life are stressful. She just lives a stressful existence, and I can't—as a partner you don't want your partner to be in pain. You want to help them.

Citizen partners cannot solve health care inequalities, create employment opportunities, or change policing practices. They know this but still feel frustration and pain as they bear witness to injustice.

Facing reality, citizen partners often thought about marriage as a means to permanently mediate illegality by opening up a pathway to legalization. After only six months together, Natalie was contemplating marriage: "I am thinking, how much do we need [to] save? . . . Whatever it is, we will deal with it. . . . I want her, I want us to be OK. . . . This is, I think, what would be giving us an easier life so that we can do our best." With little understanding of the process, Natalie longed for a "road map" and eagerly took notes as I offered a general explanation of the legalization process. I recounted the barriers that I traced in chapter 2 and detailed the risky and exhausting process covered in chapter 5 to show that this pathway is more complicated than most think.

Many clung to the hope that their partner would legalize. Camila and Luis Escobar recounted how he would have to return to Mexico to process his legalization petition and risk being separated from his family for up to 10 years. Realizing this after they had married over a decade earlier, Camila explained, "We thought the best decision would be to put it off until we were better prepared. . . . The worst-case scenario would be he'd go there and stay there for 10 years. Well, we can't do that in the middle of his education." Once he finished college, they delayed because she was pregnant. They held out when the federal DREAM Act was close to passing in 2010 and then again once DACA was announced. As couples hoped for immigration reform, shared consequences and mediating roles began to weigh on relationships.

"IT'LL TAKE ITS TOLL": SHARED STRESS OF IMMIGRATION STATUS DIFFERENCES

Previous research has focused on how immigration status differences become sources of vulnerability for undocumented partners. For example, Joanna Dreby documents how citizen partners' efforts to mediate illegality—by being the financial safety net, driving, or filing a petition for a partner's legal status—make undocumented partners dependent, fostering inequalities from the unequal division of household labor to domestic abuse.[6] Given the focus on severe examples of inequality, we know little about the thought processes that precipitate inequalities and infuse stress into the everyday lives of most mixed-status families.

Both citizen and undocumented partners recognized that their respective immigration statuses created unequal opportunities to contribute to their family's upward mobility. Angel Padilla, who was living with his undocumented partner of almost a year, noted, "Certain days . . . it'll take its toll. But other than that, I think he knows things are going to get better. And I know things are going to get better. So we're just kind of living on hope." Hope and love fueled many couples as they worked together to manage everyday immigration status barriers. Still, this amassed an emotional toll when negotiation strategies strained citizen partner's limited resources, reshaped relationship dynamics, and stressed both partners.

"I Should Do Something": Gendered Stress and Dependency When Mediating Illegality

Couples' stress increased as citizen partners more actively mediated illegality. Xochitl recalled her concerns from when Chuy had been unemployed:

> I guess I have guilt-tripped myself . . . during a time when we were going through economic hardship and I think I was a little bit hard on him. How much we were doing to provide? And not to say he should provide more or equally or whatnot. Just to provide [something], you know? And I kind of stopped myself and I thought, like, It's not as easy for you to go get a job. . . . So I just kind of, like, took a deep breath and tried to figure out how we were going to do it.

Like Xochitl, citizens often assumed a responsibility to draw on their privileged position to help their undocumented partners negotiate barriers; this was their duty, no matter how unwelcome and stressful. Such negotiations also strained undocumented partners by triggering feelings of dependence. For undocumented men, this translated into feelings of undesirability from unmet gender expectations (similar to those discussed in the previous chapter). For undocumented women, these instances triggered fears about the possibility of being trapped in an unequal, or potentially abusive, relationship.

Citizen partners, regardless of gender, felt a responsibility to help; citizen men, however, often did more because of their own gendered expectations that they should provide for and protect their partners. Sol Montes, who had been dating her citizen boyfriend Rigoberto for over six years, recalled, "He was driving me everywhere. Literally." He drove her over an hour to school for most of the four years she attended college. When our first interview ran long, he waited patiently in the car to take her home; this happened frequently since she was always running late. Rigoberto felt this responsibility for both Sol and her undocumented parents: "I feel like I should do something. So like just taking their car and driving it for them because I have a driver's license." This not only took a substantial amount of time out of his day, but it also distracted him at work and when in class at a local community college.

Citizen partners often accepted the stress of their responsibilities because they saw their actions as mutually beneficial. Dante Chavez and Yvonne Zepeda, his undocumented girlfriend of almost five years, both struggled to pursue bachelor's degrees. Dante shared how he saw their educational journeys as linked:

Obviously, she has to pay for school and stuff. When I was working, it was kind of hard for me. I guess the two years she was there [at the university], I was paying for it. Basically paid most of it, like 70 percent maybe. A good chunk. . . . Instead of focusing on my studies, I was thinking about how to get money to pay for my schooling [and], more importantly, hers. And that kind of affected my grades. Actually, I failed classes too over there. I was about to get kicked out twice, but then I just kind of had to toughen up, I guess. Discipline myself.

Dante's support of Yvonne's education could be seen an investment in their future. But his sense of responsibility cost him an extra year to complete his degree. He insists that he "could've been done earlier" if he had not had to balance school with working to cover both their educational expenses.

Despite Dante's good intentions, his help stressed Yvonne by making her feel dependent. She already felt trapped in a frustrating cycle in which she could not find a stable job that would allow her to complete her college education, but not having a college degree kept her from finding a stable job. Only one term away from graduating, she felt "stuck" and did not think she would be able to finish soon: "I'm in another economic situation. . . . My boyfriend gives me money, but I won't take it. I had to take it last time. I didn't want to take it. But he just, he pushed me. He's like, 'Here, take it! Go to school, finish, get out!'" Similarly, Sol remembered feeling frustrated when her boyfriend bought her textbooks and once took out a loan to help her cover tuition. Both women prided themselves on their independence and being able to provide for themselves. In light of their gender ideology, their partners' help made them feel beholden, creating additional stress and frustration.

Strained relationships were most common when the undocumented partner was unable to contribute to the household and the citizen partner struggled to build a stable foundation on their own. Daniela Sanchez explained how her undocumented status held her and her citizen husband back:

Just our income and our living situation has to be limited because it's what he can make, what he can do. Whereas if it was kind of like fifty-fifty or I could get a part-time job and kind of help out. . . . Because he feels like he should take all the responsibility. But I feel like I'm inadequate. I'm just no good to put [in] my half.

Ineligible for DACA, Daniela continued to struggle with underemployment. For years she had worked only a few hours a week, first as a massage therapist and later in various capacities caring for pets. Her inability to contribute to the household had recently forced her husband to take on two jobs: one as a security guard and a second at a restaurant. She confirmed the shared stress: "He does say I wish you could work, I wish you could get a job, I wish—so we wouldn't struggle as much. And we know it. I know it. And I wish it too." She was four months pregnant when we talked, and she feared that the stress would only worsen once their son was born: "Because I'm going to be like, I want to drive my kid to the doctor's appointments. I don't want to have to wait for him to get off of work. And for him, instead of having to do 20, 30 things in a day, it's just doubled. Because everything is just leaning on him. And again, there's only so much I can do." As their family responsibilities mounted, her dependency and his stress exacerbated their frustration. They separated within the year.

Such responsibility and dependence can set the stage for uneven relationship dynamics and conflict. Tanya Diaz had struggled for years in community college, taking one or two classes a semester while working full time in customer service. Once DACA was announced, her citizen boyfriend of three years offered to help her pursue a more fulfilling career by paying her tuition for a private cosmetology school. As a single mother with aging undocumented parents, she had carried a heavy economic burden alone for over a decade. Tears streamed down her face as she remembered feeling relief: "He's so willing to help! I've never had that help before." As she neared the end of the 18-month program, though, she realized that their relationship had become emotionally abusive: he demanded that she stop using Facebook to post pictures of herself modeling her hairstyling skills. He barged into a school event to confirm she was not lying about where she was. She recalled that in the midst of an argument, "he actually threw my school in my face. One of the things he said—that was very hurtful—was 'You owe your education to me.' . . . I was like, 'Wow! This is why I didn't want you to help me.'" In the wake of these ongoing fights, they had recently broken up.

As their relationship was unraveling, Tanya received notification that her DACA application had been approved. This infused her with a sense of independence, and she was now looking for a part-time job while she finished school:

> Even when we first started this, I told him I was going to pay him back for my school. . . . Because I don't want him to throw that in my face ever again. Because he hasn't been putting in those hours, and he hasn't been putting in the work, he hasn't been cutting his fingers cutting hair. So it's not him, it's me. And I don't like that he's trying to take that away from me.

It was precisely this type of abusive situation that undocumented young adults, particularly women, worried about when their partners offered help.

"A Little Bit Held Back": Guilt over Citizenship Privilege

In addition to feeling compelled to use their citizenship privilege to help their undocumented partners, many citizen partners wrestled with how their citizenship privilege allowed only them to participate in activities. Ariana Guerrero explained that her fiancé longed to travel. His comments do not prompt her for help, but rather highlight their different immigration statuses: "I feel sad for him and I feel bad that I can do it and he can't. That's why when I was planning my trip [to Mexico], I wouldn't really bring it up as much 'cause I didn't want him to feel like, Oh, I can't go." Negotiating diverging opportunities often left citizen partners feeling guilty. Jimena Santiago remembered deciding to go out to a club when her fiancé, Rafael, could not: "He didn't have an ID. And I was like, 'Well, I can't go with you. I'm gonna go with my friends.' And that made him feel bad. So I had to be more sensitive about it. Like, sometimes I wouldn't go out [with friends] and I would just stay home." Others were preoccupied with their decisions to travel, particularly when leaving the country, because there was no way that their partner could join them.

As these barriers emerged, citizens sought ways to protect their undocumented partners from feeling left behind while also easing their own guilt. Like Ariana, some partners de-emphasized their privileged activities. Others opted out. Amelia Prado explained, "She's undocumented, so we can't travel outside of the country, obviously. And I like to travel. So I'm aware that I can go. But like I told her, 'I wouldn't go without you. I'm not going to go to Mexico or wherever else I want to go without you.'" She was careful to frame this as her decision and to assert that it was not her partner's "fault" that she no longer traveled.

Regardless of the management strategy, undocumented partners also felt guilty. Ariana's fiancé, Enrique Escobar, reflected on how he thinks she perceives his undocumented status's impact on their relationship:

> *Enrique:* I think maybe she would want me to be able to—I guess travel with her or just to—I don't know. . . . I think just my status probably keeps her a little bit held back from stuff that she wants to do too.
>
> *Interviewer:* So how does that make you feel?
>
> *Enrique:* Just a little upset in a way and selfish somewhat, I guess—but nah, I don't know. I guess just mainly a little upset that I can't—I guess give her some of the stuff that she wants or she might enjoy more. In a way we keep it a little limited to what we do.

Enrique struggled with the idea that his undocumented status held Ariana back, both in terms of traveling and in everyday activities. These feelings amplified existing anxieties that he would be unable to provide for their future, which pushed him to avoid proposing marriage for years. These guilty feelings pervade individuals' feelings about their performance as partners, introducing doubts about if they are holding up their end of the bargain.

When asked the same question, Ariana confirmed her awareness of Enrique's guilty feelings: "He feels like he's holding me back in some things. Like, if I wanted to go somewhere, he's not able to go with me. Or getting a house or things like that. . . . Maybe he feels like he's not contributing as much as he would like to." She asserted, "I think it's not a big deal to me. Like, we're happy together, and I don't expect him to do, like—I don't know, I don't see it as a big thing. Mostly, I just feel bad for him." For most couples, guilt did not present a threat to their relationship, but it did require them to invest emotional energy as they sought to manage their own and their partner's feelings.

One partner's guilt sometimes feeds the other's. Jimena shared, "He always told me, 'It's hard with me. If you wanna leave me, I completely understand. I wouldn't wanna be with my own self.' He tells me, 'I don't have money a lot of time and I'm struggling.'" As her partner voiced these feelings of guilt, she developed negative feelings about herself: "It made me feel selfish because I was just thinking about how I want to be and what I want and not really thinking about what he's facing." Like Ariana and Enrique, Jimena and her fiancé had to invest energy to reassure each other that they were happy with their relationship and would find a way to overcome the barriers.

In a few cases, conflict emerged when undocumented partners activated guilt by highlighting their citizen partner's privilege to persuade them to embrace opportunities. Madeline Velasquez recounted how her undocumented partner makes her feel guilty when he implores her to take advantage of educational opportunities: "He tells me, 'You have papers. At least you have papers and you can do so much. You can go to school, you can get financial aid and you know that I can't. It is harder for me than it is for you. I don't know why you are not doing right.'" Although Madeline was frustrated, she felt guilty because she recognized that her partner had a point. She planned to return to community college.

A few reported that relationships dissolved when citizen partners perceived these urgings as condemnation. Karen Rodriguez remembered her citizen ex-boyfriend's reaction to her insistence that he value his privilege:

> For example, he had a car and he crashed his car. He lost his car. He had a bazillion tickets. And to me, that was just like, Why do you not take advantage of what you have and use it for a good way? . . . And that would come in conflict a lot. Because in my view it's like I never had all of that. . . . And in his eyes it was like, Well, I've always had this 'cause I was born here. . . . We just fought a lot.

Together, complex emotional dynamics of stress, dependency, and guilt took a cumulative toll on relationships.

If negotiated effectively and openly, however, these shared experiences could have positive outcomes. As my research assistant and I interviewed Luis and Camila Escobar on opposite sides of a busy restaurant, they independently shared how their struggles had brought them closer together:

> *Camila:* In a positive way I feel that it has strengthened our relation-
>   ship. We've had to learn about each other in a very differ-
>   ent way than most couples. And we've had to endure more
>   stressors, earlier in our relationship than most couples have.
>   . . . We've really had to become each other's rocks.

> *Luis:* She had her depression and I had my undocumented status.
> So she knew my struggle, and she helped me through it. And
> I knew her struggle and I helped her through it. . . . I think
> what connected us, that we were both hurting, [like we were
> each] missing a leg. . . . So I think what helped was that we
> both made it through . . . [by] walking together.

Over 11 years, Camila and Luis had faced more than their share of challenges as they were more financially stressed and flooded with guilt than most of the couples I spoke to. But they had figured out how to support each other, communicating their needs and working together to solve their problems. In the end, their experiences brought them together instead of tearing them apart.

"I AM AFRAID TO ARGUE": GENDERING IMMIGRATION POLICY'S ROLE IN ABUSIVE RELATIONSHIPS

The inequality and stress in mixed-status relationships can lay the foundation for undocumented partners to experience abuse. Previous research suggests that having an immigrant background can exacerbate abuse or make it more difficult to seek help because of limited language fluency, isolation from one's family and community, lack of access to dignified jobs, and experiences with authorities in their origin countries.[7] Undocumented immigration status intensifies these factors, particularly in mixed-status relationships in which power differentials abound. Apart from this, gender inequality increases women's likelihood of victimization.[8] As a result, most previous research has focused on undocumented women's risk of abuse because of their dependence, isolation, and difficulty interacting with law enforcement and social services.[9] But the few undocumented young adults I spoke to who had experienced intimate partner abuse suggested that immigration policies complicate the traditionally gendered scholarly narratives of abuse. Rather, undocumented women, undocumented men, and those in the midst of legalization processes had distinct views about the complex webs of dependence and inequality that shaped their risk of and tolerance for abuse.

A few undocumented women reported previous abusive relationships and suggested that undocumented status intersected with other forms of inequality to foster abuse. Valeria Torres shared how her undocumented status was one way that her citizen ex-boyfriend had laid a foundation for abuse: "He would use it [my undocumented status] as a way of putting me down, as a way of him feeling superior. . . . Because, you know, he's a citizen, then he gets to have the opportunities [and] resources, and I am unable to do that." Undocumented status became one of many ways to foster low self-esteem and dehumanize her. Alternatively, Norma Mercado, who had recently left her undocumented husband of 10 years, felt that gender inequality ultimately precipitated her abuse: "I was abused physically and emotionally. I guess you can say that my self-esteem was really low. . . . I just thought my life was over, that I had to be a wife and had to dedicate myself to working on the marriage." One day she opened her door to a Jehovah's Witness and began to learn that "women are not made to be slaves but they're made to be partners. . . . That's when my self-esteem started to become more positive. . . . I just got the courage to say [to myself], You need to leave. I need to live because my kids need me." Rather than pointing to her undocumented status, Norma credited ingrained gender roles, marrying young (at 19), and having children early on with making her believe that she was stuck with "who she picked." Immigration status may have played a role by stressing Norma's husband enough to precipitate abuse or lower her self-esteem; her characterization suggests, however, that multiple forms of inequality enabled the abuse. Overall, these women's experiences suggest that undocumented status does not single-handedly cause or ensure abuse; rather it is another factor that can facilitate abuse because of the stigma, dependence, and stress it carries.

Notably, several undocumented men worried about how gendered deportation threats increased the potential consequences of being involved in a domestic dispute. Ben Melendez explained why he ended a relationship: "He grabbed me once. And I told him, 'Get off!' And I freaked out because he held me like this." Ben grabbed my forearm. "What if he hits me and I try to defend myself and I hurt him? That can get me deported. That's what the law says." Undocumented Latino men face intersecting racial and immigration status identities marking them as criminals and making them disproportionately likely to experience deportation.[10] With domestic violence being a deportable offense, undocumented Latino men worried about accusations of intimate partner violence, even if accidental or false.

The intersection of race, gender, and immigration status produces distinct power dynamics that can lead undocumented men to tolerate abuse. Pablo Ortiz, an undocumented man in a five-year cohabitating relationship with a citizen woman, was the only participant whose discussion of conflict suggested he was currently in an abusive relationship:

> She has the power to deport me. And I do get afraid. You could say that I'm in a kind of very possessive relationship in a way. So yeah, I am afraid to argue with her. Because according to her—see, I'm a very passionate person, and sometimes my tone of voice . . . [leads to] miscommunication. One little thing could turn and could get into a big argument. And next thing you know, she's—it's hard for her to go beyond the whole negative image that she has about the immigrant community sometimes for her too. . . . So I do, I do get afraid. . . . I have read many stories on the newspapers. A lot of immigrants have been deported for, I guess, spousal abuse. And anybody could make that claim, and it doesn't have to be true or anything, but you could still go into the police department, and even though it's not true, with Secure Communities and all these other stuff that's going on, you end up [in immigration custody].

He explained that he tries to "de-escalate the conflict," frequently giving in to her demands. This gives way to objective forms of abuse: For years she has refused to petition for his legalization. She once turned off all the utilities when she got upset that he left to work out of state for a few weeks. More recently, she took their three-year-old daughter away for a month. He felt that "she took advantage of that [undocumented status] because she knew that I wasn't gonna call the cops because she knew that I didn't wanna deal with those people." Wanting to be near his daughter, he convinced her to move back in and try to work it out. But he still felt at risk: "It almost got to that point where I didn't want to be in this relationship because sometimes I'm scared of her, I'm scared of her that sometimes I feel like she tries to push my buttons so I can lose my cool."

Pablo's story could have easily come out of the lips of an undocumented woman. Indeed, scholars report similar stories among undocumented, first-generation immigrant women in relationships with citizen/documented men who establish control by threatening deportation or abandonment of legalization opportunities.[11] Ben and Pablo, though, both worried that their criminalization as Latino men increased their risk of being perceived as abusers and subsequently deported.

Although women also feared their status could precipitate inequality and abuse, they did not share men's fear of deportation because of domestic conflicts. Rather, some saw immigration policies as offering them relief after they left abusive relationships or survived sexual violence. The Violence against Women Act allows victims of domestic violence perpetrated by a U.S. citizen or permanent resident family member to apply for legal residency on their own, preventing abusers from using an immigration petition as a form of control. Further, U visas are available for victims of certain crimes—including sexual assault and abuse, domestic violence, incest, and rape—if they help with investigating and prosecuting the perpetrator; these visas later open up a pathway to legalization. Perceptions of women as victims of abuse can help them avail themselves of these laws; indeed, I spoke to three women who obtained U visas for cooperating with police after reporting domestic abuse or sexual violence. On the other hand, men, in general, underreport abuse and have difficulty accessing domestic violence services.[12] Thus, it is likely difficult for men to provide the necessary documentation to substantiate abuse-related immigration petitions.

Notably, legalizing through marriage crystalizes the risk of abuse because of the process's dependent and risky nature. Take the examples of Diego Ibáñez and Valeria Torres, who were both single at the time:

> Diego: [My ex-girlfriend], she told me I should marry [her], "I'll fix your papers." . . .
>
> Laura: So why didn't you do it?

> *Diego:* For my honor. . . . 'Cause I don't like for people to tell me, in a few years from now, "I was the one who legalized [you]." I don't like that. . . . And also it makes me feel like I need to stay with them. And what if I don't want to stay? I can't risk my freedom.
>
> *Valeria:* Once you get married to this person, what if he uses that as a way of manipulating you? So, you know, there is a lot of other things that come along with that. . . . You know, like, now you're married to me, therefore you have to do whatever I say because otherwise I'm gonna take you to [immigration authorities]. I'm gonna tell them, "Hey, you know, she's just using this marriage to just [get papers]." And [then I] get in trouble.

Pursuing legalization through marriage carries significant legal risks. Like most, both Valeria and Diego worried about how this ultimate form of mediating illegality would disrupt power dynamics. The specifics of their fears are gendered, however: Diego, like other men, worried primarily about how becoming dependent could jeopardize his honor, power, and freedom. Most women, though, worried about how this could further tip the gendered scales of dependence and potentially lead to manipulative or abusive relationships.

The cases of those who pursued legalization through marriage suggest that the risk of abuse is real and cuts across gender. Malena Landeta noted that her husband would invoke his petitioner status when they fought: "If I got upset with him about . . . him going out with friends . . . he would say, 'If you continue like this, I'll just forget about that [applying for your legal status]. We'll just stop the classes.' . . . It is a bad thing that he said that, but I understand that when someone's upset, we say a lot of things." Five years into their marriage, Javier Espinoza still feared his wife might accuse him of using her for papers:

> *Javier:* You're still with that fear factor that if you don't go through it, she might just take it back and you might just lose your papers.
>
> *Laura:* Even though you were in love . . . you give in when there's fights?
>
> *Javier:* Yeah, just in case. *[Laughs.]* "Qué viva la paz [Let peace reign]." . . . I was talking to her [my wife] about that, you know, "I give in in a lot of fights and I let you get your stuff because I feel afraid of losing my papers."

Both Malena and Javier were now legal permanent residents in genuine marriages, but immigration law still haunted their relationships. They insisted that these were not frequent feelings or comments, but their partner's citizen status gave them power that they could use to explicitly or implicitly regulate their actions during disagreements.

The risk of abuse multiplies in strategic marriages in which the undocumented partner has a valid fear of being reported to authorities for marriage fraud. One such case of abuse emerged: Dulce Puente married an old high school friend who then petitioned for her legalization. While they had agreed that it was a strategic marriage, she realized later that he expected it to turn romantic. He got a tattoo of her name a few weeks after they married. While she initially entertained the idea of pursuing a romantic relationship, she felt as though she were walking a tightrope: "He's told me that he's in love with me, and I told him I don't have feelings for him. So it's a lot of pressure, and I try to keep my distance from him because of that. . . . I'm very thankful for what he's done for me, but I don't want to end up hurting him." In her second interview, Dulce revealed that her marriage had worsened. She recounted what had happened a year earlier, about six months before the needed to jointly apply to remove the conditions on her permanent residency:

> One day we were supposed to go out, and I was too tired. I told him to stay in, and I cooked dinner and we watched a movie. . . . Then the next day when I got home, he was in the shower, and I checked his phone and he had text messages with his cousin saying that he was so mad at me, that he wanted to punch me and calling me a bitch. . . . [I thought], like, What do you wanna do to me? Do you wanna kill me? . . . I didn't feel comfortable anymore.

Dulce began to fear for her safety when he punched a wall after she confronted him about the texts. She moved out, but her conditional residency status required her to recontact him, so she could apply for permanent residency. He agreed to help, and she recognized that "he was trying to manipulate me. . . . He started telling me about getting back together and all these things. And I started going with it, [even] when I knew that I didn't want to, just because I wanted him to help me." Feeling trapped, Dulce once again entertained the possibility of pursuing a romantic relationship in an emotionally and potentially physically abusive situation. Her application was approved, and she was granted permanent residency and no longer needed to maintain the relationship. But she still felt a sense of helplessness and fear: "When I was doing all the [renewal] paperwork, it said that they could investigate you even after approving you. And sometimes I think about that. But there's really nothing I can do [to fix the relationship] if he's out of state and we're not really working out." Though there is a provision to allow petitioned spouses to apply to remove the conditions on their residency on their own, few know about this process, and it requires being able to substantiate that the marriage was bona fide at the time of their petition and why it ended.[13]

It is important to recognize that most romantic partnerships did not devolve into serious conflict, abuse, or violence. Further, when abuse emerged, it was not simply because of immigration status. Rather, unequal relationship dynamics—triggered by undocumented immigration status, gender inequality, and other social locations—intersect with immigration policies to create a complicated web of dependence and inequality that can increase the risk of and tolerance for abuse.

"THERE'S A LITTLE BIT MORE SECURITY": SHARED BENEFITS OF DACA

As mixed-status romantic partners adapted to life in a context of illegality, immigration policies seeped into citizen romantic partners' lives and structured helpful *and* harmful relationship dynamics. By the time DACA was established, long-term citizen partners had already established negotiation strategies and experienced shared consequences. DACA did not necessarily alter relationship trajectories, but rather eased the everyday consequences of illegality. For example, Xochitl and Chuy had been dating for almost a year when he received DACA. Xochitl did as much as possible to help Chuy manage immigration-related barriers. Obtaining DACA altered their relationship by reducing Chuy's dependence on her and allowing him to contribute more equally to their relationship. DACA thus enabled an important shift in relationship dynamics, leading this supportive immigration policy to spill over into the lives of citizen partners.

Obtaining employment authorization through DACA allowed undocumented partners to more equally contribute to the couple's pursuit of upward mobility. In his first interview, Chuy reported earning $800 a month after leaving his job manufacturing picture frame samples and opening his own small framing shop. Within weeks of receiving DACA, he secured a job in a framing department of a chain store. Within a few months he became a department manager, making $2,000 a month. He felt more economically stable: "There's a little bit more security. I can buy the things that I want. . . . It's a different mentality." Xochitl felt the same:

> We saw it [DACA's impact] initially with our income. Because [before DACA] the fact that he wasn't able to have a secure job, we were basically managing with whatever came into his shop and whatever I was doing through my minimum wage [job]. . . . [We had to] be spending conscious. . . . Now that he has his job . . . there's just much more things that we can access. We're able to invest now rather than just get by.

This economic stability made it much easier for them to envision and plan for a brighter future together.

Economic stability also reduced the potential for conflict. Chuy could be more independent, and Xochitl did not have to carry the stressful responsibility of mediating illegality. Chuy explained that his stable income made him finally feel comfortable spending money on a new truck. No longer afraid of being pulled over for driving without a license or incurring the costs of having his car impounded, he became more independent. This also made Xochitl's life easier: "Now we have two sources of transportation. We didn't have to be figuring that whole commute process. How we were going to share the car and whatnot." Other citizen partners of DACA recipients noted similar feelings of security:

> *Max Aguilar:* It feels liberating. I feel a lot safer. She could be on my [car] insurance. . . . She could be registered [with the car and] everything under her name. Everything's fine. So all of that really helped out.

> *Jimena Santiago:* He could do things without asking me to do it. Like the cell phones, it was always under my account 'cause I was the one with the Social Security [number]. And now he's able to open that. He has credit cards so [it's] less worry [for me].

Like Xochitl, Max, and Jimena, most citizen partners reported that their responsibilities and worries decreased with DACA. This lessened their stress but did not alter their relationship's trajectory because most had willingly taken on these roles.

Despite DACA's positive shared effects, both partners remained preoccupied with illegality and the need to maintain DACA protections. Chuy thought about his status more frequently, especially as the expiration date on his work permit neared:

> That date it expires is always in your mind, you know? . . . So you've got it for two years and maybe you're good the first month, the first year. But the second year comes around and you're starting . . . a countdown. . . . So I have to reapply. Because I'm like four months away now from my thing being expired. So in order to keep my job, I have to stay on top of that.

Citizen partners were equally concerned, and Xochitl frequently reminded Chuy about the upcoming deadlines: "I need to make sure he's on top of all the other stuff to make sure he's secure here" to avoid plunging them both back into uncertainty and instability.

While most undocumented *and* citizen partners felt their worries melt away with DACA, a few suggested that their fears have simply transformed. They were no longer afraid of sudden unemployment or deportation, but they worried about whether their DACA protections would not be renewed or if the program would end. Camila Escobar explained that most of her pre-DACA fears were gone, "but now we have these new ones":

> Right now, the worry and fear is, What's gonna happen in a year when . . . his DACA is over? Are we going to be able, from now till then, [to] fix his residency finally? . . . If it [the legalization application] doesn't go through, what's gonna happen? What's going to happen to us? Are we gonna start from zero again? Is he gonna get started on a deportation proceeding? If we don't resolve this by the time his DACA expires and we reapply, what if he gets denied the second time?

At the time I was conducting interviews, the first wave of DACA recipients were beginning to apply for renewals. With no clear understanding of the process, couples worried. Yet DACA renewals proceeded smoothly as less than 1 percent of the renewals were denied.[14] But the rescission of DACA in September 2017 and the legal complexities of subsequent court injunctions on its termination likely escalated fears about what will happen if one's DACA protections expire.

It was only with permanent legal status that mixed-status couples felt that they had achieved ultimate family stability. Estefania Gutierrez-Estrada and her citizen husband, Anthony, had been married for eight years but were unable to apply for her legalization because she had entered the United States without inspection and faced the 10-year bar. After spending two years as a DACA recipient, Estefania applied for and received advanced parole, giving her permission to travel to Mexico to visit her ailing grandmother. Allowed to reenter the United States with inspection after this trip, she was able to apply for legalization without risking consular processing and a 10-year bar on her reentry.[15] They both reflected on the impact of her impending receipt of permanent residency:

> *Estefania:* Just stability, honestly. Peace of mind. . . . I know that it's not something that I have to renew like the DACA every two years or so, or they might take away the program. . . . I feel like it took so long, and now I feel it's finally moving, finally moving.
>
> *Anthony:* That just opens up a lot of options for her that she can explore and also have an impact on our finances in a positive way. It's just so many more open doors. . . . I'm looking forward to . . . [when] decisions that we have to make are not limited because of her immigration status.

DACA had provided them with some stability because Estefania could safely drive their children around and secure well-paid employment to supplement the family income. But permanent legal status would erase any fears that they might regress in the future. Both partners were excited about the opportunities permanent residency held for their family. Yet, as I will show in the next chapter, the legalization process creates new enduring consequences.

CONCLUSION

As mixed-status relationships progressed, citizen partners recognized that the context of illegality was seeping into their lives. Surrounded by marriage myths and rhetoric that marked undocumented immigrants as undesirable partners, they were invested in denying that immigration status played any role their relationship. But their everyday experiences tell a different story about how immigration policies limited them as well.

Both undocumented and citizen partners experienced illegality as a shared burden that determined their individual and collective futures. Committed to their relationships, they worked together to negotiate immigration-related barriers. Although this decreased routine risks and fears associated with everyday life, it ensured that both partners experienced feelings of dependence, responsibility, and guilt. Relationship dynamics changed and, in some cases, enabled unequal and abusive relationships. By the time DACA was implemented, most couples had established effective ways to negotiate illegality and its consequences; their lives improved, but they remained solidly situated in their relationships. As with dating, DACA's impact on recipients' relationships was tempered by couples' having already identified ways to negotiate illegality and minimize shared consequences.

If DACA is rescinded, and there is no other form of immigration relief, citizen partners will likely find themselves solidly situated in a context of illegality. They will return to an everyday reality haunted by threats of family separation, limited opportunities for upward mobility, and stressful relationship demands. Their citizenship status will not shield them from the inequalities bred by immigration policies.

"It Was Time to Take That Step"

Pursuing Legalization through Marriage

So much of your life is dictated by your legal status already. Why would you let a fractured system dictate who you're gonna share your life with or when you're gonna take that step? No! They already decide way too many things.

—REGINA CASTRO

Regina emphasized that she had always opposed the idea of legalizing her status through marriage. Immigration policies had already touched too many aspects of her life. It had dictated her educational trajectory and informed her career choices while also preventing simple everyday activities. She refused to let it also take precedence in the most intimate decision of marriage. But after marrying her citizen partner in her early 20s, Regina began to rethink her position:

> [He saw] how sad I was. . . . I felt so unhappy with my career and not being in school and all that stuff. It's emotionally impacting for your partner because he is very limited in what he can do for me, so I think that part is tough. . . . I had to take a step back and realize how he was feeling and how he was doing.

Regina's undocumented status took a toll on her husband as he helped her negotiate her undocumented status, witnessed her frustrations, and provided emotional support. Setting her pride aside, she agreed to consult a lawyer.

The lawyer repeated what she already knew: her legalization hinged on proving that she entered on a valid visa. Many establish this through entry stamps in their passport or electronic copies of their admission record. Regina's case was complicated; she needed to find the actual slip of paper they had given her. If she didn't, she would be able to legalize her status only if she underwent consular processing in Mexico and risked facing a 10-year bar on her return. Luckily, Regina's mom unearthed the paper a few months later.

Regina and her husband filed their application and began to prepare for their interview. Fearing that the immigration agents would suspect marriage fraud, they amassed evidence of its legitimacy. Whether opening up a financial account, identifying an emergency contact, or making decisions about their future education and careers, both considered how their actions would support or endanger their initial legalization petition and subsequent applications to renew her permanent residency and later seek U.S. citizenship.

Legalizing one's status presumably removes the consequences of illegality and fosters integration. Indeed, Regina's transition from undocumented immigrant to permanent resident improved her life: she moved into more stable employment at a nonprofit, eventually reenrolled in college, and accessed prestigious internships to further her career. Immigration law, however, ties this opportunity for upward mobility to a romantic relationship. This complicates marriage as the next step in family formation—discouraging it in some cases, encouraging it in others, and infusing all relationships with emotional baggage.

Scholarship has traced the intricacies of immigration policy and the limited pathway to legalization through marriage. Focusing on those who entered without inspection, Ruth Gomberg-Muñoz exposes the complexities of consular processing, including the risks and realities of experiencing a 10-year bar to reentry.[1] Such state intervention separates families or expels all members from the country, punishing both undocumented immigrants and U.S. citizens. This work, however, presumes that undocumented immigrants like Regina, who face straightforward pathways to legalization, are left unscathed. This chapter challenges this assumption, detailing the enduring consequences that emerge even when the process is relatively straightforward and successful.

Focusing on 22 formerly undocumented young adults who legalized their immigration status through marriage, I trace how immigration law required couples to establish, construct, and perform their relationship in specific ways to achieve their legalization goals. All undocumented and citizen partners felt disciplined by this process, but it was most intense for those who underwent consular processing in Mexico. Years after they achieved legalization, the process still haunted couples, as it had seeped into the foundation of their marriage. Despite the positive material benefits of legalizing one's immigration status, the process produced new and enduring social and emotional consequences for both undocumented and citizen partners.

"IT WAS A FEELING OF DESPERATION": ADJUSTING MARRIAGE AND WEDDING EXPECTATIONS

The marriage myths that I traced in chapter 2 loom large for undocumented young adults and their romantic partners as they discuss pursuing marriage and legalization. Messages that she was a "magical citizen wife" encouraged Nicole Davis to raise the possibility. She remembered prodding her undocumented partner into considering marriage after six months: "He was kind of hesitant at first when we discussed it because . . . he didn't want it to be about that stuff. But my feelings [were] kind of like, If we're gonna do this eventually, we should do it now."

All undocumented young adults were wary of embarking on this stigmatized and legally complicated pathway. But those who felt extremely excluded began seriously considering legalization through marriage. Deciding to do so affected the very foundation of their relationship as they aligned immigration law with romantic notions.

"Let's Do It": Marriage Decisions

Economic barriers, including not having enough money, a good job, and savings, dissuades many from marriage.[2] As shown in chapter 3, these same concerns often contribute to undocumented men's disrupted family formation. Yet the intersection of these economic barriers with the particularities of family-based immigration law establishes a unique situation in which economic immobility can have the opposite effect on marriage—driving it rather than preventing it. Marriage carried a promise of legalization and the amelioration of barriers to upward mobility; this decision, however, carried long-term consequences by dictating the progression of romantic partnerships and marriage timing.

Love and Legalization: Moving toward Shared Stability. Shared consequences pushed long-term couples to raise the possibility of marriage as they hoped to find relief from punitive immigration policies and to secure their family's stability. Manuel Serrano's wife, Carmen, remembered that his undocumented status was not an issue when they were dating: "It was never a problem. It was not a high topic [of conversation]. Then we moved in together [and] I got pregnant. And that's when I was like, 'Oh crap, you might be losing your job again?'" Carmen realized the severity of Manuel's economic barriers when he was offered a supervisor position at the store where he worked. Her reaction was "Do it! It'll be good if you get more money." He reiterated that he would likely be fired because the promotion would prompt them to attempt to verify his Social Security number. Carmen realized, "Shoot, it's going to affect me directly. Before I would know about legal and nonlegal status, but it was never something that affected me until I depended on that." Now that Carmen finally saw how Manuel's economic limitations translated into family-level economic immobility, her immediate thought was "Should we get married legally and help you out?" Driven by marriage myth messages, she and Manuel married a few days later.

I spoke to several couples whose story reflected Manuel and Carmen's decision-making process. Some married quickly, while others planned a wedding. Many filed legalization paperwork around the same time as their marriage, but some had to wait to save up the $3,000–$5,000 they would need for application and legal fees. In some cases, including Manuel's, marriages were not always followed by immediate legalization; couples learned afterward that the legalization process would be more complicated than they had anticipated. Despite the specifics and outcomes of their cases, immigration law dictated their relationship progression.

Fast-Forwarding and Being Strategic: Addressing New Threats to Individual Opportunities. A segment of undocumented young adults saw marriage as a foothold to pursuing upward mobility through legalization. After living the majority of their lives jumping over hurdles raised by their immigration status, they encounter ones that they cannot overcome alone. Dolores Inda had fought to pursue her college degree—paying her full tuition out of pocket and navigating an institution that was not prepared to meet her needs. "I had recently graduated from [college] and I wanted to do something. I wanted to get a job. I wanted to apply my degree." Intent on becoming a nurse practitioner, Dolores recognized that her immigration status posed an insurmountable barrier. It would be impossible to get loans to pay for the program, and she could not apply for her license or be employed in the field because she lacked a Social Security number.[3] Although her family's pending legalization petition had recently been approved, she had turned 21 and was no longer included. Being the only remaining undocumented family member "just hit me, hard. . . . I knew something had to be done. Desperation, it was a feeling of desperation." In these extreme moments, marriage offered a glimmer of hope, making undocumented young adults feel that they *needed* to get married, even if they were not necessarily *ready* for marriage.

Some had been dating their partner for a short time and decided to fast-forward their relationship to marriage. When her anxiety peaked, Dolores had just started dating her boyfriend. Conversations about her desperation to legalize arose periodically over the year until "one day he said, 'Let's do it. I'll help you.'" They soon moved in together and married in a civil ceremony. Wanting to minimize the impact on their relationship, they told only immediate family members and agreed that they were still boyfriend and girlfriend. This complicated the relationship. When I asked if theirs was a real marriage, Dolores responded slowly, concluding, "It's a gray area." They were in love and committed to pursuing a relationship, but they were not ready for marriage, and "it was strictly going for me to get my papers." She explained,

> My partner and I both highly value marriage and the traditions that came with it, and we wanted to both be able to experience that. So we tried—and it's hard to completely accomplish this—but we both tried very hard to not see it as marrying. Because we wanted to be able to one day get married and be able to embrace all the things that come with having a marriage and having a ceremony.

She admitted that they struggled to negotiate the transition and "definitely had a bumpy ride . . . because we did expedite it." Their relationship blossomed into a stable partnership, but three years of being technically married had blurred the lines they had drawn. They were now in a place where they might have otherwise married but never seemed to get around to it.

Single individuals similarly found themselves pushed into marriage. Betty Calderon had successfully navigated immigration status barriers until she was a year away from graduating from college: "I had a decision to make whether I was just gonna wait around and hope for a miracle . . . or actually do something about it. And get to where I wanted to be and where I needed to be before I finished my education." Facing the prospect of not being able to use her degree, she felt "impotent" and became susceptible to marriage myths. Not in a romantic relationship, she approached her best friend: "He wasn't married. . . . I felt comfortable with him. I started telling him that I wasn't legalized . . . and then I asked him, 'This is gonna sound really weird, but will you marry me?'" He agreed, and they held a civil ceremony two months later, and she filed for legalization soon after.

Changing Laws: Capitalizing on New Opportunities.   Many undocumented young adults in committed relationships were eager to file a petition, but legal barriers prevented it. When we talked in 2011, Carlos Almanza had just graduated from the University of California. He was working as a legal assistant and thought law school might be next. He felt "unaccomplished. Like, I feel like I should have a good job. I don't know. I feel like I'm not doing anything with my degree. I'm learning a lot where I work at, but—I hate to sit behind a desk, and answer the phones, and talk to people. I don't know. I don't know. I want to do something more." Longing for legalization, he spent his days preparing immigration paperwork for clients; he fantasized about adding his name to one of their petitions or arranging to be a victim of a crime so he could get a U visa.

When we discussed the idea of legalizing his status through marriage in 2011, Carlos joked, "I'm gay. Otherwise I could've gotten married [for papers] a long time ago." Same-sex couples could not then petition for their spouse's immigration or legalization petitions. It was not until 2013, when the Defense of Marriage Act (DOMA) was declared unconstitutional by the U.S. Supreme Court, that same-sex partners could petition for immigration benefits for their spouses. Carlos explained that this ruling influenced his and his citizen partner's discussions of marriage: "He's always said, ever since [the] DOMA [decision] went through, we had that option [of applying]." They both entertained the idea but knew that Carlos had not entered with inspection; they would not risk his 10-year banishment to Mexico.

Receiving DACA changed the equation. While not a pathway to legalization, DACA enabled recipients to apply for advanced parole to travel outside the United

States for educational, work, or humanitarian purposes. This facilitated a legalization application by providing a recent legal entry and removing the threat of a 10-year bar.[4] At the time of our second interview, Carlos's advance parole application had just been approved, and he was preparing to travel two weeks later. He and his partner were discussing marrying after he returned. Within a year of his trip, they had married, and he had become a permanent resident. Their case exemplifies how recently changed policies may catalyze marriage decisions within long-term committed relationships of both same-sex and heterosexual couples.

"Legally Married" and "Married Married": *Strategic Wedding Planning*

Linking legalization and marriage requires mixed-status couples to align law with romance. Most aspired to have some version of a fairy-tale wedding: a ceremony and reception complete with white wedding dress, gorgeous hall, and long guest list. These ideals often stem from media representations that create social pressure to perform extravagant wedding rituals. Such images permeate popular culture, spanning from children's toys to TV show and film plots, and fueled by a burgeoning wedding industry.[5] These hegemonic ideals permeated couples' wedding expectations, but their legal reality created time and financial constraints that made it relatively impossible to quickly move toward legalization while fulfilling these desires. Many couples thus planned for two weddings: a civil marriage ceremony for the legalization process and a traditional wedding ceremony and reception to fulfill their romantic ideals.

Those who employed this strategy did not see their civil wedding as a *real* wedding. Brandon Erickson, who fast-forwarded his relationship to marriage, and Rosa Lopez, who had been with her partner for eight years before marriage, shared:

> *Brandon:* We didn't end up getting married in a way . . . either of us
> necessarily wanted. . . . I think if we would have waited longer and had, like, a real wedding—ceremony and reception and everything. It's because of this [immigration] process that it became just [like] we need to get to the courthouse.
>
> *Rosa:* We didn't have a wedding when we got married. We just went to the court—me, him, my mom, my dad, and his parents. . . . At that time we weren't ready to have a wedding. We didn't want to spend the money. And our family, you know, when you start saying, "Oh, I'm going to get married," everyone just expects [all this stuff].

Regardless of how their marriage aligned with their relationship's progression, most couples wanted to pursue legalization quickly. Often, this meant that there was no time or money for a conventional wedding. Planning two weddings helped them strategically negotiate their desperation for legal status and romantic notions while also reducing the perceived impact of immigration law on their relationship.

This strategy had consequences. Brandon's wife, Cindy, confided that "it took away the romance from it because it wasn't a usual marriage." She thought her wedding would be a "monumental thing in your life," complete with "bridal showers and dresses and rings." Even though both their families were present for the civil ceremony, Cindy struggled to accept that they did not have "a big white wedding." Two years later, they still hoped to find the time for "an actual ceremony."

Hoping to guard against these consequences, Rosa and her partner, Agustin, hid their civil marriage from their friends and extended families. They filed his legalization paperwork and had the "real" wedding a year later, after Agustin had legalized his status and "when there was money." Similarly, Santos Castellanos and his citizen partner hid their civil ceremony and de-emphasized its importance, referring to it as when they "signed the papers."

Having two weddings can be an effective management strategy, but it establishes a marriage on shaky ground. Some couples struggled to talk about their weddings. Santos stumbled over his words as he tried to make a point about how long he had been married: "Well, actually legally married for four years—but *married* married—or I guess religiously married." Exasperated, he shook his head dismissively and said, "You know what I mean." When I spoke with Agustin and Rosa, they struggled when I asked when they married. Agustin picked up a silver picture frame from a nearby table—showing me the wedding picture it held and reading the engraved date on it. He smirked, saying, "It's always here so I won't forget." But Rosa shook her head and said, "No, but, see, that's the wedding. We didn't have a wedding when we got married. We just went to the court." Struggles to pinpoint marriage dates may seem innocuous, but anniversary celebrations, getting-to-know-you conversations, and other moments indefinitely remind couples of their complex relationship trajectories and past legalization struggles.

This wedding strategy can also affect relationship dynamics. Ricky Montoya had married his citizen wife in a civil ceremony three years earlier and was caught up in a complex legalization process that had stranded him in Mexico for almost two years while she remained in the United States. He recalled, "At first, she was happy that she was going to get married. But in the long run, she hates me, because I gave her this fake wedding, in her eyes." Unable to live up to the promise of providing a "real" wedding made Ricky feel that he had failed. He added, "Most of her friends are getting married, and they're having nice weddings and all that. So now she feels like she got robbed." Although his wife did not mention these feelings, Ricky's perceptions shaded how he felt about their relationship and his role in it. Unlike Ricky, Santos was able to provide his wife with her dream wedding because he was able to quickly adjust his status and secure a high-paying job afterward. They had a large ceremony and reception at a golf course, complete with a cocktail hour, three-course meal, salsa band, and photo booth. His wife, Sofi, admitted that she would have been resentful if he had not: "Maybe I wouldn't have expressed them explicitly or maybe I would've. I don't know. But 100 percent [resentful]."

Conflict also emerged as couples tried to manage their family members' opinions. Javier Espinoza, a recently legalized participant, explained that he and his wife continue to hide their civil ceremony from his wife's parents even though it had been over five years: "It felt like I betrayed them 'cause they're such an amazing in-laws. . . . I don't know when I'm going to tell him [her dad]. I don't know if I should. I think my wife said not to ever tell them." This choice maintains a distance between him and his in-laws and has also created tensions with his wife. Even when parents knew about the two-wedding strategy, tensions sometimes emerged because it did not match their cultural or religious desires for a traditional wedding ceremony.

In all, immigration law complicated mixed-status couples' marriage decisions, and then they worked hard to find a way to align their wedding ideals with their legal realities. The emotional labor they poured into these decisions continued to follow them as they married and began the legalization process.

"YOU HAVE TO LEGITIMIZE YOUR RELATIONSHIP": PERFORMING LOVE IN THE LEGALIZATION PROCESS

After marrying, couples embarked on the complex process wherein the citizen spouse sponsors the undocumented partner's adjustment of status application. Both partners painstakingly fill out multiple forms with over 40 pages of detailed information, including immigration and citizenship history, residence and employment histories, income, assets, and three years of tax information. They gather copies of required eligibility evidence, including birth and marriage certificates, tax documents, and passports. If the petitioning spouse's income is not high enough, they must find someone who will serve as a fiscal sponsor and have them fill out forms.[6] The undocumented partner undergoes an official medical examination, and they both take passport-style photos. All this paperwork is submitted along with required fees, which in 2019 totaled at least $1,760.[7]

Couples then anxiously await an appointment notification to interview. If they entered with inspection or are otherwise eligible, they report with their spouse to interview at a local U.S. Citizenship and Immigration Services (USCIS) office. If they entered without inspection or are otherwise ineligible to adjust their status within the United States, they are summoned to appear alone at the consulate office in their country of origin.

As they prepare, couples recognize that they will have to counteract marriage myths. They and their relationship documents must perform their love for the benefit of the immigration officer, who is charged with "determin[ing] whether the marriage is bona fide" and "was not entered into solely for immigration purposes."[8] Those who deviate from expected relationship patterns risk further interrogation, delay, or denial because of suspicion of marriage fraud. I explore here the interview experiences of couples who adjusted their status in the United States because both spouses attend the interview and must participate in relationship performance.[9] Regardless of where the interview takes place and if both spouses are present, the process breeds long-term consequences by requiring couples to portray a conventional and recognizable relationship to immigration officials.

Preparing Materials to Prove One's Relationship Is "Real"

Anticipating the need to prove their love, couples set out to gather as much proof of their relationship as possible. The interview appointment notice from USCIS contains a checklist of required documents, including a directive to bring "supporting evidence of your relationship, such as copies of any documentation regarding joint assets or liabilities you and your spouse may have together. This may include: tax returns, bank statements, insurance documents (car, life, health), property documents (car, house, etc.), rental agreements, utility bills, credit cards, contracts, leases, photos, correspondence and/or any other documents you feel may substantiate your relationship."[10] This notice, however, is usually received only a month or two before the interview. All participants reported preparing much sooner, often as soon as they decided to pursue legalization, by seeking advice from people who had gone through the process, internet forums, and/or lawyers. This head start was necessary to negotiate the frustrating bureaucracy involved in getting multiple names on an account and collect a longer history of documents. Remembering the experience, Cindy Figueroa sighed heavily. "Oh, God! I'd rather individually pluck my eyelashes out!"

During the 10 months between their wedding and filing her application, Mia Ochoa began building up strong institutional evidence of their relationship; she believed this entailed performing a conventional marriage with joint finances. Feeling that they needed "papers under our names, like the bills," they moved out of her parents' house and put all their bills in both their names. They made calculated decisions about "opening credit so they can see that we both are joined in our accounts. That is when I closed my bank account, because we had separate bank accounts, so we decided, 'OK, let's put them together.' And that way they are going to see, 'OK, they are married.'" Mia did this out of a need to perform their relationship but would have preferred to keep their finances separate. Indeed, over a quarter of millennial couples, aged 23–37, keep their finances separate.[11] She recalled, "I was scared because my sister had a bad experience with her husband, so I didn't want to go through that. There was times when she would tell me, 'I earn more than him, so he is using my money.'" Finances are fraught with potential for conflict, and many worried about the cascading consequences of financial intermingling for their relationships' power dynamics. Despite this, immigration law pushed them forward.

Couples also amassed evidence of their romantic history to perform a conventional relationship trajectory. Mia prepared an album with six years' worth of photos to prove the length of their relationship, since "you can see in our faces we are different [ages]." She unearthed a notebook of letters they exchanged in high school. Others pulled out similar evidence—scrapbooks, notes, cards, wedding pictures—documenting their relationship's progression. These forms of evidence often relied on having a relationship that followed a traditional timeline. Further, it was available only to couples who had publicly performed their relationship in expected ways; others were at a disadvantage.

Several couples struggled to perform a conventional marriage. Javier Espinoza spoke about how he and his wife struggled to document their shared finances: "I was so broke, so I was living with my parents. So my parents wrote a letter [that we live there together]." Living at home meant that joint rental agreements and utility bills did not exist. Limited incomes also made it unlikely that couples had accumulated other joint bills, assets, or insurance. Such difficulties were most common among couples in which both partners reported low incomes because of underemployment, low education levels, or being enrolled in school.

Couples who had shorter relationships had to be creative. Regina Castro remembered, "We got married before we even reached one year of being together in our relationship. So in terms of filling out this gap of all these years of knowing each other, we didn't have that. . . . We just had our joint bank accounts, we had some credit cards together. . . . We didn't have a lot of pictures." Their lawyer worried about their lack of proof and instructed them to get letters from friends corroborating their relationship and their good moral character. They strategically deployed their connections from being politically engaged during college. She explained, "I got a statement from a state congresswoman [I had worked with], and he got one from the [state] senator he worked for. When we went to the interview, once they saw those two letters, they just asked us what our name was and how we met, and we walked out the door with our stuff." Few individuals, though, have such powerful connections to counterbalance their limited proof. Such couples must rely on their ability to successfully perform the relationship during their interview.

Portraying a "Real" Marriage in the Immigration Interview

During the interview, immigration officials ask questions about the relationship to determine if it is real. I asked similar questions during my interviews: How did you meet? When did you marry? Often there was variation in how couples recounted their stories. Mia's husband could not remember the year they married, laughing: "This is the problem with men. They forget." Retellings often differed as partners forgot dates and details; assuming that this would look suspicious, couples practiced portraying a clear relationship history that matched hegemonic preconceptions.

Fearing scrutiny, many couples reviewed interview questions meant to assess if they had common knowledge of each other, their relationship, their home, and their daily routines. Mia remembered thinking, "Oh my God! I have to get to know him," even though they had been together for six years. "We even sat down and we started asking each other like, 'What is your favorite drink?' We knew, but we just wanted to make sure that it would be the same." In the weeks before their interview, Regina and her husband walked through their apartment and made mental notes about mundane details: the microwave was on top of the refrigerator, her husband had used a Sharpie to change the brand name from MagicChef to MagicChief—an inside joke. They clung to these trivia as evidence of their love.

Both undocumented and citizen partners developed anxiety about effectively portraying a legitimate marriage. Manuel Serrano, a recently legalized participant, and Rosa Lopez, the citizen partner of another participant, shared,

> *Manuel:* I was sweating. . . . I was so scared that I couldn't even—I was thinking, "I'm not going to be able to answer the questions because I'm so nervous. And then he's going to notice that I'm so nervous and he's going to think there's something wrong."
>
> *Rosa:* You hear stories and people tell you these things. And you start thinking, "Oh my God, what if they don't believe [us]?" . . . I knew deep inside like they can't prove that I'm lying because I know this marriage is true. . . . But at the same time you wonder, "What if they really don't believe me?"

Both Manuel and Rosa had strong cases. Manuel and his wife had been married for three years and had a daughter before they even applied. Rosa and her husband had been together eight years before they married and filed his application. Yet the depth of their relationship did little to allay their fears, and they overprepared for the interview.

In many cases, couples remembered their interviews proceeding quickly and smoothly because their evidence performed their relationship for them. Manuel's wife, Carmen, remembered that they were asked only a few questions: "Who introduced you guys? How did you guys meet? When did you guys move in together?" Manuel added that they asked him how often his wife was paid, which was compared to the joint bank statements they provided. This portion of the interview was over in minutes. Hypothesizing why, Manuel compared himself to friends who had received much more scrutiny and had to answer more personal questions: "It's because they don't have kids or because they got married on a weekend, then the next week they submitted the [legalization] paperwork." Couples who had constructed clearly interconnected lives—financially though joint accounts or socially through children—often reported a quick and easy interview.

Couples were scrutinized when they did not have sufficient institutional evidence. Ramón Le, Cindy Figueroa, and Javier Espinoza—all individuals who fast-forwarded their relationships to pursue legalization—provide examples of the type of questions that emerged:

> *Ramón:* They asked, "How come you don't have more [wedding] pictures?"
>
> *Cindy:* He came in asking us about our relationship from beginning to end. Asking about our bathroom—what does it look like. I go in the bathroom every single day, but I can't really describe it. . . . He's asking like, "When you turn the [cold water] faucet on, is it left or right?" And I'm going, "Oh my God! I don't know."
>
> *Javier:* He asked me questions—which side of the bed she sleeps on, what kind of underwear she wears. . . . It was really awkward for me. . . . And then he was just asking me sexual questions. I just refused to answer those questions.
>
> *Laura:* Like what?
>
> *Javier:* Like what's her favorite [sexual] position and that kind of stuff. The guy was getting real kinky with me.

Their relationships had not followed a traditional trajectory. Ramón and his wife, both ethnically Chinese, had employed a two-wedding strategy and so did not have traditional photos the immigration agent associated with typical Chinese wedding ceremonies. Cindy and her husband had a nontraditional relationship progression, having dated on and off for years. Javier and his wife had few financial accounts because of their struggling socioeconomic situation. Unable to present a traditional relationship through their documents, Ramón, Cindy, Javier, and their partners were forced to perform their relationship.

It is important to recognize that all couples' successful performance of their relationship was likely informed by their social positions as acculturated 1.5-generation young adults, many of whom had pursued higher education. This likely shielded some couples from suspicion and gave others the tools they needed to negotiate this complex interaction.

Presenting LGBQ Relationships in a Heterocentric Institution

Although heterosexual couples anticipated scrutiny, lesbian, gay, bisexual, and queer (LGBQ) couples expected additional complications as they prepared to participate in a heterocentric institution. I spoke to three such couples as they were going through the legalization process. All were concerned about how homophobia may be infused into the process, both explicitly through prejudice and implicitly through the use of conventional relationship archetypes. At various points in the process, they realized that the immigration system was not prepared to deal with same-sex couples.

Crys Carvajal, a queer-identified U visa recipient, recalled how she and her partner faced homophobic microaggressions when initiating their application:

> When I was calling the law office, I was like, "I'm going to be sponsoring my spouse when I'm doing my LPR thing [adjustment]. Her and I would like to come in for a consultation." [They were] like, "Oh, when is your husband going to be available?" I'm like, "I told you that it was a woman already, right? Why do you keep pushing male pronouns?"

Crys was used to advocating for herself and had the cultural capital to challenge the office staff and complain to the managing attorney. Though these comments were angering and invalidating, her savvy ensured that they did not deter their application. Wearier LGBQ applicants, however, might abandon the legalization petition if they cannot even get their lawyer's office to recognize the basic nature of their romantic relationship.

Some wrestled with building relationship evidence, especially if they are not fully open about their sexual identity or their relationship. A common strategy for navigating homophobia within Latino communities and families is to cover one's sexual identity or relationship status.[12] This can present a problem because the USCIS field manual lists "family and/or friends [being] unaware of the marriage" as a potential indication of fraud.[13] Evan Grande, a citizen petitioning for his husband, explained that his family does not know he is married: "I mean, I haven't gone to the first step of telling them I'm even gay. So now that I just jumped to married. That's gonna be a nice surprise for them." He conceded that this could become a problem if their case was investigated: "I don't really know exactly if immigration comes to talk to our parents unless they suspect fraud. So maybe then it might be a problem." Evan's partner, David Soto, explained that concealing their relationship from Evan's family "just happens to be the process of our commitment to one another." He recognized that individuals who are not familiar with the specific experiences of LGBQ Latinas/os/xs might be confused by their choice.

Though no couples had attended their USCIS interview at the time we talked, they feared that homophobia might endanger their petition. David hypothesized, "If we get someone that's homophobic, they could give us a really bad attitude, they could judge us differently." He posited that if homophobia and transphobia exist in schools and workplaces, it's going to exist in USCIS offices. "So take the homophobia piece and somebody that's already skeptical of the system [looking for fraudulent relationships]. Those two factors could lead to something really bad." LGBQ couples have long faced structural inequalities that routinely invalidate their relationships. With same-sex marriages being so recently recognized, it seems doubtful that they would be understood and affirmed by the state. Further, stereotypes about same-sex relationships as short-term sexual escapades can cause further damage by casting same-sex marriages as less real relative to heterosexual ones. Indeed, David's lawyer confirmed these intersecting inequalities, telling them that "the officers are really digging deep and are asking a lot of questions" for LGBQ applicants.

To combat these compounded barriers, David and Evan's lawyer encouraged them to keep "building your memories together" and develop institutionalized proof, like adding Evan to David's apartment lease. They both worked diligently to document their relationship. Yet it seems probable that LGBQ couples who live in highly homophobic contexts may find it difficult to put official documents in both their names or may feel unsafe with a public performance of their relationship, preventing activities like taking pictures together.[14] It may be additionally difficult for couples who do not conform to heteronormative relationship expectations.[15]

David was angry about having to validate his relationship. We talked for a long time about the pressure to prove his relationship with Evan: "It sucks that as LGBT folks going into this process, you have to legitimize your relationship . . . and your commitment to one another." Though he credited this need to validate their relationship to their status as a same-sex couple, I recognized this anger from heterosexual couples and pushed him to explain what felt unique:

> There's a lot of privilege in being heterosexual and embarking on this [legalization] process. . . . [I] walk into that room already feeling like the underdog and for the longest time being discriminated for being LGBT, for being undocumented, for being Latino . . . having to validate your experience . . . so walking into that room, it's already like boom, boom, boom, boom.

There are many similarities between the experiences of LGBQ and straight couples who are going through the legalization bureaucracy—both have to prove their relationship and can feel angry and overwhelmed. As David aptly noted, however, experiencing a lifetime of homophobia, and anticipating more from a USCIS agent, can add layers of difficulty and trauma for LGBQ applicants.

"PUNISHMENT": VARIED CONSEQUENCES OF RISKING A 10-YEAR BAR

Most participants encountered the relatively straightforward legalization process described above because they had overstayed tourist visas or had long-pending legalization petitions that protected them from undergoing consular processing.

Although they stressed about gathering paperwork and feared suspicions of fraud, most were confident that their application would be approved. The smoothness of this process led Dolores Inda to think of her interview as "a joke" because "it was just sad and depressing that it was just so simple." She and the others who were privileged to complete the process in the United States usually had permanent residency within six months of filing their application.

Six participants, however, underwent the more complicated and risky process of consular processing. They returned to Mexico to file their petition, not knowing if or when they would return because they faced a 10-year bar on their reentry. The only way to avoid this punishment was to prove that their 10-year absence would place "extreme hardship" on their citizen spouse, who would remain in the United States during their absence or live with them abroad. Extreme hardship is ambiguously defined as "hardship [that] must exceed that which is usual or expected" from any 10-year separation or move; expected emotional distress and financial deprivation are not sufficiently extreme.[16] Their uncertain fate lay at the discretion of whichever immigration agent pulled their case. Given the high risks and difficulty proving *extreme* hardship, few pursue this route; only about 65,000 consular cases were processed in 2010–15.[17] Those who take the risk often have strong cases; close to 80 percent of these waiver petitions were approved.[18] I trace three successful cases here to show the diverging strategies for undergoing this process and how each had different consequences.

Going Together: Blanca and Pedro's Material Risks

After eight years of marriage, Blanca Marín and her citizen husband, Pedro, finally decided to risk the 10-year bar to pursue her legalization. Their lawyer was confident that their legalization application would be approved but felt they had little to demonstrate extreme hardship. Blanca remembered, "[The lawyer] said there was a good risk that they could leave me there for a couple of years, the maximum 10 years."

Despite the risks, they felt that this was a necessary step to "succeed together as a couple." Unlike most of my participants, Blanca had migrated at age 15 and fondly remembered life in Mexico and had strong ties to her family there.[19] They decided that they would travel together, so that her husband "could stay with me" and she could continue to care for their two children. They spent two years saving up money so that they could afford living expenses for the first few months while they looked for jobs.

Luckily, Blanca's application was processed quickly, and her waiver petition was approved. She recounted their risky move as more like an extended two-month vacation. They had saved enough that neither had started to look for work. They never got around to enrolling their children in school. Because they were not gone that long, their reintegration after returning to the United States was relatively easy since they were able to return to their old jobs—she as a sales agent and he as a security guard. Theirs was truly a best-case scenario.

Blanca's process proceeded quickly and successfully. Their waiver, however, could have easily been denied. If this had happened, her family likely would have faced financial, educational, and emotional trauma. Given the state of the Mexican economy, Blanca and Pedro would probably have been unable to find well-paying jobs to sustain them once their savings ran out. Their children stumbled with Spanish, and she believed that it would have been hard for them to go to a school where they would have to speak a "new language." Indeed, journalists and scholars confirm that Mexican schools are unprepared to support the children of returnees who have had no formal Spanish-language instruction.[20] Further, these children have a hard time adjusting to the new cultural context and suffer emotional trauma from leaving their U.S. lives behind.[21]

Going Alone: Nicolás and Elisa's Emotional Strain

Unlike Blanca, Nicolás Fernandez chose to travel alone, risking the emotional trauma of family separation. Nicolás decided to finally get his "stuff straightened out" when Elisa became pregnant. They married and prepared the application as they awaited the birth of their son. A lawyer prepared their hardship statement, weaving together how Elisa would struggle to care for both their infant son and Nicolás's parents, who had health problems.

Tears welled in Elisa's eyes as she remembered Nicolás boarding a bus to Mexico. Her voice shook: "I've always thought of myself as a strong person, but when he got on that bus, I was like, 'What if something [happens]?' . . . And you start thinking if anything happens to him, I would have rather he'd been here. Undocumented, but here. So that was scary, that was really scary." She kept these fears bottled up inside because she "didn't want [Nicolás] to worry" and felt "helplessness . . . 'cause nothing is in your hands at that very moment. You just have to wait and see."

Elisa felt lucky to be in a relatively comfortable situation while Nicolás was gone. She had graduated from college and was working for an international firm that paid well enough to sustain them. She lived with Nicolás's parents, who helped with childcare and household activities. But she also felt stuck. She "hated" her job but had to continue: "I kept thinking like, Ah, maybe if I get a flat tire or little small accident, maybe I won't have to go to work. But I had to 'cause I had responsibilities and he was out in Mexico." This also had longer-term consequences: she "put things on hold" and delayed her return to school to obtain her teaching credential and master's degree.

While Nicolás missed Elisa for the three months he was in Mexico, he remembered that the worst part was being unable to see his son: "I left and he was already verbalizing, but not like articulate. And then I would Skype with him and all the things he would say! And I'm like, Oh my God, I'm missing all this. It was probably by far one of the most difficult things to try to endure." Children learn new skills every day, and their one-and-half-year-old son grew into an entirely different person during his absence. Elisa witnessed how this was also hard on their son: "He knew that his dad was gone, and but he was still small enough where he'd get distracted with any little thing. But there was definitely times [when he was like,] 'Where is dad?' Or when he came back, he [our son] was like . . . 'Who are you?'"

In the end, Elisa and Nicolás felt that the legalization process had punished their whole family. They count themselves lucky that their waiver was approved, their separation lasted *only* three months, and their son was so young that he does not remember. Still, three years later, the pain of their separation was palpable and had shaped their family's trajectory.

Stuck: Ricky and Isabel's Two-Year Pause

When Ricky Montoya left for Mexico, he expected a process much like Nicolás's. He began the process at the consulate and was referred to a psychologist as part of his medical exam: "Since I have dreadlocks, they gave me a big old hard time. . . . I got a lady and she was just asking me about why I have dreadlocks, if I have a drug problem, if I was in a gang. All this nonsense that didn't relate to me." While this was annoying, he didn't think it was a problem. Two days later he went to his interview, in which the immigration agent flatly told him, "'Your punishment for this is one year.' And I was just shocked. I was like, for why? . . . He was just like, 'Well, I don't know. It's not my fault. I'm sorry. According to the person that interviewed you, she thinks that you have a drug problem.'" Confirmed drug use would have made Ricky inadmissible. It seems most likely that the immigration officer adjudicating Ricky's case used his discretion to allow him to reapply in one year if he could prove he was clean. He immediately regretted their decision to be counseled by a *notario,* a notary public who illegally practices law, often leading to grievous errors like this one. His wife, Isabel, hired a real immigration lawyer, only to learn they had no legal recourse. They resigned to spending a year apart before they could reinitiate his petition.

When I interviewed Isabel, they were almost two years into their separation. Before we even got settled for the interview, she launched into the saga. She was upbeat, but her pain was unmistakable. "We've had some arguments and ups and downs, just from the pain of being separated. There's times where I'm broke and I would get angry at him 'cause if he were here working, it wouldn't be so hard on me." She talked about "being lonely" and "not being able to do the same things you used to do when you were together." Further, their separation set them "behind in our life," and she hinted that she had wanted children by now since she was in her late 20s.

On a Skype call with Ricky, he sighed heavily when I asked how they managed the separation:

> She's lonely. . . . I talk to her every night. But there's points where she breaks and she just feels like she can't do it anymore. And recently, she's been telling me that she can't handle anymore being lonely, she wants to come live over here with me. She wants to pretty much drop her whole life over there. . . . It's just hard to keep [telling] her to have patience, just try to keep her calm.

As part of the process of establishing "extreme hardship" for their waiver petition, Isabel had visited a psychologist to confirm a diagnosis of depression and anxiety. Acknowledging that this makes their case stronger, Ricky still felt "awful. I feel like [her pain is] all my fault."

Throughout our conversation, Ricky continually referred to the financial burden the process placed on Isabel. He concluded that he is not a good husband: "I think to be a good husband, obviously you need to be the man in the relationship. And pay the bills. And you know, be there with your wife when she needs you." He sent her the money he earned working construction, but it was not much. He admitted that when work slows down, "I get super depressed. And anxious. There's been five, six times where I've been thinking I'm just going to go and try to cross illegally."

They clung to the hope that they would be separated only a few more months. His reinterview went well, and they had recently been allowed to submit their 10-year bar waiver. Three months after I interviewed them, Ricky's petition was approved, and he returned home. Both were trying to look on the bright side when I spoke to them a few months after his return. Their readjustment seemed to meet Isabel's early expectations: "I think our relationship will be different in a positive way. I think we'll be a lot stronger, a lot more aware of the way the world works. And we'll just appreciate each other a lot more." They were spending a lot of time together—eating breakfast, going out, and reconnecting with friends and family.

Yet negative consequences loomed. Ricky's long absence and limited employment history in a tight job market meant that he was still unemployed after almost two months of looking. Having been pretty quiet, he exploded when we started talking about their financial situation: "Right now, I still feel frustrated. . . . I still feel how I used to feel before I left. She's still paying for rent and everything. And I want to help her. And it sucks because like I say, it's all still a waiting game. A waiting game that's still not over." He recounted how he had been applying for countless jobs and not getting called back for even minimum-wage jobs at chain stores like Target. While Isabel continued to work at her office job, she admitted, "Now I'm spending more money on food 'cause I have another mouth [to feed]. The money is going quicker now that he's here than it did before."

In the midst of Ricky's continuing frustration with being unable to financially provide, these barriers will likely pose challenges to their family formation. They insisted that their relationship survived their separation unscathed:

> *Isabel:* I feel like we just kind of waited for each other, though.
>
> *Laura:* Like life stopped?
>
> *Isabel:* Yeah.
>
> *Ricky:* That's the way I see everyone too. I came back and I thought everything was going to be different, friends and things. Everyone's the same—just apparently everyone has kids now.

I asked if they had thought about becoming parents. Ricky quickly and definitively responded no, but Isabel hedged: "I kind of get the baby fever." Ricky referenced their financial instability: "I need to get my life back on the—" before Isabel jumped in, "That's mainly why." Immigration law delayed their having children for two years while Ricky was out of the country and they continued to postpone as they picked up the pieces.

All these cases could have easily gone another way. Rejection would have left families to choose between abandoning the United States or undergoing long-term separation, both options compromising all family members' economic and socioemotional stability.

UNANTICIPATED CONSEQUENCES

Legalization through marriage offers an opportunity to transform one's life circumstances—but it ties this to a sustained romantic relationship. Couples who successfully navigated the immigration bureaucracy found that their lives improved to varying extents after legalizing the undocumented partner's status. Doors opened to educational and employment opportunities, allowing some to pursue upward mobility, while others struggled to find their way back to school or into better jobs. Some felt their fears of deportation melt away, while others suffered "posttraumatic stress" from a lifetime of surveillance. Some continued to avoid bars and other age-restricted spaces, while others joyfully entered. Despite the material, psychological, and social benefits of legalization, it carried unanticipated effects, often at a cost to their relationships.

Positive Impacts: Building Stronger and More Stable Partnerships

Recently legalized young adults who had already completed their higher education or were on the brink of career opportunities were best positioned to foster their family's collective mobility. Three years after his legalization, Nicolás Fernandez and his wife were solidly middle class. Before adjusting his status, Nicolás had graduated from college but continued to work two jobs at a gas station and a fast-food restaurant. As a permanent resident, he got a job with an after-school program and returned to school to pursue a teaching credential and a master's degree in education. He quickly found a full-time job as a teacher and began earning about $45,000 a year. With Nicolás making a decent salary, Elisa quit her job to pursue her teaching credential. Reflecting on these transitions, Nicolás exclaimed that their economic situation was "a billion times better!" He hypothesized that both their careers and joint economic situation would have suffered if he had not legalized; he could not earn that much while remaining undocumented, and they wouldn't have been able to afford Elisa's returning to school. Further, he suspected that a worse economic situation would have prevented them from having a second child. Nicolás was able to achieve such rapid upward mobility thanks to his pursuit of higher education; others, particularly those with limited education, saw less.

The economic mobility and physical security that accompanies legalization also allows couples to plan for their future together. Economic stability relieved financial stress while also allowing couples to plan for their financial future, like buying a house and saving for retirement. Arturo Molina connected this to his relatively low risk of deportation.[22] He no longer felt "stuck in that position of like, we can't plan for the future because we don't know . . . if you will be here then."

Going through the legalization process can also offer couples an opportunity to bond. Recalling their application efforts, Arturo Molina felt that "it was special. We are both doing it together and both going to the interviews or to the [lawyer's] appointments to put it together. It was nice. I think we got to learn a little bit more about our families." Filling out mundane paperwork and looking for documents allowed them to ask questions about their past and their families. According to his wife, Nicole, the interview also helped her better understand his life as an undocumented immigrant. She recounted how the immigration officer hounded Arturo for having tickets for driving without a license. He sat there silently while Nicole got increasingly "pissed off. Is this how we're treating people? . . . But then I realized this is how these [undocumented] people are treated all the time. This is just the normal." Witnessing this interaction, Nicole better understood Arturo's previous experiences and his undocumented family members' outlooks. Although it was a negative experience, they both focused on small instances in which they were brought closer, united against a common enemy—the U.S. immigration system.

Partners often grew closer when they shared in the emotional labor of the process. Crys Carvajal, a formerly undocumented woman who was recently granted a U visa, was preparing to petition for the legalization of her undocumented partner, Monica Zambrano.[23] I asked Monica how she felt about this prospect: "I have a lot of feelings," she joked. As we laughed, her jaw began to tremble, and tears welled in her eyes: "She's really great at supporting me and helping me work through my feelings and my concerns about what this means."

Crys knew the emotional turbulence well from her own experiences applying for a U visa, grappling with the rollercoaster of emotions the accompanied her transition out of undocumented status. This pushed her to support Monica through the process. In one instance, Crys took the day off to accompany Monica to an appointment with the lawyer, despite her insistence that she could go alone. As expected, Crys saw Monica's "anxiety building up in her" as they waited in the office: "We couldn't even talk. It was just silence." Anticipating this, Crys had helped Monica develop a list of questions, all of which Monica promptly forgot to ask until Crys gently reminded her. Throughout the process, Crys provided key forms of instrumental and emotional support that helped Monica feel comfortable and prepared. Though most petitioners did not have Crys's intimate experience with the immigration system, a few other partners tried to actively support their undocumented partner and engage in the process, bringing them closer together.

Negative Impacts: New Responsibilities and Haunted Relationships

Linking legal status to the establishment and maintenance of a marriage also had negative consequences. Any marriage can be troubled with instances of regret, unrealized goals, and conflict. Here, though, immigration law shaded partners' understanding of these struggles. This was particularly common in fast-forwarded or strategic relationships in which legalization reshaped their relationship trajectory. In most cases, immigration law created enduring consequences by limiting one's ability to pursue new opportunities, creating emotional baggage that emerged at times of conflict, and stunting romantic lives.

"Marriage Took Over": Limiting the Pursuit of New Opportunities. Legalizing through marriage opened up opportunities for upward mobility while also creating competing responsibilities. In most cases, undocumented young adults' desperation mounted as they approached critical life junctures, like finishing college. Javier Espinoza spoke longingly of finishing a few remaining classes to obtain his bachelor's degree; this was one of the main reasons he chose to marry. His goal, however, remained unrealized after five years primarily because "I was also married. So marriage took over. As supportive as my wife has been and as amazing as she is, the fact that I'm married . . . I had to work." He turned his attention away from school, which would have been more affordable because of his newfound ability to access financial aid. Instead, he threw himself into his new job as a financial planner, often working late. This sense of responsibility also meant that Javier could not travel, even though he could now leave the country. He laughingly quoted his wife: "Pues, paga los billes y paga la luz [Well, you gotta pay the bills and pay the electricity]." He softly added, "Man, that sucks I can't really travel the world."

Citizen partners shared these newfound responsibilities. Having married in her early 20s, Sofi Castellanos believed she and her husband would have been able to "grow up a little bit more" if they had waited longer:

> I think we built our careers while being married. And maybe [it would be better if] we would've done it previous to [getting married]. . . . [So] he doesn't have to sit at the office at six o'clock thinking, "Oh my gosh, I have to go home to my wife and my dogs." *[Laughs.]* . . . He could've just stayed focused on his job and I could've done the same. Instead of [me] being at work and thinking, "Oh my gosh, I have to go back home and cook and do this and do that."

Notably, Sofi said that she *and* her husband, Santos, had to navigate these new competing demands. Most dual-career families struggle to balance their career with family life.[24] But couples directly attributed these frustrations to the power that immigration law held over their marriage decisions, forcing them to take on marriage responsibilities prematurely.

By contrast, those who legalized their status through long-awaited extended family petitions were significantly more likely to pursue new opportunities. Alejandra Sanchez legalized her status as a child dependent on a petition that her father's employer filed in the 1990s. She was 20 and halfway through college. Having legal status paved the way for completing college and pursuing several career-relevant jobs. With no familial responsibilities, she simply quit her job when she was ready to get her master's degree and moved to the East Coast to enroll in a top program.

This differs sharply from those who legalized through marriage. For Regina Castro, marriage meant that she had to "plan her future in conjunction with" her husband's. Though she legalized around the same point in her life as Alejandra, doing so through marriage limited her pursuit of various educational and career opportunities. When she pursued opportunities, it stressed their relationship as they found themselves living on opposite sides of the country. When they separated, almost five years later, she felt as if it lifted a "weight off her shoulders," because now she could move wholeheartedly in new directions, without feeling guilty for not supporting her husband's goals.

"Did You Marry Me for the Papers?" Emotional Baggage from the Marriage Myth.   When couples are in the midst of establishing their life together, the marriage myth often reemerges in times of conflict. For Javier, working long hours to take advantage of his newly legal status showed his commitment to ensuring their financial stability. Yet his wife struggled to understand why he was never home. He recalled a fight: "She was like, 'You abandoned me. You don't have time for me no more. Did you marry me for the papers?'" While any partner may feel abandoned in such a situation, Javier's wife questioned the strategic timing of

their marriage, showing how they continued to grapple with how immigration law molded their relationship.

Marriage myth messages often exacerbated underlying relationship conflict. Elena Loera married her citizen partner after five years and became a conditional permanent resident about eight months before our second interview. This had been transformative: "By him marrying me, . . . [it] gave me wings to be better." A senior in college, Elena was able to accept a prestigious engineering internship. She spent substantial time at school studying and participating in career-building activities to make up for her previous lack of opportunities. She knew this would be the only way to succeed as a woman of color in a field dominated by white men. These activities, however, created marital problems: "Now that [opportunities are] there, it's like he can't deal with them." With him not pursuing college, she recognized that their prospects would diverge: "I mean, he works, but . . . for a guy to know 'my wife's gonna make more money than me.' That's a threat to them." Although she had been attending school throughout their relationship, gaining legal status gave her the wings that would allow her to fly farther than him. He seemed to resent that reality.

Elena recalled how her husband began relying on marriage myths as their relationship soured. She sighed, "He was the one that would encourage me. . . . But now it's like he doesn't wanna be with me. He said I only married him just for the papers." This hurt her deeply because she had delayed their marriage specifically to avoid these accusations: "He offered at the beginning, four months into our relationship. And I said no. . . . I'd [rather] struggle by myself forever. I would never marry for that. So him knowing that and telling me I did it just for that, it breaks my heart." Unable to recover from these accusations, they separated.

While complications emerged early in Javier and Elena's marriages, Santos explained that these feelings could endure. He recalled that they would have "small fights day in, day out" about "married couple stuff," and "after two, three years, you just get fed up." These fights led them to question their relationship: "At some point, you think it's not going to work out, so you start questioning what went wrong. And obviously one of the options she's going to think is 'Well, maybe you're not in it. He just wanted this [legalization]. So now you got it, you can walk away.'" He explained that these accusations leave him "very frustrated," because "you don't know what to say because how can I prove it wrong?" He continued, "If I do walk away, we do split up, people are gonna think that [it was for papers]." Both were still negotiating these suspicions years into their marriage and past the point at which Santos needed to remain married for legalization purposes.

"Love Life on Hold": Stunted Love in Fast-Forwarded and Strategic Relationships.   Fast-forwarding a romantic relationship or engaging in a strategic relationship produced additional romantic consequences. One participant who had

fast-forwarded his relationship believed that this had prevented him from fully evaluating if this was the right relationship. Marrying in their early 20s, straight out of college, meant that they had not grown into their adult selves:

> I don't think she ever saw me as an adult until we were living together, which is kind of too late. Right? So you had that growing pain, a lot of conflict. [If] we would've waited two years, when I was 25 [or] 26 . . . I would've learned everything I know now about myself. . . . She would have seen that and been like, I'm in or I'm out. And it would've been the same for me.

He knew this when they married but rationalized it: "You're always going to lose in life. So, you know, the best decision is the decision that gives you the least losses." Surprised, I asked if he felt he had settled; was his marriage just about minimizing loss? He responded bluntly, "That's correct." Glancing across the coffee shop at his wife, he added, "Don't tell her."

Those in strategic marriages found that this arrangement limited both partners' pursuit of true romantic relationships. Dulce Puente recounted how a man she was interested in was unwilling to overlook her strategic marriage: "I actually told him that I was still married. He was Christian, and he just felt that it wasn't right, so he left." Lena Gomez avoided dating until she became a citizen because she felt her situation was too difficult to explain: "I did briefly date someone, two people. . . . They get a little jealous at the beginning and kind of like, 'Are you sure there's nothing else going on?'" Lena reflected on whether this also affected her friend and husband: "I feel like it's harder for him, which kind of sucks. Like, he doesn't tell people he dates that we're married. And [even] then I remember when he was dating this girl, she came over to the house [and] she was like, 'Your roommate's a girl?'" Lena's very presence created problems.

In some cases, strategic marriages can also prevent more serious relationships. Dulce was now dating someone who accepted her marriage but felt "like it can't get serious just because of that. I feel like I can't start something new until I end that chapter. . . . So it kinda puts my love life on hold." Worried about getting divorced too soon after the removal of the conditions from her permanent residency, she continued to live her romantic life in the shadows of an immigration policy that should have led to her social integration. Similarly, Lena's boyfriend remarked that her strategic marriage disrupted their marriage prospects: "First she has to get divorced before that can happen and maybe [then] I'll start thinking about time."

Having to maintain the illusion of a marriage for two years can come with heavy social costs. Miriam Velez explained how her fear of detection by immigration officials led her to socially withdraw:

> I don't even have a Facebook account because I'm so afraid that someone is gonna find out something. I don't really talk to people at work about my personal life.

I don't really talk to my friends about things that have to do with this. So it's kind of like . . . you're keeping secrets from one person and keeping secrets from others, it's very difficult.

She noted that her friends do not know that she is married and think she lives with a friend. She minimized the lies and half-truths by avoiding others. Lena similarly watched her digital footprint: "Hell no, I can't put anything on my Facebook about any of that stuff. I'm very careful about that, I'm very careful about pictures, I'm very careful about texts, I'm very careful about emails." While it is unclear if this suspicion was warranted during their applications, USCIS announced in September 2017 that it will collect social media data for all immigrants entering the country and applying for permanent residence or naturalization.[25] This policy will likely increase social costs.

CONCLUSION

U.S. immigration law purports to value familial relationships, but regulations and practices simultaneously disrupt families. Contemporary immigration, legalization, and deportation policies often separate family members, producing disastrous economic, social, and emotional consequences. I have shown here that consequences even arise in the best-case scenarios of people who experience relatively easy transitions into legality.

Mirroring previous findings by Cecilia Menjívar and Sarah Lakhani, I find that immigration law produces transformative effects in undocumented young adults' family structures, specifically shaping their marriage decisions.[26] These effects also extend into relationships' psychosocial aspects. Relationships are stressed in a myriad of ways when they become the key to legal status and the opportunities it brings. Undocumented young adults and their citizen partners repeatedly acknowledge the connections between marriage and legalization. Laws forced couples to fast-forward relationships, sacrifice their social and romantic lives for a strategic marriage, or continually validate their long-term romantic relationships. The legalization process required both undocumented and citizen individuals to make sacrifices, suffer indignities, and move their relationships in directions they may not be ready for. Although legalization improves the lives of undocumented young adults and their loved ones, these benefits come with enduring psychosocial costs.

6

―――――

"It's a Constant Struggle"

Becoming and Being Parents

[I kept telling myself], "I don't want to have a baby."... [Then I thought]
if I had papers, how do I see myself? I was like, I definitely see myself with
a baby by 29.... That fear and guilt feeling [from being undocumented] was
preventing me from having the future that I wanted.

—LUIS ESCOBAR

In their late 20s, Luis and his wife wanted a child, but he still felt unprepared for fatherhood. His undocumented status left him unable to find stable, well-paid employment, even after obtaining a college degree. Unable to provide, Luis often felt like a bad husband, and he feared things would only get worse with fatherhood. He put it simply: "You do feel like a drag if you're undocumented." Aware that he may never feel prepared, he decided not to let his undocumented status hold him back. Their daughter was a little over a year old by the time we first talked.

Luis made it painfully clear that his fears were being realized. They struggled financially as he pieced together part-time jobs: working at a restaurant, teaching Zumba exercise classes, coaching children's acting and dance classes, and selling Herbalife products. He had never recovered from being fired after his longtime employer tried to confirm his employment eligibility, pushing him to move his wife and infant daughter into a motor home in his in-laws' backyard. When I asked if being undocumented affected his ability to be a good father, he made an exception for his undocumented status: "No, no, when you put all of our restrictions aside, which is money, life, car, and bills ... outside restrictions, that doesn't make anyone better or less of a mother or father. So, I feel like I'm the best father ever. And I'm gonna keep striving to be that." But he admitted that it was difficult: "The way society has treated me [as an undocumented immigrant], it's a constant struggle to find a time to be with her and make enough money. And keep looking for the jobs that are gonna take me and the stress of not knowing what's gonna happen in the future." Luis was left feeling like a failure.

Previous research on mixed-status families has focused on how parental undocumented status constrains children's development.[1] I turn attention to parents to explore how these shared consequences affect their experiences. Luis and the 43 other undocumented parents I spoke to highlighted that immigration policies shaded their transition to parenthood. Restricted employment options, limited incomes, and inadequate time produced family-level economic instability. These material barriers collided with intensive parenting ideology. Grounded in middle-class realities, these ideals demand the investment of material and emotional resources to ensure children's proper development and future mobility. They are also tightly intertwined with gendered expectations: mothers are expected to perform intensive care work, while fathers provide financial support. Though there are class differences between parents' understanding of and methods for intensive parenting, they share an overarching commitment to prioritizing their children's needs and promoting children's future mobility.[2]

The parents I spoke to mostly had citizen children under age 10. They aspired to advance this next generation's upward mobility by providing a stable childhood: meeting their children's basic needs, spending time with them, and providing developmental opportunities to ensure future success. Immigration policies prevented some from feeling prepared to meet these ideals, disrupting their transition to parenthood. Material barriers and cultural ideals intertwined to shape the experiences of parents and parents-to-be, leaving many to feel inadequate. While receiving DACA opened up opportunities for improved family stability, these transformations were not guaranteed. Socioemotional barriers emerged throughout the transition to parenthood as undocumented young adults attempted to meet parenting ideals and realized they could not live up to their vision of what parenting should be.

"I WANT TO BE ABLE TO GIVE MY KID A GOOD LIFE": DECIDING TO BECOME A PARENT

The transition to parenthood begins with the decision to have a child. Some participants intentionally pursued parenthood, while others welcomed unplanned pregnancies. Often they were in established romantic partnerships and felt socially and emotionally ready to become a parent. Others delayed; like their citizen peers, they aimed for financial and relationship stability first.[3] Many identified ideal childbearing ages; often this aligned with educational attainment so that those who were pursuing higher education imagined becoming a parent once they completed their education and established financial stability. Wrapped into their decisions was the reality that undocumented status may complicate their ability to live up to parenting ideals. As they contemplated this transition, they all considered how immigration policies would affect their ability to parent, decided if they would allow this to influence their decision to have children, and identified how they would negotiate economic instability.

Delaying Parenting, Seeking Stability

Many undocumented young adults who were not parents but wanted children were discouraged by the instability their undocumented status created. This reflects previous work that finds that the implementation of local and state immigration enforcement lowered childbearing among undocumented women by 6.3 percent.[4] Similarly, I find that limited incomes and deportability drive parenting delays; this group often longs first for the stability provided by legalization.

Most pointed to financial concerns. Enrique Escobar, 26 at the time of his first interview, asserted that he had wanted children by the time he turned 25. He pushed his timeline back to 30 so that "hopefully by then I got my stuff set and I got a good job." He reflected on whether he would have children while still undocumented:

> *Enrique:* I mean, it's possible to bring out a decent living, like you will be able to at least eat. But unfortunately [you need] to have papers to provide a better living. . . . I have to pay rent, I have to pay the phone, I have to pay car insurance, everything. So it's not like there is a lot of money. . . . And then when you have kids, then it's way more money. It would be way harder to not have papers. You probably need to do three jobs or something. . . . With three jobs you probably build up [enough income] to [equal] one of the good jobs.
>
> *Laura:* You think you would still have kids while being undocumented?
>
> *Enrique:* I don't want to. I don't want to.

Despite having worked his way up to manager at a tire shop and earning a little over $20,000 a year, Enrique did not feel stable enough to support a family.

Some considered the possibility of deportation and family separation. Gabi Rivas Silva, in her late 20s and married for 10 years, commented, "If I had a kid right now, and we were going through this immigration issue, and I were to get deported, that wouldn't be good. . . . I just kind of think, once my life is stable—or if it ever is stable—then maybe [we'll have kids]. But at this time, no." She recited a statistic she heard recently: "There's like 50,000 kids in foster care right now whose parents got deported." She acknowledged that most people "never sit there and think, What would happen to my kid if I were to get deported?" But this report had confirmed for her that she did not want to raise children while remaining undocumented: "You don't want to make your kids suffer. You don't want them to be going through that. It would be horrible."

These young adults actively delayed parenthood. While some were inconsistent or practiced ineffective forms of birth control, those committed to delaying parenthood readily accessed and used contraception.[5] One reported having an abortion. In her early 20s, Daniela Sanchez was struggling to pursue community college and could find work only for a few hours a week. When we began to talk about her plans for having children, she lowered her voice so that her mom wouldn't hear from the next room. She rounded her hand over her belly and mouthed, "I was pregnant." She whispered,

> For me, in my situation, what I had to offer, I felt like there's no way [I could have a baby]. . . . It was the hardest thing I've done so far. . . . Just being undocumented, any situation it just makes it a little harder for anything. When you're dealing with your own life, you work it through. But when you have somebody else and . . . their life is depending on you, you can't just be [like], "Oh, we'll just see what happens."

Ultimately, her decision was driven by fear that her child would be drawn into a shared world of uncertainty.

Embracing Parenthood, Negotiating Instability

Conversely, a number of parents shared that they did not think about their immigration status as a barrier as they broached parenthood. Take three examples:

Nancy Ortega: Five years after living together, that's when we decided it was time. . . . [We] just felt like we wanted a baby with that person.

Maria Loya: I don't really think like that [about my status]. That doesn't really come to my mind. I just know that I want to have kids like everybody does.

Aaron Ortiz: You only live once, you know. You can't wait on the government to live your life. [If] you wait on the government—it's like waiting for Jesus Christ, he might never come back. [Laughs.]

These parents did not perceive their status as an insurmountable barrier to parenting. In fact, many had previously refused to allow immigration policies to alter their family formation, rejecting marriage myths and partnering with other undocumented immigrants. Feeling otherwise ready to have children because of their age and relationship commitment, some actively pursued parenthood (like Nancy), while others welcomed an unplanned pregnancy (like Aaron). Many, like Maria and her partner, framed their pregnancy as a combination of the two: a planned surprise, since they had been talking about having a baby but had not intentionally pursued pregnancy.

Others delayed parenthood until forced to decide if they would let their immigration status dictate this aspect of their life. Celia Alvarez remembered turning 27:

> My family was like, "Oh, you're getting old, you know. You're falling behind. You should have a kid already. You're married, you have a house." But I'm like, "How am I gonna have a kid if I'm undocumented?" [My family says], "You don't need to have papers to have a kid." And I'm like, "No, but I want to be able to give my kid a good life. And if you're undocumented you can't do that." So they're like, "So that's why you're not gonna have kids?" And I started thinking, Why am I gonna have this ruin my life? I gotta fight it. So then I decided to have a kid.

Celia initially reacted much like those who were delaying—she worried that her status would limit her ability to provide a stable life for her child. While fear dictated her initial decision, later conversations made her reconsider her position and pushed her to embrace parenthood.

Despite refusing to let immigration policies control their childbearing decisions, these parents-to-be still had to devise strategies to negotiate status-related instability. When they decided to have children, Nancy and her partner were both making below minimum wage. To prepare for the expenses and her unpaid maternity leave, Nancy remembered that they "tried to save up as much as we possibly could" in order to feel ready. In a subsequent pregnancy, her partner took on a second full-time job to make up for her lost income. Although most would-be parents have to consider financial costs, undocumented parents see financial stability as elusive because of legally embedded barriers to employment and economic mobility.

"I'M MORE AWARE OF IT": EMERGING LIMITATIONS DURING PREGNANCY

Pregnancy was a key turning point when parents were forced to recognize that immigration policies have family-level effects. This deeply influenced participants' feelings when expecting a child. I interviewed Abby Zamora a few weeks after she found out that she was pregnant. Having kids "was something that I wanted" but "it was unexpected." She lamented, "I wanna give my child a better future. . . . [I] cry about it. I'm more aware of it [my undocumented status] now than before. . . . It kind of puts me feeling kind of blue." She aspired to use her recently completed GED to start community college and improve her employment opportunities so "I could provide for my kid better." Abby was one of the few women who felt acutely aware of the limitations her status would place on parenting. In most cases, parents-to-be realized that their undocumented status would present material barriers as they negotiated pregnancy-related social service institutions without legal status.

Prenatal Care

Although immigration status had varying impacts on individuals' feelings about having a baby, all 30 undocumented mothers I spoke to asserted that it had not affected basic access to prenatal care. California provides all low-income women, regardless of status, with restricted-scope medical insurance that covers pregnancy-related services.[6] Sylvia Cortez remembered,

> [I was talking to] my friend who was pregnant before me. . . . I'm like, "What am I gonna do? I don't have money for my pregnancy or anything like that, no medical [insurance]." They're like, "Oh, they help you in the clinic. . . . They get you Medi-Cal." . . . They did help me. They gave me some program to apply and see if I was eligible.

Embedded in undocumented social networks and a medical system prepared to offer social services to low-income and undocumented mothers, none reported difficulties obtaining Medi-Cal coverage.

Yet some believed that they received unequal care. Estefania Gutierrez-Estrada, a 31-year-old college graduate who was eight months pregnant with her second son, compared her prenatal experiences to that of her citizen friends: "They're always posting [on Facebook] about my doctor. He saw me and we're gonna have another ultrasound. And I only get limited, I only get like two or three throughout my whole pregnancy.[7] And us obviously having to wait for hours before the doctor would see us. It was kind of sad." Pregnant with her fourth child, Janet Godinez recounted negative treatment from the office staff at a recent checkup. Even though she called ahead to confirm, the receptionist insisted when she arrived that she did not have an appointment and refused to let her inside the clinic. This happened so often that Janet had learned to get the name of the person she spoke to in case there were problems when she arrived: "It frustrates me! Because they think, OK. Since they don't have a status or a Social or they're not from there, we're gonna treat her like that." While low-income citizen mothers are seen in these same clinics and share these experiences, undocumented mothers attributed these affronts to their immigration status.

Estefania, Janet, and other mothers began to feel that their immigration status was already shaping their parenting, preventing them from caring for their babies before birth. Scarce ultrasounds were a common complaint. Filling this vacuum were commercial ultrasound services. When I shared that I was also pregnant, several expectant parents asked me if I had gotten ultrasounds "at the mall." Seeing my confusion, Daniela Sanchez, who was six months pregnant, quickly pulled out a brochure showing me a variety of packages in which customers could watch ultrasound videos and buy photos and merchandise. She had her eye on a teddy bear that would play audio of her son's heartbeat. While all parents, regardless of status, long for opportunities to bond with their unborn children, undocumented parents perceive their inability to access these opportunities as tied to their status and inability to acquire higher-quality insurance.

Concerns about unequal access were more pronounced when parents tried to obtain specialized care. Julián Salinas recalled wanting alternative childbirth options after watching the documentary *The Business of Being Born*. Filled with fears about skyrocketing medical interventions, forced C-sections, and negative outcomes associated with common birthing drugs, they wanted a home birth under the care of a doula and midwife. This was not covered by their insurance, and their lack of funds forced them to have their son in a clinical setting.

Similar concerns arose when participants faced infertility. Daniela Sanchez recounted her health care experiences after a doctor diagnosed fertility issues: "I was kind of upset for a little bit. Because I was like, Why would they say that? Why wouldn't they make sure before they put somebody through this?" When I asked for clarification, she rolled her eyes and pointed to her pregnant belly, "Obviously they weren't sure because they were wrong."

> Every time you go, you get a different doctor. So the first doctor that told me about it didn't even really tell me about it. She gave me a Post-It with the name of it—polycystic ovarian syndrome. She said we found this in your test. Again, they're trying to rush you. . . . But when I got home and googled it, I was like, "Oh my gosh!" And literally the first thing you read is "leading cause of infertility." . . . But then the third doctor was like, "Well, it's not a for-sure thing, you still have these options."

Daniela also believed that her status would have prevented her from pursuing fertility treatments *if* she had needed them. Indeed, Rosa Lopez, the citizen spouse of a recently legalized participant, noted the high cost of her fertility treatments. She and her husband believed that the cost and lack of medical coverage would have prevented them from pursuing treatments if either of them had remained undocumented. Further, the high costs of adoption, in vitro fertilization, and surrogacy raise similar barriers for undocumented members of LGBQ couples who desired to have children.

Maternity Leave

Maternity leave was also infused with status-related concerns. Celia Alvarez, who had her daughter a few months before our first interview, remembered thinking that her undocumented status made her ineligible for maternity leave. She recounted the stress:

> I was always afraid of going on maternity leave. You have to turn in paperwork, and I'm like, What if they ask for more stuff [like a Social Security card]? . . . And I talked to some of my coworkers, and they were like, "Oh, I have a friend that works in the office, let me ask her." So my coworker would ask her, "Hey, I have a friend that this, this, and that," but they wouldn't say it was me just in case. And then the friend would be like, "Oh, don't worry about it. She could do it."

A counselor at the clinic also assured her, "Oh, don't worry. We deal with cases like that all the time."

All the women I spoke to had successfully claimed their right to maternity leave, but their status precipitated financial concerns. Janet Godinez noted that it was unpaid. Currently on maternity leave from her job as an office assistant, she shared, "I feel good because I know that when I go back, I'm gonna have my job. I have my job secure. But at the same time, I don't have money. I can't go to the unemployment or disability to help me with something." This prevented some from taking the full 12 weeks they were entitled to.

Job security was not necessarily guaranteed. Celia was finding it hard to return to her job as a security guard because "they can't find me a building" to be posted at. While she had previously worked during the day and close to home, they were offering her faraway assignments at undesirable times—on the swing shift, 4:00 p.m. to midnight, or graveyard, midnight to 8:00 a.m. She turned these offers down because they were incompatible with raising a three-month-old child and because she feared driving so far without a license: "Now they are pressuring me, that if I don't pick something soon, they are going to have to let me go."

While the women I spoke to had accessed maternity leave, there are likely many undocumented women unable to fully claim their rights. Nancy Ortega's employer pressured her to return soon after the birth of her second child because his business was suffering without her. She felt able to advocate for herself, but many may not. Speaking about her coworkers at a fast-food restaurant, who were mostly first-generation undocumented adults, Sol Montes shared,

> When a few of my coworkers got pregnant, they asked for maternity leave and they almost got fired because of that. I admire those women because they're hardcore women with this big ol' belly working the whole kitchen, holding their pee. When they gave birth, like their milk dripping [because] they had to pump, and they don't let them go pump because it's so freakin' busy.

Undocumented workers' labor rights are routinely violated.[8] This can prevent mothers from taking time off before and after the birth, or caring for themselves and their children's needs after birth. Financial strain can also dissuade undocumented parents from taking advantage of maternity or parental leave. Fear of retaliation may limit their willingness to claim accommodations.

"I WANTED TO RAISE MY CHILD A CERTAIN WAY": CONSTRAINED PARENTING

The shared barriers associated with illegality crystalized when participants became parents. Pablo Ortiz, who had a three-year-old daughter, explained that his undocumented status pushed him into work as a solicitor, earning a variable income of $800–$1,000 a month. Although his citizen partner worked, the birth of their daughter stressed their already-precarious finances: "Before, if I [only] ate a 99-cent burger from a fast-food restaurant, it wasn't a problem for me. Before. But now, it has to be more than that because I have to be a father to my daughter and I have to provide for her as best as I can."

Imagining the childhood he wanted to provide for his daughter, Pablo felt that he had fallen short. His low income, lack of a Social Security number, and absent credit history had previously forced them to live in a substandard apartment: "That place was very polluted. We have a video recording of that place when our baby was really little, and we see the sun[light] reflection going into our place and you could see all this dust." They lived in a small back section of the house; a hallway had been closed off with drywall to separate it from the front half. Although the house was meticulously clean, it was small and cramped—belongings piled in the corners because it lacked storage space. His partners' citizenship status and higher income could not relieve this barrier. "[It] was really hard to find [a new place] because a lot of the places that we were trying to move into, they wanted my Social Security [number] or they wanted my credit history and all that stuff, and I don't have none of that stuff." Having also recently looked for apartments in the neighborhood, I agreed; even the most rundown apartments had required official rental applications and were unwilling to overlook a lack of a Social Security number. Although most participants identified problems with their housing and living situations, parents were particularly concerned about how this affected their children—pollution, undermaintained facilities, much-needed pest control, limited space to play, poor schools, and dangerous neighborhoods. Now that Pablo's daughter was older, these financial barriers became even more apparent. He longed to fulfill her desires for toys while also meeting his personal commitment to maximizing her educational opportunities.

Like Pablo, most parents were unsatisfied with what they could provide, prompting negative feelings about their parenting that could be traced directly to the financial barriers raised by their undocumented status. Most managed to meet their family's basic needs, but they aspired to more. Like their citizen peers, they harbored intensive parenting ideals that pushed them to prioritize their children's development and future upward mobility by spending time with them, raising them well, and providing for their educational success.[9] Gendered expectations shaped their specific commitments: women were expected to provide care, while men expected to provide financial stability and support. Those who could not meet these ideals often felt, and were seen by others, as "bad" parents because they could not meet these middle-class expectations. In all, hegemonic parenting ideals and constrained circumstances jointly shaded undocumented young adults' parenting experiences.

Falling Short: Raising Children in Line with Parenting Ideals

Undocumented parents' limited employment options often left them feeling as if they could not parent in the way they would like. Elias Ruiz, the undocumented father of two sons, ages four and five, reflected:

> I would love to find another job where it would be less hours and I have time . . . to dedicate more time to my sons. I am taking time to work 11- or 12-hour days. And when they go to school, I am at home, and when they come home, I am at work. And I can't enjoy the weekends. Only Sunday, because Saturdays also I have to work.[10]

He and his partner, Nancy Ortega, felt financially stable; he made $2,000 a month working at a warehouse, and she made slightly less. But they both worked long hours, six days a week. Both longed for more family time, and Nancy worried that this was hurting their relationship with their sons. For a while, the kids preferred spending time with their grandmother. While parents like Nancy and Elias strove to meet their parenting ideals, their undocumented status constrained their parenting opportunities.

Multigenerational households were a common and effective strategy for maximizing the ability to meet basic needs on a limited income; this strategy, however, could frustrate parenting. In Yessica Martinez's case, our conversation about housing was prompted by her mom arriving home with her three-year-old son and eight-year-old brother. The small apartment erupted with commotion as the kids ran in, chasing each other and pulling out toys. When her son emerged from a bedroom in tears, she admitted wanting him to be able to enjoy his own space so that he was not constantly fighting with her brother.

Zoe Miranda reported more intense parenting problems: "I need to get help. I'm bad [at being a mother] because I have an anger problem. And when I get angry, I start yelling at him instead of communicating with him. . . . Not like really bad, like psycho. But I do yell. And I don't like yelling at him." She credited this to her strained relationship with her mother, whom they lived with, and their constant arguing: "I'm 29, and I still feel like she sees me like I'm 15." These frustrations led her anger to build quickly and continue a cycle of what she believed was dysfunctional parenting.

Many multigenerational living situations did not create conflict, but they could tax parent-child relationships and parental self-esteem. High childcare costs prompted parents to rely on family members. Yessica explained that this was a key reason she continued to live with her mother and was grateful for her help. Some, like Edgar Gonzalez, found it mutually beneficial to pay his mom to watch his five-year-old daughter. While confident that their children were well cared for, some worried about how their children were being raised. Sara Romero, however, was frustrated to have her ex-boyfriend's mother care for their son:

I know his grandma takes really good care of him, better than any day care will. But he's, like, really chiquiado [spoiled]. He's one year old, and he does not know how to drink from a straw. . . . No, sit him down and teach them. If you don't carry him when he wants to, he'll start crying and screaming.

Sara desperately wanted "more time off work and more time with him so I can raise him my own way. Right now she's raising him the way she raised his dad, and we're going to have a problem." She feared that her son might turn out like her ex-boyfriend, lacking motivation, unable to keep a job, and disrespectful toward women. Finding an affordable and quality day care seemed to be the only way out, but it felt nearly impossible on the limited income she earned working nights at a bar.

Unable to rely on family members, other parents sought affordable childcare. Most relied on babysitters, often immigrant women who watched several children in their home without any accreditation or training. Nancy's two sons had a babysitter near their school. Although they had been mostly satisfied, they sometimes worried about the conditions. For example, when her youngest son was an infant, he came home covered in inexplicable insect bites, presumably because the babysitter lived in low-quality housing. With another babysitter, her eldest son, then around five, let slip that the babysitter's 20-something son was pushing them around and threatening them. While angry, she was stuck until they could find alternative childcare.

Some mothers found it more effective to stay home, forcing the household to sacrifice an additional income. Nayeli Valencia, the undocumented partner of a DACA recipient, explained,

> Right now I am not looking for work because of the illegal state that I'm in. I am not going to find a job that pays me well. And so it doesn't make sense to go to a job where they pay me the minimum [wage], because I have two kids and I would have to pay for a babysitter for them. And if I make the minimum, it doesn't make sense. I am going to work only to pay the babysitter.[11]

Nayeli and several others elected to become stay-at-home mothers, particularly when their children were young. Highlighting how this was linked to her undocumented status, Nayeli aspired to be able to legally work so "we would not be buried economically." She explicitly connected this to her ability to parent: "If we could have a little more for the kids to have enough clothes, because they're growing."[12]

Low-income citizen parents share these concerns. Indeed, research suggests that one adult working full-time for minimum wage cannot earn enough to provide for a modest standard of living. In California, about 40 percent of one full-time, minimum-wage income is needed to pay for a four-year-old's childcare.[13] While there are government programs to increase the affordability of quality childcare for low-income families, undocumented parents struggle to access these programs because of ineligibility, fear of interacting with social service institutions, or a desire to avoid being seen as a public charge, which could endanger future legalization options.[14]

Further exemplifying the unique aspects of undocumented status, Elisa Fernandez, the citizen partner of a recently legalized permanent resident, believed that their ability to meet parenting ideals depended on their legal status. Her husband's legalization had fostered financial stability, enabling them to move out of her in-laws' house and improving her sense of parenting:

> One of the most frustrating things for me is that I wanted to raise my child a certain way, but when you are living at home with that many people, then everybody has some kind of input whether you like it or not. . . . I still take my son [there] 'cause my babysitter is my mother-in-law, and I appreciate her so much. But once we moved out, we, I feel like we felt a sense of power over our own immediate family.

While low-income citizens also face strong constraints on economic mobility, undocumented young adults must contend with legally imposed barriers. As Elisa suggests, documented status opens up the possibility of mobility and is seen by most undocumented parents (perhaps unrealistically in some cases) as a game changer that would allow them to parent in the way they would like.

"Bad" Parents: Gendered Expectations and the Pressure to Provide

Both mothers and fathers initially asserted that their immigration status did not affect their ability to be a good parent. Adán Olivera explained, "That is just a paper, and not [about] being a person." Financial barriers, however, run up against gendered expectations, disrupting aspirations for a life in which status does not matter. Fathers feel pressure to consistently provide for their children's basic needs and wants, while mothers focus on caregiving, including meeting intermittent costs related to children's education, health, and personal growth. The different level of financial resources needed to meet these expectations continued the gendered consequences of illegality identified in chapter 3, consequences in which men have a higher risk of disrupted family formation. Still, both mothers and fathers risked feeling that they were, or were perceived to be, "bad" parents.

Most mothers felt that they were meeting gendered parenting expectations because they cared for and spent time with their children. Sylvia Cortez saw herself as a good mother to her toddler: "[I] take care of him, raise him as a good boy [to] be respectful with other people . . . be there for him when he is sick." A single mother earning $1,200 a month as an office assistant, Sylvia experienced many of the constraints discussed above, but she, like most mothers, felt that she was raising her son well despite these barriers and frustrations. They sought the best options within their means, spent their available time with their children, and nurtured them. Citing these caregiving activities, most felt that they were "good" mothers.

Yet immigration status and employment situations prevented a few women from meeting gendered expectations. Sara Romero recounted how her job prevented her from performing key caretaker responsibilities: "Sometimes my mom would be like, 'You're a bad mom because all you care about is work, and on your days off all you want to do is sleep.'" Sara struggled to meet mothering ideals because her undocumented status made her take the only stable job she could find: working nights at a bar, which entailed getting home at 3:30 a.m. As a result, she was unable to put her toddler son to bed and struggled to wake up with him in the middle of the night and early morning. Consistent with other studies on working mothers and transnational mothering,[15] Sara attempted to reimagine herself as a good mother by focusing on her ability to provide financially. As a single mother, working hard to make ends meet came at the expense of not meeting others' expectations of how she should mother her son. Her parental self-esteem plunged.

Conversely, most fathers struggled to meet fathering expectations and felt negatively about their parenting. Pablo Ortiz shared, "Now I'm also a father, and therefore I've got to provide for my kid. Those stereotypes have affected me because I feel bad about myself. That I can't provide for my kid." In his second interview, he reflected on how he felt as a father as my research assistant rushed to drive him to the train station so he could begin his two-to-three-hour commute home from work:

> *Pablo:* Immigration status takes [away] my right to be a full-time father. . . .
>
> *Interviewer:* Do you feel like your immigration status affects your daughter and yourself?
>
> *Pablo:* Oh yeah, how it affects me as a provider like—ahhh, I wish I could—'cause our car just broke down not too long ago. I wish I could just go to a dealer and say I wanna buy a car. So we could go and take my daughter to day care, so she could use it to go to school . . . so we could minimize the dangers from my daughter in the streets, riding the bus and all that stuff. As a father figure, I wish I could take my daughter to Legoland or SeaWorld or some of these places, you know? But sometimes I can't, and I just try to turn the TV off for her *[laughs].*

Pablo anxiously longed to have the financial flexibility to provide his daughter with a safe, comfortable living situation. He also acknowledged the importance of spending quality time with his daughter—turning off the TV to limit her screen time—and doing activities together. But he lamented that his immigration status and precarious financial situation sometimes prevented him from even doing that well. As his partner planned for an upcoming trip, he worried about "how to tell my daughter that maybe I won't be able to go" because he could not miss work.

Ray Guzman explained that these negative self-conceptions are often reinforced by others' gendered parenting expectations:

> As a father, I feel worthless. . . . I'm 28, and when I go apply for something for my kids or [at their] school, they want to know what I'm doing [for work]. They look at me a lot different. They tell me, "Oh, well you're not doing nothing. How do you provide for your family?" I do side jobs. And they say, "Well, you don't have a stable income?" . . . I feel like I'm handicapped in some way.

Despite spending quality time with his children every day, Ray's intermittent work as a handyman made him feel inadequate. These concerns are reflected in his belief that he was also an inadequate partner given that his children's mother covered rent and bills. Although Ray's circumstances were worse than most, many fathers felt similarly constrained and judged.

Adán Olivera was one of a few who felt he was a good father because "I take them places like Disneyland, to the park. I buy them anything that I didn't have. . . . Every time we go out, we'll just buy them something." Adán internalized the paternal provider role and found that he could live up to expectations because he'd secured work as a salaried office employee earning $2,400 a month, despite lacking a Social Security number. His was one of the highest reported incomes. He admitted that it would be significantly harder to be a "good" father if he had a minimum-wage job similar to those of his undocumented friends, "because it would not be providing me enough money."

The intersection of gendered parenting expectations and economic limitations led to divergent consequences because mothers and fathers negotiated different levels of financial demand. Fathers focused on the relatively high costs of consistently providing for basic needs, while mothers emphasized lower costs that limited their caregiving. Luis Escobar and Aida Mendoza were both married to their citizen partners, living with their parents, and had infant children at the time. Despite being in similar situations, expectations differentiated how much they internalized negative feelings:

> *Luis:* [I'm supposed to be] this male provider [who's] strong. And the fact that we lost our place and now I'm [living] with my in-laws and it's hard to find a great-paying job. And I have this uncertain future for myself. . . . It makes you feel guilty that you have a family and that you have a baby.
>
> *Aida:* Just recently he got very sick. He needed a humidifier, and we had to look around with people that we knew to see who could lend it to us [because we could not afford one]. . . . It breaks my heart that I can't do anything for him.

While Luis and Aida both reported negative consequences, they confronted different levels of financial need with distinctive frequency. Luis felt the pressure to consistently muster over $1,000 a month to cover rent and bills, while Aida worried about a one-time, relatively small $30 expense. Yet both parents conducted considerable emotional work as they felt guilty about the limitations that their immigration status placed on their children. Fathers, however, experienced these negative feelings almost daily in response to broader provider demands, while mothers noted isolated incidents related to caretaking.

The gendered nature of social service structures reinforces such differences. Undocumented parents are not eligible for welfare and other government support programs, such as the Earned Income Tax Credit, that many working parents depend on to make ends meet.[16] The social programs they are eligible for cater to mothers' caretaking, while there are few resources helping undocumented fathers (or single mothers) afford basic expenses like rent and bills.

Luis was the only father to discuss using social services to close financial gaps. When recently unemployed, he visited a local food pantry. He struggled with this decision and felt it reflected poorly on him as a father. Yet all mothers reported easily accessing California's Women, Infants, and Children (WIC) program, which provides monthly healthy-food vouchers to low-income pregnant women, breastfeeding and postpartum mothers, and infants and children under age five. In 2016, WIC benefits provided an average $61.24 worth of food to qualified family members each month.[17] Most participants enrolled simultaneously with their application for emergency Medi-Cal during pregnancy. Mothers embraced this and other social services, including Medi-Cal coverage for their citizen children. They interpreted it not as a maternal failing but a critical tool to help them provide for their children's health and well-being. As their children aged, mothers often identified low-cost, after-school activities to help them meet their goal of providing for their children's development and educational success.

Further highlighting the role of social service structures, single mothers reported that they struggled to file for child support. While they did not perceive accessing child support as a personal failing, many felt that they were choosing between increased financial security and the potential threat of deportation. Tanya Diaz recounted her interactions with her son's father:

> He would give me money before, but it wasn't consistent. I've avoided going to court . . . because I don't know how that will affect [me]. He could get mad and be like, "Well, she's not even a citizen here." And I don't know how that would play out in court. But it's that fear that you don't know. . . . I think it's because he knows I can't do anything about it. . . . My son's dad would try to scare me before when I was younger. He'd be like, "I'm taking you to court, and I'm gonna keep my son anyways because you're gonna get deported" and things like that.

For years, Tanya struggled to assert her right to child support out of fear that her ex-partner would file for full custody. Although she knew she had a right to child support, she refused to demand it to minimize conflict and reduce her risk of deportation.

Sara Romero was planning a similar tactic until she reached someone at the child support office who informed her that her status does not matter. She explained, "It did stop me at first, because when you call the child support offices, the first thing they ask you for is 'OK, what's your Social Security number?' And you're like, 'Really? Great.' But they told me you don't have to worry because it's not going for you, it's going for him [my son]." Armed with this information, she felt safe enough to demand that her son's father meet his financial responsibilities. Their examples show that undocumented status can dissuade parents from accessing social services that can help them meet children's needs, particularly if they are not embedded in a system designed to serve undocumented immigrants. Notably, these social services are still primarily set up to meet mothers' needs, further contributing to gendered consequences.

CONDITIONAL IMPROVEMENTS: FAMILIAL FINANCIAL STABILITY THROUGH DACA

Obtaining DACA removed immediate barriers to undocumented young adults' socioeconomic mobility by providing employment authorization. These gave undocumented parents an increased sense of financial security and flexibility, facilitating their transition into and positive feelings about parenthood. This change, however, was not available to all parents; it depended on their being able to use DACA's work permit to gain a higher-paying job and a secure pathway to upward mobility.

"That Changed a Lot about How I Felt": Financial Stability and Flexibility

Receiving DACA enabled undocumented young adults, particularly men, to feel more confident about becoming parents. Enrique Escobar, who had delayed having children because of his undocumented status, recounted the pressures: "From my family, since all my brothers, pretty much they all have kids. They're like, 'When are you having kids? You're getting old already. Her family, I think it's probably about the same thing. They'll even come to us and ask." These questions have prompted him and his fiancée to think about when they would have children. He explained, "Before I didn't even want to have kids." He credited this change to obtaining DACA: "Just being able to—or having that confidence and being able to support and . . . take care of a family. That changed a lot about how I felt."

For those who were already parents, DACA opened up slightly better employment opportunities and provided the financial flexibility they needed to more easily cover their children's expenses and meet parenting ideals. Zoe Miranda, who moved from a customer service job at a gas station to one at a major department store, reflected on her newfound ability to provide for her three-year-old son:

> I was able to buy him the clothes that he needed. 'Cause we were struggling financially. . . . So I was able to get him his shoes because he didn't have shoes. I was able to get him pants, shirts, sweaters, everything that he needed. Toys that he would go to the store and tell me, "Mommy, I want this." And I'm like, "No, papas, I don't have money right now." I was finally able to be like, "Get it. It's OK."

Her slight increase in disposable income made taking her son to the store significantly more enjoyable. "It just felt so good" because she was finally able to give him the things that he needed *and* wanted. This also made her feel better about herself as a mother: "People are not looking at me. Like, 'Oh my god! She can't get him that?'" Now the cashiers aren't rolling their eyes, other customers aren't judging her with side-eyed glances, and her son is happily feeling provided for.

Receiving DACA also allowed undocumented young adults to achieve some additional financial flexibility by getting a credit card. Despite receiving DACA relatively early on, in October 2012, almost two years before his second interview, Adán Olivera kept the same office job and reported earning $100 more than during his previous interview. Despite few changes, he believed that DACA had improved his economic situation: "It's better. Before, we didn't have a backup with the credit card. Now we have a backup. If we need something, we have this credit card." Although credit cards are a risky way to make ends meet, it allowed him to manage his family's larger expenses: "We can buy the kids more stuff. Before, it used to be paycheck by paycheck. It's not enough. But now with the credit cards we would pay this." Pausing, he continued, "Kind of like Christmas. For Christmas, we'll get a credit card, and we're gonna spend $1,500. That's it. And then we'll pay it off. And before, those $1,500, we didn't have it, 'cause it was just the paycheck." This unanticipated benefit of DACA allowed Adán and his wife to feel like better parents and access some of the financial management strategies that citizen parents could.

Along these lines, DACA also enabled parents to access improved housing. Julián Salinas, his wife, and their two children shared one bedroom in an apartment that they rented with his mom and uncle. Describing it as "a little crowded for us," he recalled how they had been unable to find another place when both he and his partner were undocumented: "We'd tell the manager we don't have papers, [but] we could give you references, we have bank accounts, we can do this, and they were like, 'No, you're not [legal]. You can't do that.'" Now, with Social Security numbers and California IDs, they could follow the official rental application process. Currently looking for apartments, Julián shared, "I have more freedom to choose wherever we want to live. . . . Before we had to go to the Latino neighborhoods [because] . . . they are more open to negotiate." Although they had yet to move, Julián already felt a sense of freedom and possibility, which he directly attributed to DACA. This translated into feeling like a better parent because he and his partner desperately want to move their children into a better neighborhood with more space. His partner mentioned wanting them to have a yard so that their kids could play outside whenever they wanted. Once they began looking at places, his daughter excitedly asked, "Oh, can I have a pet? Can I have a dog? Can I have my own room? When we move out, can I have my own room?" They both looked forward to being able to provide their children with these experiences.

Though receiving DACA enabled parents to develop discretionary income and financial flexibility, it also brought new fears and risks of spoiling children. Adán Olivera credited DACA with allowing him to provide his children with small luxuries that he did not have growing up. He now takes his children out on activities every weekend:

> I do it because I didn't have any of that. My parents couldn't afford none of that stuff that they [my kids] have. . . . I talk to my kids. I tell them why they have this—"You have a PS3 [video game console], you can have a little car which you play with every day." And they kind of understand where I'm coming from. Like, I didn't have this, but I want you to have it. But . . . you gotta be good in your grades, you behave, everything. Be respectful, and, as of now, it's been really good with them.

He boasted that this has been an effective parenting strategy. In a recent parent-teacher conference, his seven-year-old son's teacher told him, "He's good, always participating. He's really good to have in the class, and he's always helping other kids." His nine-year-old daughter is "always helping [her teacher], passing papers and doing her homework, everything." Like Adán, many parents measured their success by being able to disrupt the financial limitations that they experienced as the children of undocumented parents.

"It Takes Time": Persisting Barriers to Family Mobility

Not all parents could capitalize on DACA to change jobs and improve their socioeconomic status. Some recipients did not see substantial changes in their employment situations. As she cradled her two-month-old daughter, Maria Loya explained that her ability to provide had not changed. She kept the same job working as a floor manager at a fast-food restaurant: "Right now it's kind of hard to find a job. So like, when I see that there's more job opportunities, then I would probably try to apply to a better-paying job." Like Maria, others mentioned a slow economy and limited job opportunities as reasons why they had been unable to improve their financial situation. This was most common among parents who did not have college degrees or strong social networks to help them gain access to better jobs.

A handful of parents thought about or had returned to school for additional certifications or degrees to improve their chances for finding a better job, but they struggled to balance this with family life. Nancy Ortega, who continued working in the same office after having DACA for almost two years, explained that she was trying to finish 150 hours of training to become a licensed insurance provider so she could open up her own business. Although she thought it would take her only a few weeks to complete the hours via an online course, it had been over six months:

> It's just lacking time that I work [on it]. At work, I was only able to do it for about 10 to 15 minutes. So even though I tried, it was kinda hard for me to do it at work and then come home and do it, take care of the kids, and the homework and our whole routines. I would do it for another 10 to 15 minutes. And 30 minutes a day, you know, for a hundred and something hours, it doesn't—it takes time.

Similarly, Celia Alvarez returned to community college, but her husband commented that it was difficult, "Trying to match it [her school] with our daughter's schedule. . . . Both of us trying to be good parents and trying to be there as much as we can . . . she's held down by us [me and our daughter]."

In several cases, the passage of time hampered pursuits of economic mobility. Undocumented young adults had been in the same job for years; they were older and did not have the employment history, professional skills, or certifications needed to move into more lucrative employment. As Nancy and Celia noted, they had taken on additional responsibilities, building a home with their partners and raising their children. They had both struggled to balance work and community college in their late teens and early 20s. This juggling act was significantly harder now that they had family commitments.

Finally, obtaining DACA did not remove the threat that parents may once again be plunged into instability. Erick Godinez and I discussed his attempts to save money now that he received DACA and was earning more at his job with a moving company. When I asked if he was saving for something specific, his face lit up: "My girlfriend is pregnant!" He continued, "I'm saving for the baby. Yeah, she is four months [pregnant] right now. We found out it was a baby girl, so we're so happy!" Caught up in his excitement, I shared that I was also four months pregnant. Following our excited laughter, congratulations, and baby shower discussions, the conversation naturally paused. His face suddenly dropped as he quietly added, "That is one of the things I'm afraid of."

> They give us DACA for two years. I know that I can renew it, right? I'm afraid when Obama leaves, what's going to happen? That's a big question mark for me. I'm not afraid, but what's going to happen? But I tell my girlfriend . . . it's too much people to cancel the thing, so I think they are just going to renew it every two years. So, it's one of my worries.

Erick's past fears about being unable to provide transformed into worries about the future, framing his feelings about becoming a father. His hypothetical foreshadowed immigration policy changes to come with the rescission of DACA a few years later under President Donald Trump.

CONCLUSION

As we wrapped up our second interview, Luis returned to the same question: Was his immigration status affecting his parenting? He was still struggling with the idea that spending time with his children was just as important as financially providing for their future well-being. Receiving DACA had allowed him to obtain a new job at a nonprofit. This dramatically improved his ability to provide financially, but it required long hours as he tried to make up for lost years without a professional career. He had little time for his family. Comparing himself to a younger nephew who had become a permanent resident and bought a house, Luis lamented that he had been unable to use his college degree or work permit to achieve such mobility. He wondered if perhaps it was not his generation's turn. Maybe he was meant to slave away like his parents so that his daughters could do better.

Uncertainty, financial instability, and persistent worry shaped Luis's and other undocumented young adults' decisions to have children, their parenting experiences, and their parental self-esteem. They struggled to live up to ideal visions of parenting but still hoped that their children's citizenship status would protect them from the worst consequences. Instead, they began to see multigenerational punishment as their undocumented status molded their children's everyday lives and opportunities.

"I Can't Offer Them What Other People Could"

Multigenerational Punishment of Citizen Children

No. At the beginning, no [I didn't think being undocumented would affect my kids]. Until I had my next child. I was like, Oh my god, I can't offer them what other people could.

—MARTA SANDOVAL

Tears streamed down Marta's cheeks as she remembered giving up on her dreams because of her undocumented status: "I wanted to be a lawyer. Or like work for a radio station. Silly dreams. . . . But then in the 12th grade, I just realized that that was the end of me." She finished high school feeling that college was not an option. Instead, she spent four years earning below minimum wage working at small stores in the *callejones*, the wholesale fashion district in downtown Los Angeles. Tired of mistreatment, she looked for another job. Chuckling at her younger self, she recalled feeling "awesome" after being hired at Disney's historic El Capitan Theater in Hollywood. They soon ran her Social Security number and promptly let her go with a small check for her training hours. Her voice broke: "I never cashed it. I still have it to this day." Gulping back air, she explained, "Because no. To me it's—special. Even though, like, a lot of people are gonna think like, That's not even a good job—but to me it was." Over the next couple of years, she settled in to work at a fast-food restaurant, married, and had her first child. Her life hadn't changed much in the 10 years since.

Despite these strong barriers, Marta believed that her children's citizenship would shield them from the pain and disappointment she had experienced as an undocumented young adult. Yet, as her firstborn grew older and she had her second and then third child, she awoke to the shared nature of her and her husband's undocumented status. The kids wanted things that she could not afford. They were in the car when her husband was pulled over and ticketed for driving without a license. They asked to travel places like their friends did. They worried about being separated by deportation. She lamented, "I can't offer them what other people could."

In this chapter, I focus on the citizen children of undocumented young adults to explore the extent to which parents' fears about their inability to provide are realized. Previous research has established that the citizen children of first-generation undocumented adults have poorer outcomes than children of documented or citizen parents. Studying children ages 0–3, Hirokazu Yoshikawa argues that parental undocumented status constrains children's developmental contexts, particularly the home and childcare settings where they spend the majority of their time; this is because parents limit interactions with legal authorities (including the use of social service programs), have few social ties, and experience poor work conditions.[1] Focusing on elementary-school-aged children, Joanna Dreby points to the enforcement context, in which deportation threats create economic and emotional uncertainty for families and disrupt children's well-being.[2] I extend my focus to 1.5-generation parents who have less fear of deportation and stronger social and cultural capital *and* to a broader age range of children up to age 15. This allows me to explore how constraints evolve as children age and how they emerge even when parents are more socially integrated.

I trace how undocumented young adults' citizen children experience the context of illegality and connect these everyday experiences to long-term consequences for their upward mobility. These endure even as their parents receive DACA, because illegality shaped children's early experiences of social exclusion and limited their mobility pathways. This is particularly clear among older children. I refer to this process as *multigenerational punishment,* wherein the sanctions intended for a specific population spill over to harm individuals who are not targeted by immigration policies. Overall, I highlight how immigration policies produce family-level inequalities that endure into the next generation as dependent social ties and daily interactions place citizen children in a de facto undocumented status.

"WHY CAN'T I DO THIS?": ECONOMIC BARRIERS TO CHILDREN'S DEVELOPMENT

As I showed in the last chapter, parents were plagued by concerns that they were failing to enable the next generation's upward mobility. They worked hard to meet their children's basic needs, spend time with them, and provide developmental opportunities for future educational success. Many found, though, that their economic instability restricted their children's development, perpetrating multigenerational punishment.

Parents' lack of employment authorization directly affected the types of jobs they could access and their ability to participate in their children's lives. Antonio

Mendez recalled working at a garment factory after high school, imagining how such labor-intensive work affected families:

> It was really demanding. My skin from my fingers was peeling. It was hard labor.
> . . . I was wondering [what] these other men and women who are working here,
> how is it that they go home and have the energy to interact with their children?
> To go to the park? To talk to them? . . . Me going in as an 18-year-old, I'm—I was
> doing cross-country and track at high school! And I'm dying, I'm tired! . . . How is it
> that this society expects these families to have healthy children?

Although Antonio did not have children, his job exposed him to the challenging balancing act that undocumented parents face. Many worked long hours, often at labor-intensive jobs. This was particularly common for fathers, including Elias Ruiz, who worked the night shift at a factory. His work left him chronically sleep deprived, so he often fell asleep in the car or at their destination during family time. Even when parents were physically present, their jobs often drained their mental and physical energy.

Parents' limited income, time, and presence ultimately hinder children's early development. Nicolás Fernandez, a recently legalized participant, was undocumented when his son was born and remembered working two jobs—at a fast-food restaurant during the day and as a gas station attendant at night:

> I didn't have time like, "Oh, let me read to you." It's like, "Well, I have to go to work."
> When you are about to go sleep, I'm already making my way to work. . . . It's not
> that you don't care about your kid, it's just that you literally don't have time to read
> to them or interact with them. . . . I was always fucking stressed 'cause it's like you
> don't have any money. I have to go to work, I have to work graveyard, I have to work
> the holidays. All these things. And the last thing that was on my mind was "Oh, let
> me talk to my child."

Now an English teacher, Nicolás was acutely aware of the importance of early literacy and language development. Other working parents also longed for time with their children, acknowledging its importance for cognitive development and emotional well-being.

Similar developmental concerns have been identified more generally among children from low-income families. Research shows that such children are exposed to 30 million fewer words by the time they are four than children in professional families; professional parents talk more, use richer language, and continue conversation longer.[3] This vocabulary gap can have long-term academic consequences. Studies show that illegality compounds these class inequalities. Yoshikawa finds that citizen children, ages 0–3, of undocumented immigrant parents experience delays in early cognitive development when compared to the children of documented immigrant parents.[4] These disparities persist in children's academic performance during preschool and elementary school.[5]

Parents quickly pointed to their undocumented status as compounding economic constraints. Nicolás believed that legalizing his status and transitioning into work as a teacher allowed him to deeply engage with his children. He now has money to buy them books *and* can consistently read them bedtime stories. Elias was more vague: "I think that it would be much easier [as a citizen]. I don't know exactly [how], but I imagine that it would be more easy."[6] In some cases illegality's structural constraints clearly emerged; in others, parents attributed economic inequality to immigration status. Regardless, illegality confounded the real and perceived socioeconomic challenges facing other low-income families.

Parents' limited income also determined their ability to afford extracurricular activities to support their children's intellectual and social development. Alfonso Rojas, a participant's undocumented partner, provided for their family on $1,800 a month before his partner received DACA and began working. They could usually afford what the family needed, but not always what their three sons (ages 4, 10, and 17) wanted: "There was a time that my oldest son wanted to play basketball, and he asked us for a monthly fee so that he could play [on a] basketball [team] in the park. It was not too expensive, but we could not cover our daily expenses and afford the fee."[7] Irene Correas declared, "Summer camps, they're so expensive! We want her to be active, but we can't really pay the tuition." Research confirms the importance of extracurricular activities for children's socioemotional development and academic performance.[8]

Many parents sought free or low-cost extracurricular activities. When Irene's daughter's friends went to summer camps, she pieced together activities. Many parents accessed free or low-cost programs, but these were often hard to find and get into. Nancy Ortega explained that she was able to enroll her two sons in a free karate class only because her sister worked for a nonprofit that helped parents access such services. A few, like Estefania Gutierrez-Estrada, tried to create their own opportunities; she recalled petitioning the local Little League baseball team to lower the cost for enrolling her son.

Parents often had to choose between earning income and having the time to support children's activities. In her first interview, Irene explained how she and her partner worked long, inflexible hours in a coffee shop, limiting their ability to participate in their six-year-old daughter's education: "Whenever they have asked us to volunteer in their schools, we can't because we have to go to work. We have long working hours, and so we can't really participate in her school as much as we want to." Like most parents, they valued education but simply did not have the time to participate in the way the school demanded.[9]

Alternatively, Delia Trujillo elected to switch jobs, leaving factory work to sell cookware door-to-door. Although this was financially risky because her income depended on a sales commission, she shared, "I like it . . . because I can take care of my kids. Because I can have time for them, their sports and everything."[10]

While she had a hard time supporting her four children (ages 4, 9, 10, and 13) on $600 a month, she could accompany them to a variety of extracurricular activities in the afternoons, including soccer, orchestra, cheerleading, and First Communion classes. Comparing Irene's and Delia's experiences suggests that most parents were unable to both make the money they needed to support their children's development *and* actively involve themselves in their lives.

Children's ages differentiated the amount of pressure parents felt to provide educational opportunities. Camila Escobar believed that her two daughters, ages nine months and four years, were not yet aware of the impact her husband Luis's undocumented status was having on their family's economic situation:

> I definitely think that the girls' lives are gonna be affected. They're being affected right now, but they don't know. They don't understand. If the situation stays this way, say, five years from now, 10 years from now, then it's gonna be incredibly affected. Yes, very much so! But right now, I don't think that it's really affected that much because I don't think they even care. As long as they have mom and dad and they get to play and get to eat, life is good. We could be under a bridge and life would be good. They don't understand yet.

She and Luis were not yet worried about the potential effects of living in a motor home and not having a stable income. But they anticipated that soon their daughters would see how their friends lived and begin asking for dance classes or other opportunities. Luis commented: "I don't see myself having her there [in the trailer] when she is five or six. She definitely needs a room by [then]. I think that is just common sense in child welfare."

Indeed, as children aged, they articulated their desires and began to differentiate themselves from their peers who had citizen parents. In her second interview, Irene shared how this was emerging with her daughter, now eight years old:

> I'm starting to see it now. Her friends' moms are either a doctor, a lawyer, an architect. They never had to struggle from being undocumented [and] not being able to work with your degree. Sometimes she asks, "Why can't I do this? . . . We just don't have money, huh?" For her, I would have to explain to her, we don't have the same situation as your friends' parents. . . . She understands. She's very good. But it's hard for her because she wants to do the things that her friends want to do.

Parents' continually constrained time and money began to instill a sense of inequality.

"WHEN AM I GONNA GO?": TRAVELING TO FIT IN AND MOVE UP

Mirroring the enduring consequences attributed to financial constraints, parents also found that an inability to travel limited their children's development. Pablo Ortiz and Alvina Villanueva shared how travel emerges in young children's lives:

> *Pablo:* Even though she's small right now, sometimes advertisements come up. Legoland. SeaWorld. She wants to go to these places. But sometimes it hurts. It hurts me to hear that because I know that I cannot take her. It's because it's on the other side of the border *[laughs]*.
>
> *Alvina:* In terms of traveling, they want to go to Mexico, but I can't go. . . . I limit their travel and knowing other places.[11]

For Mexican-origin families in Southern California, travel limitations were often experienced as being unable to travel to local vacation destinations in San Diego or to Mexico to visit family. Not only were such trips expensive, but undocumented immigrants feel a limited ability to travel domestically because of the threat of deportation and the material risks of driving without a license. Although San Diego is only two hours from Los Angeles, traveling there is risky because it is close to the U.S.-Mexico border; there are permanent checkpoints on major freeways connecting the cities and heightened immigration enforcement in the region. Recognizing this, Pablo joked that it is on the other side of the border. Further, they cannot travel internationally because they would have to clandestinely reenter the country. Although citizen children technically did not face these restrictions, their young age and dependence on their parents often translated to a shared inability to travel. Travel may be seen as a luxury, but it plays an important role in teaching children that they are different from their peers and limiting their developmental opportunities.

Feeling Different

Sitting in the same classrooms as children who have citizen parents, the children of undocumented young adults become aware that they are different. Alfonso Rojas, an undocumented partner, shared,

> The other day I was writing a story with my son for school, a story of what they did for vacation. And we didn't do anything but go to the park, to take him to play. And his classmates, he saw that they went here, they went there. And he asked me, 'Why can't we do what my friends do?' Those limitations that he has, even in school, reflects that [our undocumented status]. . . . It makes him feel less than those in the same classroom.[12]

Informal social interactions and formal class activities can prompt children to identify missed opportunities, develop a sense of inferiority, and internalize parental immigration status as a source of social differentiation. Sociologist Joanna Dreby finds that children also hide their immigrant origin, particularly when their peers include high concentrations of Latinas/os/xs, to avoid stigmatizing peer interactions.[13] Janet Godinez recounted a similar experience in which her preteen son asked her about going on vacation because "his friend and his mom and dad were gonna go to vacations together." She pointed to how these feelings of deprivation and difference emerge as children age: "Now that they're older, they see the difference. They understand more."

Although these instances surprised Alfonso and Janet, others anticipated such conversations because they reflected their own childhood experiences. Celia Alvarez worried that her undocumented status would eventually affect her daughter, who was only a few months old: "When she hears her classmates say, . . . 'We went to visit my grandma in Mexico,' she's probably going to wonder why we don't take trips like that." These questions echoed those that Celia had asked her parents as a young child. The resulting conversations were how she and other undocumented young adults often began to learn the limitations of their own undocumented status. They intimately knew the feelings of inequality and inferiority that came from being unable to participate in the same activities as their peers. They saw that their children would soon learn these same lessons of illegality.

Such feelings of difference can have lasting impacts on children's friendships and ability to fit in with their peers. As Celia predicted, Marta Sandoval's four-year-old daughter asked why they did not travel like her preschool friends: "She comes to me, 'Mom, my little friend told me her mom was undocumented too. That's so cool! We both get to spend vacation together!'" Marta's inability to travel shaped her daughter's social life, encouraging her to develop a friendship with a classmate who also had an undocumented mother. Her daughter's experience reflected Marta's own childhood as she remembered the pain of feeling "bad" when her friends talked about their vacations in Mexico. This had also shaped her childhood relationships by pushing her "to hang out with people that I thought were kind of like me"—undocumented.

Participants' specific travel desires and limitations reflect their specific context, including their Mexican origin and proximity to the U.S.-Mexico border. Similar experiences likely occur in other geographic areas and populations when the children of undocumented young adults cannot replicate their peer group's social norms.

Missing Opportunities

Parents also saw traveling as a critical opportunity for children's intellectual and emotional growth. Nancy Ortega and Daniela Sanchez explained why:

> Nancy: So they can see other places, learn different customs and traditions. Not only to San Diego [but] all around, especially in third world countries. That way they can see how easy they have it but also give them that desire to one day help [others].
>
> Daniela: For him to grow as a human . . . I want him to experience as much as he can with traveling. Because I haven't been able to

see as many things, and seeing them on TV is bittersweet. So
I would want him to kind of experience it. And realize . . . I'm
no better. My way of thinking isn't the best. . . . What I've been
taught in the school system isn't the best and the only way.
There's more.

Like other parents, Nancy and Daniela saw traveling as a key means of raising
their children to be open minded, responsible, and successful. It provides an
opportunity to generate knowledge through lived experience and build cultural
capital. Although Daniela noted that some of this can be transmitted through TV
or other media, she recognized that this is insufficient for producing a deep sense
of reflective, respectful, and critical thinking.

A few parents shared that they had sent their children to travel alone or with
others to ensure that they had opportunities for socioemotional growth. Naya
Camacho described how she recently sent her 10-year-old son to spend the summer with her sister in Mexico:

He was so, so happy. He said, "I don't want to go back [to the United States]."
Because they have the liberty to run, to play, to everything, and here you're in an
apartment. You can't do this because [of] the manager and the neighbors. . . . In his
case, I said, "OK, I'm going to give him the opportunity to go and know my other
part of the family and know where we came from." . . . I told him, "See how the kids
sleep there? If they are in need, leave your clothes there for them." He left everything.
He only brought, like, the clothes [he was wearing]. He [left] everything. He said,
"Mom, they need it more than me." And so I [did] it for that purpose, to know where
we came from, our values.

Naya beamed with pride as she shared how her son's visit helped him develop
strong values and solidify his sense of humanity. Few parents, however, could
send their children on such trips, either because they lacked funds or did not have
family members with the capacity to support such efforts.

Once older and independent, citizen children could potentially travel on their
own, but memories of these childhood differences will continue to haunt them.
Adán Olivera stressed to his two children, both in elementary school, that they
could go to San Diego when they were older: "How do you explain that you can't
go to SeaWorld? Sometimes I do try to tell them, 'You can't go because your
mom and dad can't go because we weren't born here. You guys were, so you guys
can go, but you can't go alone.'" Rather than hearing reasons like "it's too far"
or "we'll go next year," children face legal explanations and an indefinite date of
future travel. Alfonso Rojas suggested that these instances are internalized and
persist: "They are going to grow up with this limitation. In the future when they
are older, they are going to do it. . . . [But] when one has a memory like this, it is
going to affect you."[14]

"MY SON DOESN'T DESERVE THAT!": DRIVING
WITHOUT A LICENSE

Children's dependence on parents, especially at younger ages, links their physical mobility so that children share in the challenges of not having a driver's license. Cruz Vargas talked about his fear of driving with his one-year-old son: "What am I supposed to do if I get pulled over and I have my son? Some cops don't care. They're like, 'So? Take your son out and go walk.'" Extrapolating from his own negative experiences with police, he suspected that his son would share in the punishment of being undocumented—having a car towed and being stranded on the side of the road. He angrily insisted, "My son doesn't deserve that! My son's done nothing wrong to deserve that!" Thoughtfully, he continued, "I've done nothing wrong to deserve that, you know? I wasn't born and was like, 'Eh, I don't wanna have papers,' you know?" As parents sought to minimize the risks of driving without a license, they found that their children suffered through constrained opportunities for mobility and shared experiences of illegality.

As with leisure travel, parents believed that their children's development was being restricted by their attempts to limit the risks associated with local, everyday driving. Daniela Sanchez, who was six months pregnant, worried that it would be difficult to take her infant son to doctor's appointments because she refused to drive without a license. Estefania Gutierrez-Estrada found it impossible to not drive her seven-year-old son to school: "It's been an issue basically school-wise. You have to be there at a time, so we can't really rely on public transportation." Intent on minimizing the risk of police encounters, she refused to drive more than this. This limited her son's access to after-school programming and made it hard to visit public places like parks and museums where he can exercise, be stimulated, and learn new skills. These barriers became even more noticeable as children grew older and developed busier, time-dependent schedules.

Feeling pressured to meet their children's need for mobility, most parents drove unlicensed, developing strategies to limit their risks. Victoria Sandoval explained how she tried to avoid being stopped by police: "I always try to drive safely. And I'm always with my three-year-old, so I'm always careful." Many parents reported monitoring their driving behaviors: precisely following speed limits and rules about signaling, changing lanes, and making turns. Alicia Medina drives only "during the day, because the night is when they set up the checkpoints."[15] Others tried to keep track of when and where sobriety checkpoints were commonly set up so that they could avoid them. These management strategies seem to have served many well, since only a handful of parents reported running into a checkpoint with their children in the car.

Seeing parents' management strategies, older children often adopted a de facto sense of illegality as they began to look out for police cars and checkpoints. Alicia explained how her 11-year-old daughter came to understand her fear of being pulled over: "Now she understands many of the things I can't do. When I'm driving, she understands. She helps me. She says, 'Pull over to the side, Mami. Over there I see a police car.' She alerts me to dangers that come with driving without a license."[16] Citizen children thus come to adopt a similar vigilance and outlook as their parents. This can take a psychological toll on them, adding stress and fear that children with citizen parents do not have to deal with.

Parents who had been pulled over with their children in the car reported shared trauma. Janet Godinez recounted having her car towed:

> They told me that since I don't have a driver's license, they were gonna take away my car. And they see my kids crying because they were taking the car. But they [the police] don't care at all. . . . I had blankets [and clothes] because I was gonna go wash [at the Laundromat]. And they told me, "Since your situation, I'm gonna, under the table, let you take out stuff." . . . Then my kids start crying when they were taking the car in the [tow] truck. And then the cops told me, . . . "Well, we're gonna take you home."

In Janet's case, she felt the police were relatively agreeable because her children were present, using their discretion to minimize (but not eliminate) the effect on her family. In other cases, though, police interactions triggered children's fears of detention, deportation, and family separation. This was true for Ignacio Nuñez's six-year-old daughter when they were pulled over. "[She's] telling me, like, 'Daddy, they're gonna take you to jail!' I'm like, 'No, Mami, they're just checking and that's it.' But she gets scared. She starts crying." Children who experienced these types of events were left traumatized and confused about the role of police, who they thought were supposed to "serve and protect."

Parents also worried that their unlicensed driving set a bad example. Nancy Ortega laughed as she remembered a recent comment made by her two sons, ages four and five:

> They do say, "I'm not gonna drive until I get a driver's license." They say that! If they get on the steering wheel, they'll just sit there. [They] would say, "I can't drive, Mommy, because I don't have my driver's license yet." So now I have one [because of DACA], but [their dad] doesn't. How do I explain that to them, that Mommy has one but Daddy doesn't?

Given that she had never discussed driver's licenses with them, Nancy was baffled about where her sons learned about them, perhaps on TV or in a video game. Tanya Diaz's 10-year-old son knew that she did not have a license:

> He jokes around, "I can't be in the car with you because you don't have a license." That he's a law-abiding citizen. "Mom, that's not right, you're driving without a license. I can't be in the car with you, Mom." I'm like, "Fine, get out." . . . I feel like a hypocrite: "Here, son, follow rules, while I'm gonna break them." It's hard to

teach that to him. So I'm sure he's confused. Is it wrong or isn't it wrong? We'll see when he gets older, how it affects him.

Although Tanya and her son are teasing each other, she suggested that these conversations might have real implications for how citizen children will feel about themselves in relation to the law. Will her son follow the laws? Or break them unnecessarily because he had seen her do it? In extreme cases, citizen children might adopt oppositional stances because they see how the law unfairly treats their parents or that their parents do not follow it.

THE SPECTER OF DEPORTATION:
SHARED FEARS AND RISKS

Most undocumented young adults I spoke to did not express substantial fears that they may suddenly be deported. They recognized that their deportation would drastically alter their lives and believed they would struggle to adapt to life in a country they no longer remembered.[17] Yet they reasoned that their deportation was unlikely, letting it fade to the back of their minds. Parents, however, were more likely to discuss fearing deportation because it threatened their family's stability. Parents struggled with two crucial decisions: Should they talk to their children about the possibility of their deportation? What would they do if they were deported? Regardless of their specific plans, parents suggest that their children will experience multigenerational punishment through emotional trauma and threats to their upward mobility.

"Why Can't the Parents Be with Their Kids?": Fearing Family Separation

Becoming a parent intensified fears of deportation. Cruz Vargas shared, "I wake up every day knowing I don't have papers, and I wake up every day knowing it's a possibility I can get deported." I asked if his feelings had changed since the birth of his son a little more than a year earlier. He shifted his gaze away, watching his son crawl around their cramped bedroom:

> [The thoughts] they're kind of more. You know? Because now I actually have someone that really depends on me. So now I have to be way more cautious. 'Cause before [if] I get deported, I can make it on my own. . . . It wouldn't be easy at all, but a girlfriend's [just] a girlfriend at the end of the day. . . . She'll get over it. I'll get over it. . . . But my son, my son's not gonna be able to understand that I can't be here. My son's not gonna be able to understand that I can't provide for him. . . . So I have to be way more cautious with everything.

Growing up, Cruz had been aware of the threat of deportation, but it had not pushed him to change his behavior. He frequently had encounters with police. Once, he was stopped walking home with a friend late at night. He was charged—he claimed falsely—with a minor offense and served two and a half months in jail because "it was more expensive to fight it." Though he had already begun to change his ways, becoming a father increased his sense of caution.

Although parents were weighing deportation threats, many shielded their young children from this reality to protect their current emotional well-being. Edgar Gonzalez explained that he does not talk to his five-year-old daughter about his immigration status or the possibility of deportation: "She's too young to understand that stuff. I don't want to confuse her with all that stuff." Like Edgar, most parents felt that their young children were prone to misunderstanding immigration and the nuances of (il)legality.[18]

In some cases, parents' decisions stemmed directly from their own experiences being raised to fear deportation. Norma Mercado, the mother of an eight- and four-year-old, explained, "I knew since I was little that I didn't have papers and that I couldn't go anywhere. My parents would say, 'We can't go there because immigration will come.' So I don't want them to be scared [like I was]." By avoiding these conversations, Norma hoped to prevent immigration policies from reproducing emotional trauma.

Yet many parents elected to discuss deportation threats with their older children to protect their future well-being, especially if they already knew about their parents' undocumented status. Janet Godinez described her 12-year-old son's reaction to news coverage about deportation and family separation:

> When he sees that, he asks me questions: "Why are they separating the kids from the mom?" And then I have to explain [to] them: "Because they know that the mom doesn't have benefits [legal status]. And [immigration officials] went to their job [to take them] . . . And the kids have to stay here . . . because the kids are United States [citizens]." So he'll tell me, "But why can't the parents be with their kids? Because that's the only thing they want to do."

In addition to trying to help her son understand the nuances of immigration enforcement, Janet prepared her children for the possibility that immigration agents could detain or deport her or her undocumented partner:

> With my kids, what I've been telling them is that in case something happens and I don't go for them at school, to stay in school. Don't come home or don't run away. Don't get scared. Just be in school or whatever place you are, stay there until I come back. Or if you guys see someone that you know, go to them.

Similarly, Alicia Medina shared that she had similar discussions with her daughters, "as a way to not have them with eyes closed, covered. So they can see more or less reality."[19] Despite the fear this provoked, parents felt that this was the most responsible way to protect their children from emotional trauma if they unexpectedly disappeared. Their actions reflect immigration advocates' recommendations to develop a family preparedness plan that specifies who will care for children and to talk with them about the plan.[20]

Despite best intentions, awareness of deportation threats often led to fear. Alfonso Rojas, an undocumented partner, described the cost of talking with his son, age 10, about the risk:

> It affects them. One time when the police passed near the house, on a chase, there was a lot of police, helicopters, and my son was on the balcony and he hid. He was hiding. He told me that immigration was coming. He doesn't have anything to do with this. But he did it because we have talked about this.[21]

"It's Too Much": Choosing between De Facto Deportation and Family Separation

During conversations about deportation threats, parents reported that children often asserted that they would accompany their parents. Victoria Sandoval, a single mother, recounted comments from her older children (ages 11, 12, and 15): "They say, 'We're going with you. We're gonna tell them [immigration officials], "We want to go with our mom because she's the only one that we have. We cannot stay with anyone else. We have nobody else but our mom."'" These conversations made parents realize how their deportation would lead their citizen children to experience multigenerational punishment, either through family separation or through deprivation of opportunities in the United States.

Despite desires to remain together, parents struggled with the thought that their citizen children would experience de facto deportation if they followed their parent to the country of origin and lost the opportunity to pursue upward mobility in the United States. Tanya Diaz reflected on whether she would take her 10-year-old son with her:

> I couldn't. My mom was saying, "Let's just take him with us." But there is no life for him over there. I push school on him so much that I hope something good comes of it. He does put his education to use because he's a bright kid. There's no opportunities for him there. He could be so much more here.

Similarly, Abby Zamora shared, "I don't believe in family separation, [but] I wouldn't want to jeopardize my baby, taking her to a country where I don't even know how to survive." She worried about not being able to provide for her daughter's basic needs, let alone pay for her school. Confirming Tanya and Abby's fears, scholars find that the citizen children who accompany their deported parents often struggle in school systems that are unprepared to support them.[22]

On the other hand, parents anticipated that family separation would cause emotional trauma. Despite Tanya's clear assertion in her first interview that her son would remain in the United States, she said in her second interview that she would take him with her because "I cannot be without him." Estefania Gutierrez-Estrada similarly asserted that separation was "out of the question":

> I experienced separation from my parents, and it's not something pretty. It's not something that you want a child to experience. My dad was never in the picture. My mom left [to the United States] when I was 10. I went through depression. Now that I think about it, it was clearly depression. I would get sick all the time. . . . Even the teachers and report cards [said], "This child is going through a lot of emotional hardship and she needs support" and this and that. And I was just crying constantly: "I want my mom. I want my mom here for Mother's Day. I want my dad here for Father's Day." Or for the graduations or whatever. So I know what it feels like, and I can't have my children do that, you know? I can't have my children experience that. The whole separation of families, it's too much.

Estefania grounded her decision in her childhood experiences in a transnational family—her mother had migrated to the United States in search of work, leaving Estefania with family in Mexico before they reunited in the United States.[23] This economic strategy comes at a high emotional cost, which Estefania intimately remembered. Hoping to prevent this emotional trauma in the next generation, she was adamant that her family would stay together.

Only one parent shared that their child's other parent had been deported. Flor Vega's daughter, three at the time of our interview, was only a few months old when her ex-partner was deported, so she did not feel the emotional impact. Yet other scholars have documented how older children experience severe psychosocial effects, including fear and anxiety, social withdrawal, and altered eating and sleeping patterns.[24] Flor's ex-partner had also helped her financially. His absence limited her ability to provide a stable household and developmental opportunities.[25] Emotional consequences also manifested later: "She asks for her dad, and I don't lie to her. . . . She knows her dad is in Mexico. . . . Sometimes she'll see another little girl with her dad and her mom, and she'll ask me, 'Where's my dad?' I want her to live with both of her parents too, but she can't."

"MORE NORMAL" BUT "A LITTLE TOO LATE": THE IMPACTS OF DACA ON CHILDREN

Most parents anticipated that receiving DACA would catapult them and their children into a world of opportunities. Early evidence suggests that children whose mothers are eligible for DACA have lower rates of adjustment and anxiety disorder diagnoses.[26] Aaron Ortiz, who had recently applied for DACA, hoped to go back to school. "I wanna pursue a career and try to live a more comfortable life," he said. A community college graduate, Aaron aspired to complete his bachelor's degree in horticulture and become a state park employee. Without DACA's employment authorization, he earned $2,600 a month as a self-employed handyman. He was financially stable but aspired to more because he saw the multigenerational nature of inequality: "I wanna be able to have an opportunity and let my daughter have an opportunity. So that's why I want to file for that [DACA] because I really feel like I have a lot of potential in a lot of ways and I can't do a whole lot without anything [legal status]." Although Aaron and the other parents aspired to transform their family's stability and children's well-being through DACA, many found that some of consequences of illegality endured in their children's lives.

Establishing a Pathway to Integration (for Some)

After receiving DACA, some parents capitalized on their employment authorization to earn more money and afford better educational and extracurricular opportunities for their children. Luis Escobar put his college degree to use. He moved from a hodgepodge of jobs to one as a community organizer, almost tripling his monthly salary from $1,200 to $3,300. Aware of the importance of early-childhood education, he and his wife began investing in their oldest daughter's education. He felt DACA had improved his daughters' lives "200 percent!" He said,

> Just the fact that I am able to pay for a nice pre-K for her. I know I was able to take her to a regular pre-K. . . . [but] it is a reality that LAUSD [Los Angeles Unified School District] is still fucked up and they will get better opportunities [if they] go to a better school. So instead of like one teacher per 100 little pre-K kids, she is in a mini little private one with 15 kids and it is three teachers.

Though he exaggerates the student-to-teacher ratio in public schools, a well-resourced, private program will likely better prepare his daughter for educational success. Similarly, other parents discussed how moderate income improvements allowed them to afford enrollment fees for extracurricular activities.

Parents who obtained a driver's license after receiving DACA enjoyed a newfound physical mobility that allowed them to provide educational opportunities and support. Abby Zamora was looking forward to getting her driver's license. She imagined that this would open up opportunities for her toddler daughter's social and emotional development: "I'll be able to drive her around. I want her to be in sports, anything that is gonna help her learn discipline and just be a happy kid. So I wanna be able to drive her around without getting my car taken away." Similarly, Janet Godinez noted,

> I drive more confident, more normal. . . . Because before I couldn't drive all the way to school. I had to walk. . . . [If] they call from school, I'll go [there] driving, fast. I'll let them know if you behave bad, I'll go. Now they know that I have a car, I'll probably be in five minutes at their school.

She also remarked that this has allowed them to pursue activities outside the home: "With the family now we could go everywhere and we don't have to worry about 'Oh, it's going to be dark. Oh, it's going to be late. We have to go back to the house'" to avoid checkpoints and police. In most cases, a driver's license removed immediate barriers so that there was significantly less fear and more freedom to parent and attend to children's needs.

Access to a driver's license and protection from deportation also allowed parents to feel comfortable traveling locally. In some cases, travel was the main way that young children understood their parents' newfound opportunities. Estefania Gutierrez-Estrada recalled her citizen husband and then five-year-old son's reaction to her receiving her DACA approval in the mail: "The first thing that my husband said [was] 'Well, congratulate your mom. Now we can go to San Diego.' And he's like, 'San Diego! Yeah!' So that was his understanding of this whole immigration thing." Adán Olivera, who had shared his children's desperate desire to go to SeaWorld in his first interview, instantly focused on travel in response to my question about how he thought DACA changed his life:

> It did affect me in a way that before we didn't go out to anywhere, like San Diego. We couldn't drive out of state. . . . [With DACA], we started going to San Diego. I took my kids to SeaWorld, [the] Safari Zoo. We did the whole weekend . . . spend the night and three days. It makes them happy. That's kind of the way it changed me, because now we go everywhere.

Over half of the 20 parents who had received DACA spontaneously talked about traveling to San Diego. Like Adán, most beamed with pride. These trips signaled that they could facilitate their children's social integration and close some of the most tangible gaps between them and their peers who had citizen parents.

Although most parents focused on other impacts, a few, including Naya Camacho, reported that their children had less fear of family separation:

> *Naya:* They feel like, "My mom is not going to Mexico. She's going to stay with us."
> *Laura:* Did they think about that before?
> *Naya:* Yes, 'cause for a long time they were having like the redadas [immigration raids], and in my corner by my house they had a redada, and they're so afraid. They are so afraid they said, "If you go to Mexico, we're going with you." But, yeah, and now that I have DACA . . . they said they feel more comfortable.

DACA recipients' protection from deportation also likely lessened the need for preparatory conversations about family separation, decreasing the frequency of emotional turmoil.

Unmet Expectations

While some parents were beginning to see early indications that their undocumented status would no longer hold their children back, many did not see immediate and dramatic economic impacts. In many cases, illegality's enduring consequences on undocumented young adults' lives ensured that their children continued to experience barriers, particularly economic ones.

Partners Irene Correas and Julián Salinas both received DACA a year before their interviews. Irene, in her early 30s, had earned a bachelor's degree six years earlier and quickly found a job at a school district. It was a big step up from her previous job as a barista, but it had limited hours. She anticipated needing to earn a child development certificate or a graduate degree to turn it into a more stable career. Julián had been pursuing architectural training at various local community colleges for almost a decade. Now driven to complete his degree, he anticipated two or three more years of school before obtaining his bachelor's degree and being able to work in the field. In the meantime, he strung together part-time jobs in which he was quickly given raises to earn several dollars more an hour then his previous job as a barista. Like Irene and Julián, many undocumented parents saw some financial gains, but their economic integration was slow and did not facilitate their children's immediate integration.

Irene reflected on how DACA was slowly improving their family's financial situation: "little by little, we'll do more." They had committed themselves to moving their children to a better neighborhood and had enrolled their oldest, then eight, in several extracurricular activities, including "theater classes. She's taking violin classes now. She likes to play soccer outside with her little friends. She used to play basketball. Now she's trying out to swim." Yet, Irene noted that there were still differences between her daughter and her peers who had citizen parents:

> In the summer, some of her friends were going to summer camps, but it's a lot of money. It just wasn't very viable. So what I did was find this free music class. . . . She also likes to do activities on her own. Like, she has this activity book that will get her ready for third grade. She likes to read.

Irene's comments parallel those that she had made two years earlier, clearly establishing that DACA had not removed all the limitations that their immigration status placed on their children.

Persisting income limitations prevented families from taking advantage of new opportunities, like travel. A few parents shared that they were still trying to save enough to take their children to theme parks in San Diego, a minimum of $200–$300 for tickets for a family of four.[27] Several others shared that they could not afford longer family vacations, particularly ones that involved airfare. Vanessa Miranda felt that receiving DACA had changed her thought process about traveling beyond Los Angeles: "[Before I thought] I can't. What if something happens and I don't have my stuff [immigration status]? That was stopping me. Now it's not stopping me, but I don't have money [laughs]." Despite having a work permit, she continued to work in the same job as a full-time administrative assistant making $1,600 a month. This was not enough to fulfill her seven-year-old daughter's dream of going to Hawaii. Further, international travel remained out of reach since DACA allowed recipients to travel outside the country only for educational, employment, and humanitarian reasons after a long and costly advanced parole process.

Too Little, Too Late

Despite receiving DACA, parents felt it was not enough to shield children from immigration policies' far-reaching impacts. They still experienced illegality through other undocumented family members and their previous experiences with inequality.

Parents who were partnered with first-generation undocumented adults found that their children's fears simply shifted to the other undocumented parent. Janet Godinez explained, "Now they're scared of my husband getting deported." Several highlighted DACA's exclusivity, as it was available only to a select group of undocumented young adults. Children remained in mixed-status families, since their other parent or extended family members were still undocumented. In light of these persistent fears, several parents spoke hopefully of the Deferred Action for Parents of Americans and Lawful Permanent Residents (DAPA) program, which was announced in November 2014 toward the end of my second wave of interviews. Though never put into effect, DAPA would have provided undocumented parents of citizen and permanent resident children with the same benefits of DACA—a renewable work permit and protection from deportation.[28] This program would have also improved children's economic stability; estimates suggest that DAPA recipients would have increased their wages by 6–10 percent.[29]

Parents of older children found that the remnants of previous limitations remained. Children had aged as their parents waited for the opportunity to provide them with more. Tanya Diaz remembered her 13-year-old son's reaction to finally traveling to San Diego:

> We went to SeaWorld. We went to Legoland, but he was too old already. I'm like, "Damn it, babe, I'm sorry." . . . It was nice. I wish he was younger. He still enjoyed it, but Legoland for sure is for little kids. . . . Past [the age of] 12, you don't even want to go there.

Tanya's son's experience suggests that there is a point of no return, an age at which parents cannot retroactively provide experiences and opportunities. Further, there is no chance to remove the memory of this previous limitation, so feelings of deprivation can persist. Many of the undocumented young adults remembered and regretted being unable to travel to similar places when they were young. Their own children will likely have similar memories, especially if they exited childhood before their parents received DACA.

Older children had also been exposed to their parents' undocumented status longer, allowing it to shape their sense of self and way of interacting with the world.

As Marta shared earlier, illegality had already limited her daughter's social networks. After overhearing some of our conversation, Nancy's 20-year-old citizen sister shared that watching her undocumented siblings and mother had shaped her own driving habits: "It makes me drive carefully as well. [Be] a bit scared of cops. Because they may not have shown it, but they were scared. . . . [And] checkpoints, it does make me be more aware." Allie internalized their hypervigilance: driving cautiously, fearing police, and noting checkpoints. This suggests that such practices are unlikely to disappear if they have become ingrained in citizen children's understandings of and approaches to the world.

Parents with younger children believed that DACA established a pathway to integration for their children. This was true in Luis's case. He quickly transitioned into a well-paid job at a nonprofit because of his strong social network. Luckily, this timing aligned with his daughter's being preschool age. If Luis's daughter had been older, he would have been unable to start her early education in a private preschool program. Children's ages noticeably affected how much they could benefit from their parents' legal integration.

"I WANT HER TO KNOW HOW I STRUGGLE": PASSING ON DUAL FRAMES OF REFERENCE

Parents longed to protect their children from multigenerational punishment, but when they realized this was not entirely possible, many sought to instill avenues for resilience. When I asked participants to consider whether they would discuss their immigration status with their children, many were quick to note the positives. Daniela Sanchez responded:

> A lot. I think I will [talk to him about my status], yeah. Just like I think my parents did when it came to that experience with bringing us here. You want to give your kids an idea of how things are. Just different hardships that you have so they value where they're at right now. Just like I value what I have right now because of what I know from my parents. . . . Even with all of these restrictions [of being undocumented], I still can see how lucky I am. . . . So I want [my son] to know what his grandparents did, what we [me and his dad] had to do, what other people are doing.

Coming to the United States at age four, Daniela only had a few hazy memories of life in Mexico. Yet her parents' stories allowed her to develop a narrative that life as an undocumented immigrant in the United States was better than life in Mexico. She believed that this kept her "moving forward every day because you always say, 'Well, it could always be worse.'" These conversations gave her an inherited frame of reference, one that she hoped to pass on to her son. Many parents planned to use their narratives of struggling as undocumented immigrants to foster their children's growth by teaching them an appreciation for what they had, persistence in the face of adversity, and compassion.

Scholars use the concept *dual frame of reference* to capture how first-generation immigrants evaluate their current opportunities in relation to those in their country of origin. These frames often allow them to feel positively about their current situation, despite marginalizing experiences.[30] As immigrant children, undocumented young adults often do not have sufficient knowledge of the origin country to fuel such frames; rather they draw largely on conversations with their parents to develop inherited dual frames of reference. They later hope to instill similar frames in their own children via conversations about the opportunities they were denied as undocumented immigrants and children's advantages as U.S. citizens.

Most parents delicately balanced shielding their children from their past struggles while also teaching children an appreciation for their privileges. Celia Alvarez shared how she planned to achieve this with her 2.5-year-old daughter:

> I want her to know how I struggle and like all this so that she can appreciate what she has. So in a way, I do want her to know. As soon as she's of age, I'm probably going to tell her . . . what I had to do for jobs and like, and like everything. So, hopefully—

Celia trailed off, further highlighting her uncertainty about the specific details she will share. Perhaps she will discuss having to work three jobs to put herself through community college, worrying about losing her job as a security guard, or being scared to drive her daughter around in the family's new car. And, as her citizen husband believed, these stories will teach their daughter "how hard it was and how easy she has it" as a citizen.

Intent on pushing their children to complete high school and pursue higher education, parents, like Janet Godinez, highlighted how citizenship status bred better opportunities:

> They ask me, "Why can't you work on something else instead of doing [that] for the minimum [wage]?" And I have to explain to my kids, because I don't have documents. And that's what frustrates me. . . . That's why I tell my kids that they have to go every day to school. Because . . . they were born here and everything. They have more benefits and they have more help than us. Because if we go somewhere, they deny the help or they tell us, "Oh, since you don't have a Social, we can't help you," or "You can't get this benefit." That's what I talk to my kids [about]. And I tell them, "You guys have to work hard, study hard. When you guys grow up, you will have a good job. A better position instead of, you know, winning the minimum [wage] or working 10 hours and still getting the minimum, no overtime, no benefits."

Explaining the limitations that her children see and telling them about other experiences that they don't, Janet spun her negative experiences into inspiring lessons. She sought to refocus their confusion and sense of injustice into hard work and persistence so they could achieve the upward mobility unavailable to her.

Parents also anticipated drawing on their stories to teach their children compassion. Aaron Ortiz imagined what these conversations might look like when his one-and-a-half-year-old daughter was a little older: "I guess not to look people down. If a person doesn't speak the language . . . think about it, don't react just because he doesn't speak English. Or doesn't smell like chicken when you smell like chicken." We laughed, but it was unclear if his comment about chicken was his way of highlighting the ridiculousness of potential reasons children can exclude others. Or perhaps he was drawing on some deep-seated memory of lunchtime struggles, in which immigrant children are targeted for having the "wrong" kind of food. Either way, Aaron's and other parents' lessons often stressed compassion toward immigrant classmates, likely because of the teasing they experienced as immigrant children.

Finally, some parents hoped that these conversations would inspire a sense of justice. Speaking about the future he imagines for his six-week-old daughter, Bruno Reyes joked that she will become the president of the United States. Becoming serious, he continued,

> I just want her to have a good education, to think outside the books. A lot of stuff they teach you here is a lot of trash. . . . I want her to be aware and I want her to help out the people. That's why I want to teach her about my struggle. So she could be like, "Damn! People go through all this stuff. They don't teach me that over here."

Bruno hoped that his and his partner's undocumented experiences would move her so that "she will do what she can to change the law."

Irene Correas had successfully fostered this sense of awareness and activism in her daughter. She shared how she spoke to her daughter, then about five years old, about the differences between undocumented status and citizenship and why she was arrested as part of a civil disobedience action protesting rising deportation rates:

> There were images in the media and so she saw. And she's like, "Well, I saw this police officer take you. Why?" . . . And so I basically told her, my friends and I don't have the same opportunities as other people because we don't have a Social Security number. And so I kind of showed her her Social Security number . . . [and] that I didn't have that. . . . [And] some people believe that I didn't belong here and they wanted me to go back to Mexico. And there were families that will separate Mommy and Daddy and the kids.

She saw that her daughter seemed to understand these differences, and she wanted to highlight immigrant communities' power to resist, so she began taking her daughter to activist meetings and rallies: "She started to understand, 'Oh, OK, you just wanna go to college. OK, you just want to stay here with your friends.'" She proudly recounted her daughter's actions at a recent event: "While we were marching around the block, she started screaming, 'Undocumented and unafraid!' you know. 'I'm undocumented and unafraid!' And I just felt like really like—wow! She's understanding what I'm going through." While many parents hesitated with how to discuss immigration-related issues with children, Irene's example shows how honest, focused conversation can open up the potential for transformation.

CONCLUSION

As undocumented parents raise their citizen children, they see their undocumented status steadily shaping the next generation. Immigration policies effectively produce family-level inequalities as children share in the consequences of their parents' limited economic and spatial mobility. These effects crystalize as children grow up and try to make sense of the differences they see between themselves and others. Some parents begin to see parallels between their own undocumented childhoods and those of their citizen children. Ultimately, children's citizenship status does not protect them from spending the beginning of their lives subjected to many of the same inequalities as their undocumented parents.

Children's experiences suggest that the enduring consequences of illegality can be reduced the sooner their parents transition into a legal or liminally legal status. The older children were when their parents received DACA, the longer they had lived in a context of illegality. They had already begun to comprehend and internalize inequalities when they did not have the same opportunities and experiences as their peers with citizen parents. It also meant that they were unable to access early-childhood educational opportunities or participate in extra-curricular activities. These experiences define children's early development and leave painful memories; neither can be undone by DACA, or even permanent residency and citizenship.

8

Immigration Policy and the Future of Latino Families

My experiences are going to go with me.

—LUIS ESCOBAR

As he looked to the future, Luis could not help but look back. He remembered when he first arrived to the United States at the age of nine: "You think you're gonna walk into the Magic Castle and Mickey [Mouse] is going to greet you and pat you in the back." Instead, he was dropped into the harsh reality of South Central Los Angeles, living with his mom and younger brother in a plastic garden shed behind his older brothers' house. They never went to Disneyland.

It was the early 1990s, and California raged with anti-immigrant sentiment. Luis remembered that Governor Pete Wilson and California voters wanted to "flag undocumented students from high school and deport them as soon as they turn 18." This was not exactly what Proposition 187 entailed, but he and his family were scared: "psychological suppression that you gotta be afraid, you gotta hide."[1] Struggling to find a place to belong, he became involved in a community-based organization dedicated to empowering youth. He found a purpose advocating with his peers for better school resources.

Luis graduated from high school in 2001. Unlike most undocumented youth, he had mentors who knew about Assembly Bill 540, a recently passed state law that allowed him to pay in-state college tuition. He began community college. Drained by four hours on the bus each day, he invested in a car. It was almost older than he was, and he had to stop every 30 minutes to put water in the radiator. It took five years to transfer to a four-year university: "Sleep[ing] in the car in between classes, lots of coffee. Eating [only] bread and butter" to save enough money to pay tuition costs out of pocket. He temporarily left school when he was pulled over and cited for driving without a license so he could save up and pay the impound fees for his towed car.

Despite these immense barriers, he eventually earned his bachelor's degree. As college graduation approached, Luis married his girlfriend with the dream of legalizing his status through marriage. He planned to "be an engineer. . . . [with] all this money." They soon learned that he would be unable to safely legalize his status because he had entered the United States without a valid visa. Older, and a little wiser, he got "a reality check. . . . The older you get as a DREAMer, the harder it is to get a job because they don't look at you like, 'Aww, DREAMer, let me hook you up.' No, you are a grown undocumented person." He continued to push forward, but the barriers were formidable for him, his wife, and their children.

Luis did what he could to disrupt the power that immigration policies held over his family. But, at the end of his first interview in spring 2012, he was resigned: "I've given my soul, my blood, my heart, my sweat to this country. I prayed, I've protested, I've hurt my back. My family is completely damaged. . . . So now I have a daughter, and I have to do whatever it takes to make a better life. . . . If this country is gonna punish me even more, then I will have to take the punishment."

Two months later, DACA was announced.

We spoke again almost exactly two years after. Luis had received DACA and was using it to piece together a better future for his family. Picking at a plate of pancakes, he explained the mark his undocumented status had left on his life. He was one of the most upwardly mobile DACA recipients I spoke to, but he still felt vulnerable: "How do I live in that world [with DACA]? What are my new tools that I should have? Who am I now as a person compared to the person before? . . . It was really like trying to let go of that person, but [I] couldn't let go of that person." Struggling with this transition, he concluded that, for better or worse, his life would always be shaped by his undocumented status.

Memories may fade, but his previous experiences shaped his deepest self.

Choices were made. Roads were not taken.

Time marched on.

* * *

Undocumented immigrants and their families are here to stay. They are woven into the social fabric of the United States, but as Luis's story exemplifies, they are simultaneously kept on the margins. Immigration laws and policies create a context of illegality that constrains opportunities and leaves undocumented young adults and their families swirling in uncertainty. These legal inequalities develop into social inequalities as hegemonic cultural ideals transform the material constraints associated with illegality into socioemotional barriers to participation. The very nature of families and family formation ensures that these inequalities endure, stretching into future generations.

The interplay between the law, cultural ideals, and families makes illegality consequential in everyday family life. Immigration laws and policies constrain family formation by limiting who undocumented young adults date, if and how they advance relationships, their relationship roles, and how they perform their roles as partners and parents. Their citizen romantic partners and children also contend with the material and emotional costs of punitive immigration policies. These constrained circumstances shape the life course of undocumented young adults and their citizen family members so that the imprint of undocumented status remains even as they transition into more inclusive immigration statuses. The longer we wait to address these legally imposed barriers, the more irreversible the consequences will become.

CONSTRAINED CHOICES: IMMIGRATION POLICY, GENDERED EXPECTATIONS, AND ALTERED FAMILY FORMATION

Families are sites of social reproduction. Members of marginalized families share limited resources, allowing inequality to ripple through families and persist over generations. Such inequalities are increasingly produced through laws and legal institutions as the state disrupts family life, increasing the risk of long-term negative consequences.[2] Immigration policies thus alter undocumented young adults' ability to build essential family relationships, constraining their choices and limiting their ability to meet their own and others' expectations.

Illegality limits the material resources available to build and sustain families. Undocumented young adults could not always afford to go out on dates, and they hesitated to risk driving without a license. They were denied access to age-restricted spaces and were infantilized as they tried to keep up with their citizen peers and partners. They struggled to deepen relationships because their intimate moments were rushed (and rare). These same barriers remained as they built families—permanently partnering, cohabiting, marrying, and having children. They worried about their capacity to support a growing family and doubted their ability to be the partner and parent that they wanted to be.

Illegality also frames relationships as a strategic means to an end. Popular narratives about legalization through marriage to a U.S. citizen took hold, shaping whom they were told to date (or not date), whom they allowed themselves to love, and when they chose to marry. If they were lucky enough to pursue legalization through marriage, laws shaped the very foundation of their life together as they structured their relationship to support their petition.

These limited resources and unstable beginnings endanger a relationship's capacity to provide emotional support and security. Relationships began with fears of inadequacy and (perceived) suspicion, requiring both partners to invest energy to prove their love. Differing immigration statuses, and the opportunities they dictate, infused inequality into relationships. Couples struggled with feelings of stress and guilt as they tried to build a brighter future, despite limited resources. Some successfully negotiated their different immigration statuses and built a sense of unconditional love and support. Others struggled for this mutual understanding. All together, these constraints led many undocumented young adults to internalize negative feelings about themselves as partners and parents.

These findings highlight how laws and hegemonic cultural ideals jointly make immigration status consequential in undocumented young adults' everyday lives. Immigration policies codify inequality along immigration status lines, creating unequal access to material resources. This restricts undocumented young adults' ability to participate in family formation in the ways that have become normalized by U.S. culture. In particular, gendered cultural ideals transformed material constraints into socioemotional barriers that disrupted family formation experiences and altered outcomes.

Steeped in traditional gender roles, undocumented young men aspired to be the provider. Early on, this manifested as expectations that they drive and pay for their dates. They dreamed of financial stability before transitioning to marriage and parenthood. This persistent desire to provide conflicted with their limited financial resources, and it endangered many men's ability to form families in the way they desired. Some prepared for a life of loneliness while others delayed taking on the added responsibilities of husband and father. Still many pushed on, committing themselves to partners and raising children despite their constrained circumstances. Although women also negotiated material and socioemotional barriers, their gendered expectations insulated them from severe consequences, ensuring that men's family formation was disproportionality disrupted in comparison. Thus, gender and immigration status mutually construct experiences of illegality. Future work should explore how other material constraints and cultural norms invoke social locations that intersect with undocumented status and that co-construct experiences of illegality.

In many instances, the stories of these undocumented young adults reflect those of low-income, incarcerated, or racial/ethnic minority citizens, in which structural barriers restrict family processes and produce negative family outcomes.[3] I demonstrate how material constraints and socioemotional barriers come together in these marginalized families. Rather than become cultural innovators, undocumented young adults maintained hegemonic notions of family formation complete with gendered expectations, romantic images of love, and beliefs that there was a "right way" to form a family (whatever the specifics were). When illegality constrained their choices, it not only altered their ability to form families but also left them frustrated and dissatisfied that they could not live up to their own and others' expectations. This suggests that future research on marginalized families needs to deeply engage how material constraints *and* socioemotional barriers jointly (re)produce social inequalities via consequential family outcomes.

THE PASSAGE OF TIME: LIMITING THE BENEFITS OF
INCLUSIVE IMMIGRATION POLICIES

Immigration scholars have increasingly highlighted how laws and policies can restrict immigrant integration. For example, assimilation theory's use of *context of reception* highlights how governmental policy structures immigrant integration so that undocumented immigrants have lower incorporation levels.[4] Further, substantive scholarship shows that moving from an undocumented to a lawful status improves economic and political integration.[5] By focusing on the full process of family formation, I complicate the seemingly direct connection between lawful immigration status and immigrant incorporation. Rather, remnants of illegality endure, even as immigration policies change or individuals transition into more secure immigration statuses. I contend that the steady march of time pulls undocumented young adults along the life course, setting up consequences that outlast undocumented status.

Although not a formal legal status, receiving DACA reshaped the meaning of illegality overnight. DACA protections carried many material benefits associated with having a work permit, access to a valid Social Security number, and protection from deportation. Surveys show that DACA recipients moved into better jobs, had higher incomes, accessed financial accounts, bought cars and houses, stayed in or returned to school, and had better psychological wellness.[6] Indeed, many of the DACA recipients I interviewed reported similar benefits. Everyone did not, however, benefit equally. Those with less education and weaker social networks were less likely to experience substantial mobility.[7] While they may have moved into slightly better jobs, many did not have the requisite education, skills, or connections to launch themselves into the middle class. Those who had already formed families found it particularly difficult because they could not risk losing income and often lacked the time and resources to pursue new training or return for educational degrees. The same was true among the recently legalized lawful permanent residents.

Differential benefits aside, I find that the imprint of undocumented status remains because of family formation's time-dependent nature. Family formation is a key life course transition produced through a series of large- and small-scale choices that have long-term consequences because they affect subsequent life course transitions.[8] Enduring consequences emerge because immigration policies constrain undocumented young adults' choices through this process. Relationships progressed as undocumented young adults awaited legal changes. They chose partners and made seemingly innocuous, but still significant, decisions about where to go on dates, if they should drive, or if they could enroll their children in an after-school activity. They made, or avoided making, life-altering commitments to partner, marry, or have children. All these choices remained with them, even when the sociolegal context improved.

Receiving DACA helped many participants advance romantic relationships and fulfill parenting roles. Its impact was most positive when protections were acquired in time for key relationship transitions and when children were younger. Irreversible damage often remained, however: immigration policies had shaped whom they partnered with, left emotional scars, and produced internalized feelings of undesirability. For those who legalized through marriage, new consequences arose as couples constructed relationships that would facilitate the process. For many parents, legal changes came too late; they had missed their chance to provide their children with desired opportunities.

Enduring consequences likely emerge in other contexts, including education, employment, and political engagement. For example, undocumented high school and college students may give up on pursuing their education because they do not believe that they will use their degree to pursue a career and upward mobility.[9] Obtaining DACA or another form of immigration relief does not change that these individuals will be ill positioned for upward mobility in an economic system that increasingly requires educational credentials. Similarly, in academic settings, immigration issues can distract undocumented students from their studies; news of a recent ICE raid may prevent them from studying or paying attention in class as they worry about their family's safety. These small moments can have far-reaching, cumulative consequences—lowering their course grades and GPAs.[10] In these ways, past experiences forever structure opportunities because they cannot be undone after a more secure legal status is obtained.

MULTIGENERATIONAL PUNISHMENT: ENDURING CONSEQUENCES FOR FAMILIES AND COMMUNITIES

In addition to enduring throughout an individual immigrant's life, illegality's consequences can stretch over generations. Citizenship does not protect family members from the legal violence perpetrated by immigration policies. Instead, multigenerational punishment emerges within mixed-status families as social ties and daily interactions lead citizens to witness and share in immigration policy's punitive effects. Citizen partners witness their undocumented partner's exclusion, help them negotiate barriers, and face negative material and emotional consequences. Citizen children's immediate everyday lives and future opportunities are similarly limited by their parents' immigration status. This ensures that illegality endures beyond the immigrant generation and perpetuates the marginalization of Latino families and communities.

Families' multigenerational nature ensures that immigration policies perpetrate multigenerational punishment. Shared consequences emerge because citizen family members have strong social relationships with undocumented immigrants. Children are inherently dependent on their parents, and romantic partners become interdependent as they commit to building a life together. Illegality thus constrains the intergenerational transmission of resources and limits the opportunities available to future generations.

The consequences of illegality are also shared more generally within the Latino community. Close cross-status relationships can occur in any kind of social relationship leading to shared consequences that likely depend on the depth of a person's relationship to undocumented immigrants. Like citizen partners and children, extended family and community members also helped undocumented young adults navigate immigration policies by registering their cars in their name, cosigning loans, or giving rides. Deportations tear apart not only families but also the social fabric of communities, as friends, coworkers, and neighbors mourn the deportation of their undocumented friends.[11] Further, shared consequences can emerge absent direct social relationships to undocumented immigrants. Communities are socially and economically devastated when deportation removes community members and reduces remaining undocumented members' social and economic participation.[12] The racialization of illegality as a Latino issue also ensures that documented immigrant and U.S.-born Latinas/os/xs face persistent exclusion because their race leads others to assume they are undocumented.[13] This conflation can have significant population-level consequences: one study found that infants born to Latina mothers had a 24 percent greater risk of low birth weight after a large-scale immigration raid than those born during the same period a year earlier; notably, the risk increased for both citizens and immigrants.[14]

Ultimately, laws and policies that appear to target a single group actually restructure society so that the consequences of illegality extend beyond an isolated population segment. Illegality is woven deeply into Latino communities, given that almost half of the Mexican and Central American immigrant populations are undocumented.[15] Mixed-status families abound as a quarter of Latino children have at least one undocumented parent.[16] Mixed-status social relationships are also common; for example, a 2012 poll found that 63 percent of Latino registered voters nationally knew an undocumented immigrant.[17] Thus, illegality has become a defining factor of Latino integration by embedding itself in the very foundation of families and communities.

The experiences of mixed-status Latino families provide a critical lens for explaining the broader incorporation patterns of Latino and Mexican-origin populations. Segmented assimilation theory has used Mexicans as a classic case of downward assimilation, highlighting worse incorporation outcomes over multiple generations when compared to other racial/ethnic groups.[18] Comparisons within the Mexican-origin population show that there are improvements over generations, but that they do not necessarily achieve parity with whites.[19] Scholars attribute these patterns to a variety of factors, including economic structures, weak coethnic community, and racialization. More recently, research has highlighted the high propensity of undocumented immigration status to figure as an additional reason for these lower incorporation outcomes. Frank Bean, Susan Brown, and James Bachmeier point to undocumented Mexican immigrants' "membership exclusion" as a key factor that hinders their incorporation and that of their children by fostering "formal and informal exclusion and stigmatization to the point of being deemed socially illegitimate."[20] I highlight the intimate process behind this trend, illuminating how multigenerational punishment is an important mechanism driving the continued exclusion of Latino populations, particularly those of Mexican origin.

The enduring consequences of illegality likely have sweeping implications for other immigrant and racial/ethnic communities. About 24 percent of undocumented immigrants are not of Latin American origin; 12 percent come from Asia, 5 percent from Europe and Canada, 4 percent from the Caribbean, 2 percent from Africa, and 1 percent from the Middle East.[21] Notably, Asian Americans and Pacific Islanders (AAPI) are the fastest-growing undocumented subgroup, more than tripling between 2000 and 2015, and accounting for about one in seven Asian immigrants.[22] Despite racialized differences in experiences of illegality,[23] AAPI and other non-Latino families and communities likely experience similar enduring consequences.

CONSIDERING THE BROADER CONTEXT OF ILLEGALITY: DIVERGING AND SHIFTING LAWS

Immigration status is not an inherently significant category of difference, but it is made increasingly consequential by federal, state, and local government legislation. Such laws and policies produce immigrant illegality by limiting undocumented immigrants' everyday activities, decision-making, and upward mobility. Yet the stories of undocumented young adults and their mixed-status family members suggest that immigration policies extend their reach much deeper. I refer to the context of illegality to capture this dynamic and marginalizing social world constructed by immigration laws and policies. This broader focus imagines illegality as a sociolegal context to capture how it determines individual-level experiences, as well as familial and societal ones. Rather than attributing shared consequences to chance, it recognizes them as broader, systemic inequalities that have been created by immigration policies and become a source of intergenerational inequality for immigrants and Latino families and communities.

Illegality is context-specific because policies vary by place, change over time, and are implemented unequally. I focus on undocumented young adults in Southern California—a relatively protected population in one of the most supportive state and local contexts—as they transitioned into a more inclusionary form of liminal legality through DACA. Theirs is the quintessential best-case scenario.

It seems likely that the consequences I have traced here are exacerbated in more exclusionary cases.

As new federal, state, and local level policies are implemented, illegality can become more or less consequential over time and in different places. Tracing DACA recipients' experiences allowed me to show how federal-level changes to immigration policy can create a less consequential form of undocumented status that alters how these select undocumented youth experience illegality. Importantly, subfederal policies, such as college tuition equity or financial aid provisions, can intervene to create state-level differences in the extent to which undocumented young adults can capitalize on DACA to redirect their life pathways.[24] State and local policy changes can similarly make undocumented status less consequential. For example, in 2019, 13 states; Washington, DC; and Puerto Rico had laws making driver's licenses available to undocumented immigrants.[25] Some cities, like New York and San Francisco, offer municipal identification cards.[26] Several states, counties, and cities have established laws or policies that limit their cooperation with immigration enforcement officials.[27] Further, immigrants' experience and negotiation of illegality are structured by place-based characteristics such as population demographics, the immigrant economy, the capacity of the local social service sector, geography, and the organization of housing, public space, and public transportation.[28]

Subfederal policies seek to soften illegality's everyday consequences. However, just as many state and local policies strive to make immigration status more limiting—increasing collaborations with immigration officials, barring access to education and other social services, preventing landlords from renting to undocumented immigrants, and criminalizing undocumented immigrants who are present and seek employment.[29] Although these policies do not change one's immigration status, they leverage the balance of power between the federal and state/local governments to change the significance of undocumented status in everyday life.[30]

These policies can also shift over time. While California is currently one of the most inclusionary states, this has not always been the case. As Luis remembered, California has a dark, not-so-distant past of anti-immigrant legislation. The 1990s saw voter-approved propositions that banned undocumented immigrants from accessing education, nonemergency health care, and other public services.[31] California became incrementally more progressive, with the context of illegality slowly bending toward inclusion.[32]

An individual's experience of the context of illegality also varies based on their other social locations. When forming families, gender differentiates how undocumented young men and women experience illegality. Likewise, intersectional social locations—including race/ethnicity, class, immigrant generation, and sexual orientation—shape various outcomes, including educational and employment experiences, access to integrative resources and legalization opportunities, legal consciousness and activism, and deportation risks.[33] Although the general character of illegality may seem the same, individual experiences vary greatly.

In many ways, the stories I have told here are those of a unique population forming families in a distinct place and time. Specific experiences may be different in other places; for example, deportation fears may be more prominent in places where immigration enforcement strongly collaborates with local police. Interviewing the same participants under Donald Trump's presidency would likely reveal increased uncertainty because of the legal precarity of the DACA program and the hypervisibility of immigration enforcement. All this variation, however, can be traced back to immigration laws and policies that configure the specific nature of illegality and structure the evolution of its enduring consequences. As a concept, *context of illegality* invites us to move beyond the specifics of a case to envision the dynamic production of illegality and its broader consequences for families and communities.

FOSTERING INCLUSION AND RESILIENCE IN IMMIGRANT FAMILIES

In addition to erecting structural barriers, illegality manifests in everyday family life as social stigma: judgment for one's partner choices, suspicion of marriage decisions, and condemnation for not meeting partner and parenting expectations. Few openly discussed these topics, not even with partners, friends, or family. The stigma was too strong for some, and others tried to ignore the issue, seemingly hoping that this might insulate them from its effects. But those who had open and honest conversations seemed the most successful at destigmatizing the limitations created by illegality and fostering healthy family dynamics. Partners who openly renegotiated gendered expectations could imagine and pursue a future together without infusing their everyday lives with risk and resentment. Parents sought to empower children with informed understandings of the law, knowledge about their opportunities as citizens, and a sense of justice.

If we want to keep the law from punishing families, we all have a responsibility to be vigilant of the small, day-to-day ways illegality can creep into relationships. We must remove the stigma of the marriage myths by pointing a finger where it belongs—at the laws that constrain choices. We must call out jokes about marrying a citizen and demands to do so, correcting misconceptions with legal realities. We must stop invalidating and judging relationships simply because they do not meet conventional expectations. We must support parents as they make difficult decisions about what avenue might best ensure their children's physical and emotional well-being. Open and honest conversations will be critical to destigmatizing the grip that the law holds on immigrant families. This may help curtail some of the socioemotional consequences until policymakers implement changes to dismantle illegality and the exclusionary context it creates.

Policy Recommendations

The United States has not seen comprehensive immigration reform since 1986. The experiences of young adults who legalized their status or obtained a liminal legal status through DACA show that integration depends on the creation of a pathway to legalization that will facilitate the integration of undocumented individuals, their families, and communities. Ultimately, legalization is the key to ensuring that immigrant families and communities can thrive and strengthen U.S. society. The long-standing absence of such pathways to legalization has ensured the enduring consequences of illegality.

It is critical that any future policies do not foster a sense of uncertainty. DACA was always conditional—its protections had to be renewed every two years, and there was always the possibility that a future presidential administration would discontinue the program. This reality led some recipients to avoid planning or preparing for the long term. Notably, recent plans outlining pathways to citizenship propose temporary or conditional statuses and long wait times for citizenship eligibility. While these policies may put people on the path to legal incorporation, shorter and clearer pathways are critical to limiting exclusionary consequences. Conditionality will keep applicants in limbo because they are unable to envision a certain future. This will likely curtail short- and long-term incorporation.

As policymakers debate whether and how to maintain U.S. immigration policy's grounding in family reunification, I offer a few words of caution. Any policy needs to provide for the reunification of immediate and extended family members to foster healthy families and communities. But making legalization opportunities contingent on family relationships—specifically on spouses and children—can be a double-edged sword. Specifically, current policies place too much pressure on families, disrupting family relationships and changing family formation processes. By requiring citizen partners and children to petition for their undocumented family members, we reproduce inequality within and among families. Further, current laws privilege citizen family members' pain over the struggles and contributions of undocumented individuals. This is not to say that we should eliminate family-based immigration policies, but rather that we need laws that value family ties, individual contributions, *and* the humanity of all involved.

Further, we need to recognize that legalization—whether it is for DACA recipients or all 10.7 million undocumented immigrants—is not a silver bullet. It will not undo the fact that a generation of immigrants has had every aspect of their lives shaped by immigration policies. We cannot ignore the damage that has been done. After a generation of finding ways to negotiate the laws and policies that exclude them, undocumented immigrants will need to learn to be legal. Further, as seen with DACA, integration is conditional on recipients' ability to translate their new-found legal integration into individual and family mobility. Social programs are needed to help undocumented immigrants acquire these missed skills and opportunities as they adapt to life after legalization. This could include campaigns and programming around educational access and employment skill building.

As we await comprehensive immigration reform, opportunities for integration exist in integrative state, local, and institutional policies. States, cities, and institutions can become sanctuaries, limiting their cooperation with immigration enforcement officials. IDs and driver's licenses issued by states, cities, and country-of-origin consulates can facilitate spatial mobility and social integration. Cities can decriminalize activities, like street vending, that lead to consequential police interactions and limit financial security. Schools and nonprofits can find novel ways of training undocumented immigrants to pursue entrepreneurship and self-employment in ways that limit their risk of financial instability and employer abuse.

Advocates should also examine seemingly unrelated policy areas for ways to facilitate integration. For example, providing all low-income children with access to social services, such as free or reduced-price lunch and Medicare, can minimize the impact of parental immigration status on children's academic outcomes.[34] Broader social safety net programs for low-income families are, however, currently under attack. Congress's 2017–18 budget battle threatened funding for the Children's Health Insurance Program (CHIP), and President Trump proposed to slash the Supplemental Nutrition Assistance Program (SNAP).[35] Programs like these are integral to immigrant families' well-being. To limit multigenerational punishment, policymakers must ensure that all children retain their rights to these programs and that immigrants are not punished for using social services. Indeed, proposed changes to "public charge" rules threaten to expand the forms of public assistance that would make an immigrant ineligible to receive permanent residency.[36]

THE FUTURE OF IMMIGRANT FAMILIES: PERIL OR PROMISE?

Aaron Ortiz gazed into the future as he watched his 18-month-old daughter chase birds around the Los Angeles arboretum. His dreams were no longer about his own success, but hers. He shared his hopes and fears for her future. He was adamant that she attend college. But he didn't know how he would afford all the opportunities he felt she would need to prepare for college—sports, tutoring, extracurricular activities. College tuition seemed even more out of reach. Recognizing that his undocumented status would limit his daughter, he was looking even further into the future. He would work hard so that his daughter "can get an easier lifestyle, and then her babies can be immune to this." Aaron saw another generation toiling for the mobility of those to come. He took solace in the thought that his daughter's citizenship status would shield her children in ways that he could not protect her.

Aaron hypothesizes just how enduring the punishment inflicted by immigration policies may be. Exclusionary immigration policies are already being felt by the next generation of Latino citizens. Will we pass inclusionary immigration policies to ensure that their children and grandchildren are immune? Will we treat them with love and give them papers? Or will we continue to wait, leaving families and communities in the wake of destructive and exclusionary policies?

As I wrote this book, debates and proposals for immigration reform raged. The early days of Trump's presidency were filled with fear that he would live up to his campaign promise to end the DACA program. A sigh of relief seemed to sweep over the nation as weeks passed and DACA remained intact. On September 5, 2017, however, the Trump administration announced its plan to phase out the program over the next two and a half years by allowing individuals' DACA protections to lapse.[37]

Public uproar ensued as states, universities, and DACA recipients filed court cases to challenge the decision.[38] A renewed movement to pass the federal DREAM Act emerged. Seven years after its last vote, Congress considered legislation providing a pathway to legalization for DACA recipients and other undocumented young adults.[39] A decision by the 9th District Court placed an injunction on DACA's rescission, noting that the "plaintiffs have clearly demonstrated that they are likely to suffer serious irreparable harm" if their protections lapsed.[40]

Meanwhile, the Trump administration sued California for its sanctuary policies, and U.S. Citizenship and Immigration Services changed its mission from ensuring "America's promise as a nation of immigrants" to "protecting Americans, securing the homeland."[41] The world awoke to a humanitarian crisis at the U.S.-Mexico border: cries of terror-stricken detained migrant children separated from their parents filled the airwaves, and photos of teargassed Central American asylum seekers occupied the front page.[42] Trump's call for a border wall streamed across social media and instigated a 35-day shutdown of the federal government.[43]

U.S. society is positioned to move in two distinct directions. We can develop and preserve laws and policies that, like DACA, will promote immigrant inclusion (even if imperfect). Or we can adopt increasingly draconian anti-immigrant measures that will exclude undocumented immigrants and their loved ones. The direction we move in will have sweeping implications now and far into the future.

Reflections on Methods
and Positionality

Much of my early interest in studying family formation was crystalized by the scene that opened the book: three undocumented young men reflecting on the trials and tribulations of dating while undocumented. I gave this example whenever academics wondered why I asked questions about dating and marriage, because it highlighted the social impact of immigration policies. This is often where I stopped. It was only when interviewees asked me why I was doing this work that I revealed that it is also my story.

Here I provide additional details about my project methods while weaving in reflections on how these were influenced by my positionality. My hope is to reframe "me-search," a term often hurled at marginalized scholars to invalidate their work by dismissing it as too close to their own experiences. Instead, I illuminate how being close can make research stronger.

POSITIONALITY (OR MY STORY)

I met my partner in December 2008 at a holiday party hosted by IDEAS at UCLA, an undocumented student organization. At the end of our first date, he asked me to drive his car home. It was in that moment that I knew he was undocumented.

As we dated, the gendered nature of illegality emerged. I tried to help out by driving or paying for things, prompting odd looks from cashiers and friends. Once, he didn't have his wallet, and I tried to break the tension with a joke about how I would pay *again;* we didn't talk for the rest of the night. We went to a concert and were denied entrance because he didn't have a California ID. I worried about his safety when he was running late or not answering the phone. I traveled out of the country and felt bad that he couldn't come. We heard marriage myth messages firsthand. He delayed our marriage, proposing only after DACA was announced and he felt secure in his ability to financially contribute.

We anticipated having to eventually tackle the risky process of consular processing to legalize his status, but we planned to put it off until it became absolutely necessary. Our life changed because one of my interviewees told me about using advanced parole to establish legal entry. Another recommended a lawyer who had experience with this process.

We prepared an application to adjust his status as I conducted the second round of interviews for this book. I wrote research memos about the process of legalizing through marriage while surrounded by painstakingly organized piles of our own evidence—years of utility bills, bank statement printouts, taxes, pictures. I held our two-month-old daughter as we met with the immigration agent who would determine whether our relationship was real and if our family would be safe. My research ensured that I knew about a lot about the legal process, which helped us prepare. But it also meant I knew what could go wrong, knowledge that kept me on edge (and him exasperated with my lack of positivity).

As I wrote the first draft of this book, we filed to remove the conditions on his permanent residency, updating our evidence and triple-checking dates. I turned in the final manuscript just days after he successfully completed his citizenship interview. We would like to think that this will close this chapter of our lives, but this research has only confirmed what we know deep down: our family will forever be transformed because of the U.S. immigration system.

PROJECT DESIGN AND SAMPLING STRATEGY

Despite my incredibly supportive academic network, I have shied away from voicing these connections. While I never claimed (or necessarily strove for) objectivity, I wanted to avoid the insults that came with subjectivity. I had heard too many slights about people who studied themselves. But I also knew that my relationship didn't make me an insider, and I didn't know how to articulate my complicated insider-outsider perspective.

As I designed my project, it felt safer to discuss a different aspect of my positionality: my sustained involvement with undocumented immigrant youth in the Los Angeles area. For years I had been advocating for the newly reintroduced federal DREAM Act as a founding member of Dream Team Los Angeles. I pointed to what I witnessed in these spaces to guide my research questions and project design. This was around the time that research on undocumented young adults was expanding rapidly, and faculty mentors pushed me to take a new angle and focus on their romantic lives. I resisted. I wanted to study these issues, but I feared becoming paralyzed by issues that were too close to me. If I couldn't even read about deportation for class, how could I write about it? Publicly, I reasoned

TABLE A.1 Sampling strategy for first wave of undocumented interview participants (2011–2012)

	Did not complete high school	Completed high school	Previously attended a 2-year college	Attending 2-year college	Attending 4-year college	Completed 4-year college	Total
Women	7–8	7–8	7–8	7–8	7–8	7–8	45
Men	7–8	7–8	7–8	7–8	7–8	7–8	45
Total	15	15	15	15	15	15	90

that I should ask about a broad range of topics since I was going through the effort of finding people. Privately, I planned to be prepared to write a dissertation that did not deal with romantic relationships if necessary.

Thus, my dissertation—which constitutes the first wave of data—broadly focused on the educational, economic, social, and political integration of undocumented young adults. I planned 120 interviews—90 with undocumented young adults and 30 with formerly undocumented young adults who had legalized their immigration status in the past five years. This large sample ensured that I would reach saturation with about 15 interviews across two gender and six educational comparison groups (see table A.1). When my dissertation committee suggested I cut back my sample size, my experiential knowledge helped me defend the need for these comparisons. I pointed to the many times I had seen gender, current enrollment status, and level of education become relevant in the time I had spent time with undocumented young adults.

The second wave of this study emerged in response to the changing policy context brought about by the establishment of the DACA program. But it was also driven by the magnitude of family-level effects that were revealed in the first wave of interviews. I saw my story in those of my participants and began to feel compelled to uplift their voices. I was finally ready to pursue these questions, in part because I felt confident in my ability to negotiate my positionality but also because my partner had gained the privileged security of DACA.

I set out to reinterview the 123 original participants with two purposes—understanding how the DACA program was reshaping their lives and getting more details about their family formation experiences. Unable to recontact 35 of the original participants, I recruited 32 additional participants to meet my sampling quotas. I maintained the gender comparison and, based on my analysis, collapsed the education categories into two—less educated (did not complete high school, completed high school, no longer enrolled in college) and more educated (attending two- or four-year colleges, four-year college graduates). I supplemented my initial sample of LGBQ participants to reach saturation around issues of same-sex family formation.

Knowing that romantic partners had a unique perspective to offer, I conducted interviews with them as well. I asked all wave 2 participants if I could interview their current romantic partners to understand how they were experiencing immigration policies. Most who were in committed relationships agreed to introduce me to their partners, and 39 spoke with me.

RECRUITMENT METHODS

Within academic settings, I am often forced to speak about how my social networks "facilitated access" to a "hard-to-reach population." I cringe because this makes my community engagement and relationships with undocumented young adults seem inauthentic and utilitarian.

Indeed, my personal connections ensured that I could successfully carry out the study. I drew on my social networks to initiate snowball sampling with 12 participants who had varying levels of education and separate social networks. At the end of each interview, I asked participants if they knew anyone who might be interested in participating. If they did, I asked them to contact the person to describe the study and ask if they were interested. I checked back with the initial participant after a few days, confirmed the person was interested and consented to having their contact information shared with me, and then contacted them. At the end of each wave, I relied on three well-networked contacts to refer me to specific types of participants needed to fulfill my sampling quotas.

I compensated participants for the time they spent on the study. In the first wave, I used a dual-incentive technique in which participants received a $20 gift card for being interviewed and an additional $10 gift card for each person they successfully referred, usually extended family members, neighbors, former classmates, coworkers, and friends. This dual-incentive strategy was most useful in facilitating follow-up with the referring participant without being perceived as bothersome. In the second wave, participants received $15 cash.

While these techniques facilitated recruitment, I believe my positionality was also integral to my success. Those participants who were most involved in immigrant youth organizing were often the most suspicious of researchers' intentions. These gatekeepers knew me well, putting them at ease. A few even mentioned that they had previously been asked for referrals but refused; with me they felt confident that I would not do any harm to their loved ones, either as part of the interview process or with what came out of the project. Once I had snowballed out of these networks, my activist reputation did not precede me. Rather, it was positive interviewing experiences that fueled participants' willingness to connect me to others.

INTERVIEW APPROACH AND TOPICS

Like my overarching research questions, my interview questions were guided by my presence in immigrant youth spaces and my own relationship. If not for this,

I would not have known what to ask about, and my interviews would likely not have elicited such honest and illustrative examples.

Both waves of interviews asked broad questions about participation in school, work, family formation, and political/community involvement. In the first wave of interviews, one of the nine sections focused on family formation. It included broad questions about dating experiences and activities; past and current partners and why relationships ended; conversations with their partner about their undocumented status; marriage decisions; their thoughts about legalizing through marriage; plans for having children; and what it means to be a good husband or wife and good father or mother. In the second wave of interviews, half the interview focused on family formation. The questions traced romantic trajectories and dug more deeply into the previous topics. I also asked more general questions about their romantic lives—what characteristics they were looking for in a partner; what characteristics they thought partners looked for; whether they ever felt undesirable or unattractive; what they imagined their wedding would be like; what it was like living with their partner; how they managed conflict. If they legalized through marriage, we talked about their experiences with this process. Throughout, I asked questions to understand how their experiences were affected by their legal status or gender, and how they felt their experiences compared to other undocumented individuals as well as citizen friends and family members.

I designed extensive interview guides for each subpopulation, 10–15 pages divided into key sections and complete with broad questions and detailed probes. This functioned as a guide that I kept in mind but did not allow to restrict conversation. My goal was to foster a conversational atmosphere in which the participant would feel comfortable discussing the issues I had selected *and* empowered to raise their own. While I had an interview guide in front of me, I prioritized flow rather than an assurance that I asked every question. As we moved through each section, I asked the broad questions that I had memorized but jumped around and let the participant drive the conversation. I asked follow-up questions to get more details and probe the issues laid out in my guide. I reined in clearly off-topic conversations but allowed us to wander, trusting myself and the participant to lead us to relevant places. When the conversation naturally paused, I would check that we had addressed the questions in that section, asking ones we had missed or moving us along to the next topic. I trained all interviewers to do the same.

I conducted all but three of the first wave of interviews on my own and about half of the second wave. I hired a graduate student to conduct two-fifths of the second wave. Six additional research assistants conducted 24 interviews, ranging from one to seven interviews each. I interviewed most of the new participants and those whom I remembered being more reticent in their first interview. Interviews lasted an average of one and a half to two hours. Participants chose the time and place of their interview to make them feel most comfortable. Many volunteered their homes, searching out a (semi-)private space for the interview when I arrived. Others suggested public spaces they frequented—nearby fast-food restaurants, parks, favorite restaurants, or coffee shops. When they did not have a place in mind, I suggested a nearby Starbucks or fast-food restaurant.

Treating participants as equals in a conversation, rather than subjects of study, was key in encouraging them to speak so openly and deeply about very intimate issues. A few were used to sharing their stories as part of their advocacy for immigration reform, but many had never talked about their immigration status in such depth. In many cases, opening up space allowed their stories to spill out. Others were less forthcoming, but they opened up as the interview progressed and I shared about myself and offered comparisons to general trends I was seeing among other interviewees.

It was easy for me to see myself in participants' words, and I often found myself sharing my own story. In some ways this was in service to what qualitative scholars call "building rapport," practical attempts to legitimize myself, allay suspicion, and foster conversation. Sharing my own experiences also facilitated conversation, since I could offer examples for participants to react to and engage with when they could not quite articulate a feeling. It only seemed right to share my own story after they recounted theirs, so I invited participants to ask me questions and openly answered them all. Most often, undocumented participants wanted to know if they and their relationships were "normal"; I drew on my personal experiences and access to so many stories to help them put their experiences in perspective. Citizen partners often had the most questions; some were excited to finally be able to talk to someone else who shared their experiences, while others asked about the legalization process and why I had taken so long to "fix" my partner's status. Those who were experiencing relationship conflict often asked for my perspective; I sought to commiserate and validate their feelings without providing specific advice. I also answered questions about laws and policies, providing basic information and encouraging them to consult lawyers and local nonprofit organizations. I left time after scheduled interviews to allow for these questions. Sometimes postinterview conversations continued on as if between friends as we provided rides, ate, or wasted time waiting out LA traffic.

DATA ANALYSIS

All interviews were audio recorded, transcribed verbatim, and coded in Hyper-Research, a qualitative data management program. Interviewers also completed a memo for each interview, which included fieldnotes about the surroundings and participant engagement, and summaries of key points from each interview section. These memos were used to identify areas for focused coding and analysis. Two research assistants conducted open coding to identify any mention of laws and policies; this informed the selection of the four types of laws and policies I focused on. I developed a codebook of open and discrete codes to explore a set of focused research questions for each chapter. Coded passages were sorted and analyzed to identify trends and make comparisons across relevant demographic characteristics. I conducted additional rounds of coding if new questions arose.

Instead of trying to be "objective," I worked to be aware of my subjectivity. I illuminated my blind spots during data collection and preliminary data analysis by having conversations with my research assistants about the patterns they were seeing. Their various positionalities brought new perspectives to light. During data analysis, I reviewed each transcript multiple times to make sure that I was fairly representing those I had interviewed. I paid even more attention when analyzing and writing up the partner interviews for chapter 4; I wanted to be sure that my feelings were not overshadowing their words.

WRITING

Being close to my work has also raised challenges, including making it harder to tackle certain topics. When I started writing my dissertation, I began with parenting and the multigenerational punishment of citizen children. Parents were a smaller sample to analyze (making it faster to generate a publication), but underneath that strategic rationale was the fact that parenting was not my reality in the way that other parts of my data were. But by the time the article moved into publication, I was pregnant and crying over page proofs in the middle of a coffee shop. With a baby at home, I struggled tremendously to keep my focus when revising that article for this book.

I have also become incredibly attentive to confidentiality and risk. As I wrote this appendix, President Trump's administration began a campaign to denaturalize immigrant citizens.[1] This prompted some to ask whether I should fully disclose my positionality; would it put my husband or me at risk? After speaking with colleagues, legal counsel, and my husband, I elected to keep it in. The legal ramifications seem minor (if anything, this book proves that our relationship is "real"). But it also felt unethical to expose the intimate lives of my interview participants without being willing to do this myself.

This personal understanding ensured that I struck a balance between protecting my participants while honoring their stories and refusing to silence their voices. Following standard practice, all participants were assigned pseudonyms to protect confidentiality. I elected to give them both first and last names to make them seem more like real people and tried to reflect the same level of gender and racial association. Although I often provide background details to humanize participants, I avoid this with riskier cases, such as when discussing the experiences of those who had legalized through strategic marriages. I also thought about the emotional costs for couples and walked a fine line between exploring relationship conflict and airing dirty laundry. I avoided identifying the participant or their partner when discussing topics or opinions that the other may not have known about or that could create conflict.

I share these examples to establish that we have the right to do, and not do, certain kinds of research. Our positionalities may grant us a unique perspective that can make our work great, but it also increases our personal and professional risk. Negotiating this requires deep reflection, critical training, and a genuinely supportive network of friends and colleagues.

Demographic Characteristics of Study Participants

All undocumented and recently legalized respondents were Latina/o, 1.5-generation young adults who entered the United States by the age of 16. They were all aged 18 to 35 in 2011–12, when the study began with undocumented participants having a mean age of 25.66 and recently legalized participants 26.76. Reflecting the fact that an estimated 71 percent of the undocumented population in California is Mexican-origin,[1] almost all participants were Mexican-origin individuals; I had four undocumented participants from Guatemala, one undocumented participant from Honduras, and one recently legalized participant from El Salvador. All participants lived in Los Angeles, San Bernardino, or Orange County at the time of their first interview. I interviewed relatively equal numbers of men and women.

UNDOCUMENTED PARTICIPANTS

Between the two waves of interviews, I interviewed 126 individuals who were undocumented in 2011. By the second wave of interviews, they spanned the spectrum of (il)legality; almost three-quarters of the those in wave 2 had received DACA, 20 remained undocumented, and eight had pursued a pathway to legalization. I was unable to recontact 26 original participants for wave 2.

As planned, they spanned the educational spectrum from those who did not complete high school to those who had completed master's degrees. They fell relatively equally into the two educational comparison categories: less educated (did not complete high school, completed high school, no longer enrolled in college) and more educated (having attended two- or four-year college, or having graduated from a four-year college). In 2011–12, 51 percent were in the less educated category, and 48% were in this category in 2014–15. Those who were enrolled in school during wave 1 mostly advanced to a higher level or completed their degree by wave 2. Their economic situation improved between the two waves with the mean annual income of employed participants increasing more than $6,000 from $15,931 to $21,942. This is mostly because DACA recipients' incomes increased (see details in the introduction and chapter 3); employed participants who remained undocumented reported a mean annual income of $16,493 at wave 2. See table B.1 for additional descriptive statistics.

Almost every participant wanted to build a family through a committed romantic relationship or childbearing. About two-fifths of participants were not in a committed relationship. About a quarter of participants were in a committed dating relationship, ranging from less than a year to over eight years. The remaining third were in committed partnerships: cohabiting, legally married, or in married-like relationships in which they considered themselves married but were not legally married. Of those in a relationship, almost two-thirds were partnered with a U.S. citizen or permanent resident, and a third with undocumented individuals. Most were partnered with another Latina/o. Forty-four were parents—30 mothers and 14 fathers—primarily to young citizen children; one participant had a child over age 16 who was also a DACA recipient. See table B.2 for additional details.

RECENTLY LEGALIZED PARTICIPANTS

Between the two waves of interviews, I interviewed 31 individuals who had legalized their immigration status from 2007 to 2012. Twenty-two had adjusted their status through marriage to a U.S. citizen and nine through long-pending natal-family petitions filed mostly by extended family members. During the first wave, 29 of these participants were lawful permanent residents (LPRs), and two were naturalized citizens. By wave 2, most were eligible to naturalize, and four more had done so. While I sought variation, recently legalized participants were not selected by educational background; a little more than a quarter fell into the less educated category at each time point. Almost two-thirds had achieved a bachelor's degree or higher by the time of their first interview. Their economic situation was substantially better as employed legalized participants reported a mean annual income of $32,435 during wave 1, almost double the undocumented sample; this increased slightly by wave 2. I chose not to reinterview or was unable to recontact nine of the original participants for wave 2. See table B.3 for additional descriptive statistics.

During wave 2, the 16 who had adjusted their status through marriage to a romantic partner were still married to the same partner. Of the additional six who had entered into a strategic marriage to a friend, two were single, three were dating a new partner, and one was dating the partner who had petitioned them. One had divorced their petitioning spouse, and another was in the process of doing so. None of the participants who had adjusted through a natal family petition were married, and only one was cohabitating. Almost two-thirds of those who had married their romantic partner had children. Those who married a friend or legalized through family mostly did not have children. See table B.4 for additional details.

ROMANTIC PARTNERS

Of the 39 romantic partners, 28 were partnered with undocumented sample participants. There were equal numbers of women and men, and all but one identified as Latina/o. Most were U.S. citizens, usually second-generation children of immigrants. I also interviewed five partners who were undocumented, mostly first-generation immigrants, and had five additional couples in which both partners were part of the undocumented sample. Their relationship status ranged from 12 in committed dating relationships, three cohabiting, three in married-like relationships, and 10 married. One-third were parents.

The remaining 11 romantic partners I interviewed were partnered with the recently legalized participants: 10 were the petitioning spouse, and one was the current romantic partner of a participant who had legalized through marriage to someone else. Two-thirds were U.S.-born citizens, and the rest were 1.5-generation immigrant youth who had naturalized. All identified as Latina/o except for two. There were equal numbers of men and women, and most had a bachelor's degree. Two-thirds were parents. See table B.5 for additional descriptive statistics.

TABLE B.1 Demographic characteristics of undocumented participants

	2011–2012 ($n = 126$)[†]	2014–2015 ($n = 100$)[††]
Immigration status		
Undocumented	125 (94)	20 (15)
Work permit, pending LPR application	1 (1)	2 (2)
DACA recipient	—	72 (48)
U visa	0 (0)	3 (2)
Lawful permanent resident	0 (0)	3 (2)
Age at interview		
Mean age	(25.66)	27.43 (27.83)
18–19	(3)	0 (0)
20–24	(40)	24 (14)
25–29	(38)	50 (35)
30–34	(10)	19 (14)
35–38	(1)	3 (3)
Not reported	(3)	4 (3)
Country of origin		
Mexico	121 (92)	96 (67)
Guatemala	4 (3)	3 (2)
Honduras	1 (0)	1 (0)
		(contd.)

	2011–2012 (*n* = 126)[†]	2014–2015 (*n* = 100)[††]
Mode of entry		
No inspection	106 (81)	82 (57)
Tourist visa	16 (11)	14 (9)
Other visa	2 (2)	2 (2)
Unknown	2 (1)	2 (1)
Age of entry		
0–5	49 (38)	37 (26)
6–10	53 (39)	44 (30)
11–16	24 (18)	19 (13)
Gender		
Women	66 (49)	52 (35)
Men	60 (46)	48 (34)
Education level		
High school, incomplete	12 (11)	2 (2)
High school diploma or GED, in progress	4 (0)	2 (1)
GED	5 (5)	4 (3)
High school diploma	21 (18)	11 (8)
Two-year college, incomplete	15 (7)	15 (5)
Two-year college, trade certificate	2 (2)	1 (1)
Two-year college, associate's degree	5 (4)	10 (8)
Two-year college, in progress	23 (16)	15 (10)
Bachelor's degree, incomplete	1 (1)	3 (3)
Bachelor's degree, in progress	20 (15)	9 (7)
Bachelor's degree	16 (14)	24 (18)
Postgraduate degree, in progress	1 (1)	3 (2)
Postgraduate degree	1 (1)	1 (1)
Income		
Mean annual individual income of employed participants	($15,931)	$21,942 ($22,066)
Median annual individual income of employed participants	($14,400)	$19,200 ($19,200)
$0	(11)	8 (6)
$1–$5,000	(3)	6 (6)
$5,001–$10,000	(11)	7 (3)
$10,001–$15,000	(27)	13 (6)
$15,001–$20,000	(12)	19 (15)
$20,001–25,000	(9)	11 (10)
$25,001–$30,000	(3)	9 (4)
$30,001–$40,000	(1)	11 (7)
$40,001 or more	(2)	8 (6)
Not reported	(16)	8 (6)

[†] Data for the 95 original participants who were interviewed at this time period are in parentheses.

[††] Data for the 69 original participants who were reinterviewed at this time period are in parentheses.

TABLE B.2 Family characteristics of undocumented participants at most recent interview

	Women (*n* = 66)	Men (*n* = 60)	Total
Relationship status			
Single, never married	13	23	36
Single, previously married	7	4	11
Casually dating	0	5	5
Committed dating relationship	22	11	33
Cohabitating	3	8	11
Married-like relationship	7	3	10
Married	14	6	20
Romantic partner's immigration status			
U.S. citizen	22	24	46
Lawful permanent resident	4	1	5
DACA recipient	4	7	11
Undocumented	14	1	15
Foreign national, not in the U.S.	2	0	2
No partner	20	27	47
Romanic partner's racial/ethnic background			
Latina/o	42	27	69
White	2	3	5
Black	1	1	2
Asian American Pacific Islander	1	0	1
Not reported	0	2	2
No partner	20	27	47
Parent			
No	36	46	82
Yes	30	14	44
Age of children[†]			
In utero	4	1	5
0–4	19	13	32
5–10	18	9	27
11–15	12	1	13
16+	1	0	1

[†] Includes all reported children.

TABLE B.3 Demographic characteristics of formerly undocumented participants

	2011–2012 (*n* = 31)[†]	2014–2015 (*n* = 22)[††]
Immigration status		
Lawful permanent resident	29 (28)	18 (17)
Naturalized U.S. citizen	2 (2)	4 (4)
Age at interview		
Mean age	(26.76)	29.12 (29.19)
20–24	(11)	0 (0)

(contd.)

	2011–2012 ($n = 31$)[†]	2014–2015 ($n = 22$)[††]
25–29	(13)	15 (14)
30–34	(6)	7 (7)
Country of origin		
Mexico	30 (29)	21 (20)
El Salvador	1 (1)	1 (1)
Source of legalization petition		
Marriage to romantic partner	16 (15)	13 (12)
Marriage to friend	6 (6)	4 (4)
Natal family petition	9 (9)	5 (5)
Age of entry		
0–5	11 (10)	8 (7)
6–10	10 (10)	9 (9)
11–16	10 (10)	5 (5)
Gender		
Women	17 (16)	14 (13)
Men	14 (14)	8 (8)
Education level		
High school, incomplete	3 (3)	1 (1)
High school diploma or GED	0 (0)	0 (0)
Two-year college, incomplete	3 (3)	1 (1)
Two-year college, trade certificate	0 (0)	1 (1)
Two-year college, associate's degree	1 (0)	1 (0)
Two-year college, in progress	1 (1)	0 (0)
Bachelor's degree, incomplete	2 (2)	2 (2)
Bachelor's degree, in progress	2 (2)	1 (1)
Bachelor's degree	15 (15)	7 (7)
Postgraduate degree, in progress	1 (1)	4 (4)
Postgraduate degree	3 (3)	4 (4)
Income		
Mean annual individual income of employed participants	($32,435)	$34,598 ($34,598)
Median annual individual income of employed participants	($27,600)	$34,080 ($34,080)
$0	(3)	1 (0)
$1–$5,000	(1)	0 (0)
$5,001–$10,000	(0)	1 (1)
$10,001–$15,000	(3)	1 (1)
$15,001–$20,000	(1)	1 (1)
$20,001–25,000	(4)	2 (2)
$25,001–$30,000	(4)	1 (1)
$30,001–$40,000	(2)	4 (4)
$40,001 or more	(5)	6 (6)
Not reported	(7)	5 (5)

[†] Data for the 30 original participants who were interviewed at this time period are in parentheses.
[††] Data for the 21 original participants who were reinterviewed at this time period are in parentheses.

TABLE B.4 Family characteristics of formerly undocumented participants at most recent interview

	Through marriage to romantic partner (n = 16)	Through marriage to friend (n = 6)	Through natal family (n = 9)	Total
Relationship status				
Single	0	2	4	6
Casually dating	0	1	1	2
Committed dating relationship	0	3	3	6
Cohabitating	0	0	1	1
Married	16	—	0	16
Romantic partner's immigration status				
U.S.-born citizen	12	2	4	18
Naturalized U.S. citizen	4	0	0	4
Lawful permanent resident	0	1	0	1
Not reported	0	1	1	2
No partner	0	2	4	6
Romanic partner's racial/ ethnic background				
Latina/o	10	2	3	15
White	2	0	0	2
Black	1	0	1	2
Asian American Pacific Islander	1	0	0	1
Middle Eastern	0	0	1	1
Native American	1	0	0	1
Not reported	1	2	0	3
No partner	0	2	4	6
Parent				
No	6	5	9	20
Yes	10	1	0	11
Age of children[†]				
In utero	2	0	0	2
0–4	9	1	0	10
5–10	5	0	0	5
11–15	0	0	0	0
16+	0	0	0	0

† Includes all reported children.

TABLE B.5 Demographic characteristics of romantic partners interviewed

	Partnered with "undocumented" sample (*n* = 28)	Partnered with "recently legalized" sample (*n* = 11)
Own immigration status		
U.S.-born citizen	21	7
Naturalized U.S. citizen	2	4
DACA recipient	1	0
Undocumented	4	0
Age at interview		
Mean age	28.16	31.52
20–24	6	0
25–29	12	4
30–34	6	3
35–39	1	2
40+	1	0
Not reported	2	2
Racial/ethnic origin		
Latina/o	27	9
Asian American Pacific Islander	1	0
White	0	2
Gender		
Women	12	6
Men	15	5
Gender nonconforming	1	0
Education level		
High school, incomplete	4	0
High school diploma	3	1
Two-year college, incomplete	3	0
Two-year college, associate's degree	0	2
Two-year college, in progress	4	0
Bachelor's degree, incomplete	3	0
Bachelor's degree, in progress	4	0
Bachelor's degree	5	6
Postgraduate degree, in progress	1	1
Not reported	1	1
Income		
Mean annual individual income of employed participants	$21,800	$46,834
Median annual individual income of employed participants	$21,600	$48,000
$0	5	0
$1–$5,000	0	0
$5,001–$10,000	5	0
$10,001–$15,000	3	0

	Partnered with "undocumented" sample ($n = 28$)	Partnered with "recently legalized" sample ($n = 11$)
$15,001–$20,000	2	0
$20,001–25,000	3	1
$25,001–$30,000	4	0
$30,001–$40,000	2	1
$40,001 or more	2	5
Not reported	2	4
Romantic partner's immigration status		
Undocumented	3	—
Work permit, pending LPR application	1	—
DACA recipient	22	—
U visa	1	—
Lawful permanent resident	1	8
Naturalized U.S. citizen	0	3
Relationship status		
Committed dating relationship	12	1
Cohabitating	3	0
Married-like relationship	3	0
Married	10	10
Petitioned for partner's legalization		
No	—	1
Yes	—	10
Parent		
No	19	4
Yes	9	7
Age of children[†]		
In utero	1	1
0–4	7	7
5–10	5	3
11–15	1	0
16+	3	0

[†] Includes all reported children.

NOTES

1. FORMING FAMILIES IN A CONTEXT OF ILLEGALITY

1. Selena (1992). "An old car that comes honking / with tricycle wheels and a backward motor." Here and below, all translations are my own.

2. Obama (2012).

3. Gonzales (2011, 2016).

4. Applicants must be at least 15 years old. Eligibility includes (1) having been under age 31 on June 15, 2012, when the program was announced; (2) having entered the United States before age 16; (3) having continuously resided in the United States since June 15, 2007; (4) having been physically present in the United States when the program was announced; (5) having no lawful status when the program was announced; (6) being enrolled in or having graduated from high school; and (7) having no serious criminal record (i.e., conviction of a felony, significant misdemeanor, or three or more other misdemeanors) (USCIS 2018b).

5. In a 2013 survey of 2,381 DACA recipients, 59 percent reported obtaining a new job, and 45 percent increased their earnings (Gonzales, Terriquez, and Ruszczyk 2014). In another 2013–14 survey of 1,302 DACA recipients, 70 percent reported beginning their first job or moving to a new job, and 46 percent agreed that DACA enabled them to become more financially independent (Wong and Valdivia 2014).

6. De Genova (2002); Dreby (2015a); Gonzales (2016); Heyman (2013); Menjívar (2006); Menjívar and Abrego (2012); Menjívar and Kanstroom (2014a).

7. I use "Latino" to refer broadly to populations of Latin American origin; I do not mean this to be exclusive by gender. I use "Latina," "Latino," and "Latina/o" to describe participants' racial/ethnic background in accordance with their preferred gender identification. I do not use "Latinx," a gender-neutral version, because no participants self-identified with this term.

8. Ferguson and Ready (2011); Lareau (2003); McLanahan (2009).

9. Bridges and Boyd (2016); Cherlin (2014); Edin and Kefalas (2005); Edin and Nelson (2013); Gerson (2010); Sassler and Miller (2017).

10. Conger et al. (2002); Cutrona et al. (2003); Mistry et al. (2002).

11. Abrego (2014); Kim (2011); McLoyd (1998); Osborne and McLanahan (2007); Turney (2014); Zayas (2015).

12. Turney (2015, 2017); Western (2006).

13. Roberts (2002); Rodriguez (2017).

14. Rodriguez (2017).

15. Passel and Cohn (2018).

16. Passel and Cohn (2018).

17. In 2016 there were an estimated 11.6 million Mexican immigrants in the United States; six million were undocumented (Zong and Batalova 2018). In 2015 there were an estimated 3.4 million Central American immigrants; 1.7 million were undocumented (Lesser and Batalova 2017).

18. Estimates from multiple data sets suggest that 25–28 percent of the 18 million Latino children living in the United States have at least one undocumented parent (Clarke, Turner, and Guzman 2017).

19. Arnett (2000); Settersten, Furstenberg, and Rumbaut (2005).

20. Elder (1998).

21. Donato, Durand, and Massey (1992); Kossoudji and Cobb-Clark (2002); Rytina (2002).

22. Orrenius and Zavodny (2015b).

23. Amuedo-Dorantes and Antman (2016); Gonzales, Terriquez, and Ruszczyk (2014); Hsin and Ortega (2018); Patler and Laster Pirtle (2018); Venkataramani et al. (2017).

24. Menjívar and Lakhani (2016, 1847).

25. Elder (1998).

26. For my earlier theorization of multigenerational punishment, see Enriquez (2015).

27. Yoshikawa (2012).

28. Allen, Cisneros, and Tellez (2013); Chaudry et al. (2010); Dreby (2012); Zayas (2015).

29. Brabeck et al. (2016); Ha, Ybarra, and Johnson (2017); Hainmueller et al. (2017); Noah and Landale (2017).

30. Bean, Brown, and Bachmeier (2015).

31. Balderas, Delgado-Romero, and Singh (2016); Valdez, Padilla, and Valentine (2013).

32. Ayón and Becerra (2013).

33. Enriquez (2015); Schmalzbauer (2014).

34. Dreby (2015a).

35. Gomberg-Muñoz (2016); López (2015).

36. Menjívar and Abrego (2012); Menjívar and Kanstroom (2014a). See also Waters and Gerstein Pineau (2015).

37. Coutin (2007, 9).

38. Menjívar (2006).

39. For example, see Menjívar and Kanstroom (2014b, 9–11).

40. Portes and Rumbaut (2006).

41. Aranda, Hughes, and Sabogal (2014).

42. Golash-Boza and Valdez (2018).

43. DACA recipients do not have a lawful immigration status. They receive a temporary and "discretionary determination to defer a removal action of an individual," which holds certain benefits, including access to a work permit (USCIS 2018b).

44. The 1986 Immigration Reform and Control Act implemented the first employer sanctions (Brownell 2005). The 1996 Illegal Immigration Reform and Immigration Responsibility Act initiated the E-Verify program (Rosenblum and Hoyt 2011).

45. Donato and Sisk (2012); Goldstein and Alonso-Bejarano (2017); Orrenius and Zavodny (2015a).

46. Passel and Cohn (2015).

47. Bernhardt, Spiller, and Polson (2013); Donato et al. (2008); Gleeson (2010, 2016).

48. Hall, Greenman, and Farkas (2010).

49. Cort, Lin, and Stevenson (2014).

50. These jobs are similar to those identified in other studies (Cho 2017; Gonzales 2016).

51. McFarland et al. (2018).

52. When asked to describe the benefits of DACA, almost all 72 DACA recipients mentioned employment authorization, and nearly three-quarters referred to it first. The accompanying Social Security number led to the second, third, and fourth most mentioned benefits: driver's licenses, financial accounts, and California IDs.

53. For a related discussion, see Abrego (2018).

54. Lytle Hernandez (2010); Massey, Durand, and Pren (2016); Nevins (2010).

55. Armenta (2017); Golash-Boza and Hondagneu-Sotelo (2013).

56. A. S. García (2019); Hacker et al. (2011); Harrison and Lloyd (2013); Jefferies (2014); Stuesse and Coleman (2014).

57. Magaña and Lee (2013).

58. Eagly (2017). Cities, such as New York, have implemented similar policies (OMNYC 2014).

59. For a related discussion, see Enriquez and Millán (2019).

60. For a related discussion, see Aranda and Vaquera (2015); Armenta (2016); Golash-Boza and Hondagneu-Sotelo (2013).

61. Boehm (2016); Dreby (2015a); Gomberg-Muñoz (2016); Ybarra and Peña (2016); Zayas (2015).

62. Gabrielson (2010); JCC (2013).

63. DMV (2013).

64. de Graauw (2014); LeBrón et al. (2017); Varsanyi (2006).

65. Gonzales (2011).

66. DACA recipients in California and most states were immediately eligible to apply for driver's licenses. A few states announced intentions to deny access, but only Arizona and Nebraska implemented such policies; these were reversed with judicial and state legislative action, respectively (NILC 2015).

67. DMV (2017). For a summary of state driver's license laws, see NILC (2019).

68. In 2014, 64 percent of all new permanent residents were petitioned by family members (AIC 2016). For historical context, see Lee (2013).

69. Processing times were consistent from 2008 to 2016 under President Obama. They appear to be lengthening under President Trump, averaging 7.7 months in 2017, 9.7 in 2018, and 10.3 for the first quarter of 2019 (USCIS 2019b).

70. Other immediate and extended family petitions by U.S. citizens and all petitions by permanent residents are subject to annual visa caps for each country of origin, creating a backlog between the approval of an application and the issuance of a permanent resident visa (USCIS 2015c). Wait times vary by type of preference category; in 2014, USCIS issued visas for petitions approved 17–21 years earlier for Mexicans, 11–23 years earlier for Filipinos, and seven to 12 years earlier for all other countries (USDS 2014).

71. An immigration law provision known as 245(i) provides protection from the bar for those who had preexisting petitions filed before 2001 (USCIS 2011). See also Chacón (2007); Cianciarulo (2015).

72. USCIS (2009). Unlawful presence for 180 days to one year precipitates a three-year bar. There is no penalty if one is unlawfully present less than 180 days.

73. Gomberg-Muñoz (2015, 2016, 2017). USCIS streamlined this process in 2013 by adjudicating hardship claims before departure and by issuing provisional waivers; this minimized the risk that migrants would be unable to reenter after undergoing consular processing, and it shortened the time of separation during the process (USCIS 2018d).

74. A few parents had remained in or returned to their country of origin or had recently become lawful permanent residents.

75. Children are no longer eligible to be included in the family petition upon reaching age 21 (USCIS 2018a).

76. DACA is considered lawful presence, preventing the accumulation of a bar if they were minors when they first received DACA (USCIS 2018b). None of my participants received DACA before age 18.

77. Graber and Magaña-Salgado (2016).

78. Abrego (2014); Donato (2010); Donato and Gabaccia (2015); Donato, Wagner, and Patterson (2008); Dreby (2010, 2015a); Dreby and Schmalzbauer (2013); Golash-Boza and Hondagneu-Sotelo (2013); Hagan (1998); Hamilton (2015); Hondagneu-Sotelo (1994); Parrado and Flippen (2005); Salcido and Menjívar (2012); Schmalzbauer (2014); Smith (2006).

79. Abrego (2014); Deeb-Sossa and Bickham Mendez (2008); Enriquez (2017b); Montes (2013); Pila (2016); Schmalzbauer (2009, 2014).

80. Ridgeway (2011); Ridgeway and Correll (2004).

81. Ridgeway (2011, 68).

82. Christiansen and Palkovitz (2001); Eaton and Rose (2012); Edin and Nelson (2013); Gerson (2010); Hays (1996); A. R. Hochschild (2003); Lever, Frederick, and Hertz (2015); Townsend (2002).

83. Jaramillo-Sierra and Allen (2012); Katz-Wise, Priess, and Hyde (2010); Sassler and Miller (2017); Vespa (2009).

84. Gleeson and Gonzales (2012); Gonzales (2016); Gonzales and Burciaga (2018); Terriquez (2015a).

85. Choo and Ferree (2010); Collins (2000); Crenshaw (1991). For examples of intersectional approaches to undocumented immigrant experiences, see Cebulko (2018); Enriquez (2017a); Terriquez, Brenes, and Lopez (2018); Valdez and Golash-Boza (2018).

86. Abrego (2011); Cho (2017); Dao (2017); Enriquez (2019); Enriquez, Vazquez Vera, and Ramakrishnan (2019); Herrera (2016); Terriquez (2015b).

2. "IT'S BECAUSE HE WANTS PAPERS": CHOOSING A ROMANTIC PARTNER

1. USCIS (2015c). For example, in 2012—in the middle of my first wave of data collection—USCIS was issuing visas for petitions approved 16 years earlier for Mexicans and 12 years earlier for people from most other countries (USDS 2012).

2. Gomberg-Muñoz (2015); López (2017).

3. Menjívar and Lakhani (2016).

4. Gomberg-Muñoz (2017).

5. Chavez (2008).

6. Burrows (1999a, 1999b, 1999c, 2000a, 2000b, 2006a, 2006b); Ferrera (2017); Fryman (2009); Hardcastle (2009); Holland (2009, 2010); Mancuso (1995); Miller (2009).

7. Schiller (2012a, 2012b).

8. Fletcher (2009); Weir (1990).

9. Warren and Kerwin (2017).

10. USCIS (2011).

11. USCIS (2009).

12. The waiver process changed in 2013. Petitions to waive the bar are now processed in the United States, and applicants receive a provisional waiver decision before leaving the country. This eliminates much of the risk of long-term separation, since applicants know whether they will likely face a 10-year bar and can choose to abandon their application if the waiver is denied (USCIS 2018d).

13. Lynskey (1989).

14. USCIS (2018e).

15. Ezer (2006).

16. USCIS (2019c).

17. Coontz (2005); Shumway (2003).

18. Feliciano, Lee, and Robnett (2011); Vasquez-Tokos (2017).

19. Schwartz and Mare (2005).

20. *AB 540* is a term sometimes used in California to refer to undocumented students. It references California Assembly Bill 540, which allows anyone who attended high school in California to pay in-state college tuition, regardless of their immigration status.

21. Enriquez (2017a); Gonzales (2011, 2016).

22. Cort (2011); Cort, Lin, and Stevenson (2014).

23. Same-sex spouses became eligible to file immigration petitions for their partners in 2013, when the Defense of Marriage Act was overturned by the U.S. Supreme Court's decision in *United States v. Windsor* (Edwards 2013).

24. Gonzales (2016).

25. Cebulko (2016).

3. "YOU FEEL A LITTLE BIT LESS": GENDERED ILLEGALITY AND DESIRABILITY WHEN DATING

1. Dreby (2015a); Dreby and Schmalzbauer (2013); Schmalzbauer (2014).

2. Gerson (2010).

3. Eaton and Rose (2012); Jaramillo-Sierra and Allen (2012); Lamont (2014); Laner and Ventrone (2000).

4. Lever, Frederick, and Hertz (2015).

5. Lamont (2014).

6. For a discussion, see Bridges and Boyd (2016); Gerson (2010, 179–87).

7. Townsend (2002).

8. Bridges and Boyd (2016); Edin and Kefalas (2005); Edin and Nelson (2013); Gerson (2010); Wilson (1987).

9. DIR (n.d.).

10. Lamont (2014).

11. Yoo et al. (2014).

12. DMV (2013).

13. Gabrielson (2010).

14. Armenta (2017).

15. For a discussion of driving in rural areas, see Schmalzbauer (2014).

16. For a theorization of strategic gender egalitarianism, see Zhang and Fussell (2017).

17. Gerson (2010).

18. Dreby (2015a, 76–80).

19. Gerson (2010, 179–87).

20. Gibson-Davis, Edin, and McLanahan (2005); Smock, Manning, and Porter (2005).

21. Rubin (1994); Townsend (2002).

4. "IT AFFECTS US, OUR FUTURE": NEGOTIATING ILLEGALITY AS A MIXED-STATUS COUPLE

1. López (2015, 108).

2. Edin and Kefalas (2005); Smock, Manning, and Porter (2005); Trail and Karney (2012).

3. Jillson (2004, 6).

4. Cammarota (2008); J. L. Hochschild (1995); Rendón (2019).

5. Lee, Tornatzky, and Torres (2004).

6. Dreby (2015a).

7. Menjívar and Salcido (2002); Villalón (2010).

8. Winstok and Straus (2016). For recent data, see Breiding, Chen, and Black (2014).

9. Dreby (2015a); Menjívar and Salcido (2002); Salcido and Adelman (2004); Schmalzbauer (2014).

10. Golash-Boza and Hondagneu-Sotelo (2013).

11. Dreby (2015a, 59–68); Gomberg-Muñoz (2017, 53–54); Menjívar and Salcido (2002, 909); Salcido and Adelman (2004); Schmalzbauer (2014, 71).

12. Cook (2009); Douglas and Hines (2011).

13. USCIS (2018e).

14. The earliest renewal statistics are for October to December 2014, when 125,060 renewals were decided; 0.05 percent were denied (USCIS 2015a). By September 30,

2016, 593,582 renewal applications had been processed; 0.9 percent were denied (USCIS 2016).

15. For details on this legal process, see Graber and Magaña-Salgado (2016).

5. "IT WAS TIME TO TAKE THAT STEP": PURSUING LEGALIZATION THROUGH MARRIAGE

1. Gomberg-Muñoz (2015, 2016, 2017).

2. Smock, Manning, and Porter (2005); Trail and Karney (2012).

3. In 2014, California Senate Bill 1159 passed, allowing undocumented immigrants to obtain professional licenses in California. Formal employment still requires employment authorization.

4. For details, see Graber and Magaña-Salgado (2016).

5. Ingraham (1999); Otnes and Pleck (2003).

6. Petitioners must earn above 125 percent of the U.S. poverty level for their household size. If they do not, they must obtain a joint sponsor who does. The sponsor accepts legal responsibility for financially supporting the petitioned immigrant so they do not become a public charge (USCIS 2019a).

7. Couples who are eligible to adjust their status within the United States pay fees associated with forms I-130 ($535) and I-485 ($1,140, plus an $85 biometric fee) (USCIS 2018c). Consular processing requires additional fees.

8. USCIS (n.d.).

9. Research suggests that romantic performance is also heavily scrutinized in consular cases (Gomberg-Muñoz 2017).

10. USCIS (2012, 1).

11. Bank of America (2018).

12. Acosta (2013); Ocampo (2014).

13. USCIS (n.d.).

14. Barton (2012).

15. Luibhéid (2008).

16. USCIS (2019d).

17. Kowalski (2015).

18. Kowalski (2015).

19. Many participants advanced negative views of life in Mexico as a way to claim U.S. belonging (Enriquez 2016).

20. Lakhani (2015); Sánchez García and Hamann (2016).

21. Román González, Carrillo Cantú, and Hernández-León (2016); Zayas (2015).

22. Permanent residents are still deportable for certain crimes (Golash-Boza 2015).

23. U visa recipients are eligible to apply for permanent residency after holding their visa for three years. At that time, they can apply for a derivative visa for qualifying family members (USCIS 2018f).

24. Bianchi and Milkie (2010); Hochschild (2003).

25. Nixon (2017).

26. Menjívar and Lakhani (2016).

6. "IT'S A CONSTANT STRUGGLE": BECOMING AND BEING PARENTS

1. Brabeck et al. (2016); Dreby (2015b); Ha, Ybarra, and Johnson (2017); Hainmueller et al. (2017); Yoshikawa (2012); Yoshikawa, Suárez-Orozco, and Gonzales (2016).

2. Ceballo et al. (2012); Hays (1996); Lareau (2003); Romagnoli and Wall (2012); Shirani, Henwood, and Coltart (2012).

3. Rackin and Gibson-Davis (2017); Schneider and Hastings (2015).

4. Amuedo-Dorantes and Arenas-Arroyo (2017).

5. Condoms and contraceptive pills were most common. Several mothers had obtained intrauterine devices as part of their postpartum care. The most common ineffective form was "pulling out." None reported immigration-related barriers.

6. Services include routine prenatal care, labor and delivery, routine postpartum care, family planning, and treatment for conditions that complicate pregnancy or delivery (e.g., hypertension, diabetes) (DHCS, n.d.).

7. Two to three ultrasounds is consistent with recommendations made by the American College of Obstetricians and Gynecologists for normal pregnancies (ACOG 2016).

8. Gleeson (2010).

9. Ceballo et al. (2012); Hays (1996); Romagnoli and Wall (2012).

10. "Me encantaría conseguir otro trabajo donde sean como le digo menos horas y hasta tiempo . . . para dedicarme más tiempo a mis niños que les estoy quitando tiempo para trabajar once, doce horas diarias. Y cuanto ellos van a la escuela, yo estoy en la casa y cuando llegan a la casa yo estoy en el trabajo y no puedo digamos disfrutar más que fines de semana. Domingo solamente, porque sábados también tengo que trabajar."

11. "Ahorita no buscaría trabajo porque en el estado que estoy de ilegal. No voy a encontrar un buen trabajo donde me paguen bien. Pues no me conviene ir a un trabajo donde me paguen lo mínimo porque tengo dos niños y tendría que pagar como babysitter por los dos. Y si gano el mínimo no me conviene. Voy a trabajar solo para pagar la babysitter."

12. "Estaríamos más desahogados económicamente, pudiéramos tener tal vez un poquito para los niños que ocupan bastantes cosas que la ropa porque van creciendo."

13. Gould and Cooke (2015).

14. Broder, Moussavian, and Blazer (2015); Yoshikawa (2012). For details on programs and eligibility, see Matthews (2017).

15. Abrego (2014); Landry (2000).

16. For a discussion of how tax credits have replaced welfare programs to support working families, see Halpern-Meekin et al. (2015).

17. CBPP (2017).

7. "I CAN'T OFFER THEM WHAT OTHER PEOPLE COULD": MULTIGENERATIONAL PUNISHMENT OF CITIZEN CHILDREN

1. Yoshikawa (2012).

2. Dreby (2015a, 2015b).

3. Hart and Risley (2002).

4. Yoshikawa (2012).

5. Brabeck et al. (2016); Ha, Ybarra, and Johnson (2017).

6. "Yo creo que sería mucho más fácil [a ser ciudadano]. No lo sé realmente pero me imagino que sería mucho más fácil."

7. "Hubo un tiempo, de que mi niño el más grande quería jugar básquetbol, y nos pedían una mensualidad para que pudiera jugar básquetbol en un parque. Y no era muy cara pero no cubríamos los gastos para poder pagarla."

8. Feldman and Matjasko (2005).

9. For a discussion of how schools are not set up to encourage the active participation of Latino immigrant families, see Olivos and Mendoza (2010).

10. "En este trabajo, si vendes, lo que ganaste en toda la semana lo puedes ganar en dos días. No tienes que estar 40 horas para ganarte eso, pero eso es un riesgo, que no es seguro. . . . Me gusta por el tiempo, porque yo puedo atender a mis hijos. Porque puedo tener tiempo para ellos, para su deporte y todo."

11. "Si en la manera de que, de viajar, ellos quieren ir a México pero yo no puedo salir. Ahí es donde yo no los dejo, los limito a ellos viajar y conocer otros lugares."

12. "El otro día me estaba haciendo una historia [con] mi niño de su escuela . . . una historia de que habían hecho en las vacaciones. Y nomás hemos salido al parque, a llevarlo a jugar. Y sus compañeros miro que fueron aquí, fueron allá. Y me pregunto, ¿porqué él no podía hacer lo que sus amigos hacían? Son limitaciones que él tiene hasta en la escuela, se refleja eso. . . . Los hace sentir menos a ellos. En el mismo salón de clases."

13. Dreby (2015a, 133–70).

14. "Van a crecer con esa limitación. En el futuro cuando ellos estén grandes lo van a poder hacer. . . . Mientras uno tenga un recuerdo así, sí le va a afectar."

15. "Durante el día porque en la noche es cuando ponen los retenes."

16. "Entonces ella comprende muchas cosas que no puede. O cuando manejaba, ella entendía, mami, me ayudaba. Como dices, volteaba por un lado, mami, por allá se mira una patrulla, así ella me alertaba, en los peligros que podía, que trae pues si andas manejando sin licencia."

17. See discussion in Enriquez (2016).

18. See discussion in Dreby (2012).

19. "Una forma de no tenerlos con los ojos cerrados, tapados. Para que miren más o menos la realidad."

20. For an example, see IRLC (2017).

21. "Sí les afecta a ellos. Cuando una vez pasó la policía cerca de la casa, una persecución, que había mucho policía, helicópteros, y mi niño estaba en el balcón y se escondió. Me dejo que venia la migra, él no tiene nada que ver con eso. Pero lo hizo porque nosotros ya habíamos platicado sobre eso."

22. Román González, Carrillo Cantú, and Hernández-León (2016); Zayas (2015).

23. For a discussion of transnational families, see Abrego (2014); Dreby (2010).

24. Allen, Cisneros, and Tellez (2013); Chaudry et al. (2010); Zayas et al. (2015).

25. For a discussion of "suddenly single mothers," see Dreby (2015a, 31–41).

26. Hainmueller et al. (2017).

27. In 2015 a one-day ticket for SeaWorld cost $69 per person. The San Diego Zoo or Safari Park cost $50 for adults and $40 for children.

28. USCIS (2015b).

29. EOPUS (2014).

30. Suárez-Orozco and Suárez-Orozco (1995).

8. IMMIGRATION POLICY AND THE FUTURE OF LATINO FAMILIES

1. California Proposition 187 prevented undocumented immigrants from accessing health care, public education, and other social services. Legal challenges prevented most it from going into effect.

2. Roberts (2002); Rodriguez (2017); Turney (2017).

3. Bridges and Boyd (2016); Cherlin (2014); Conger et al. (2002); Edin and Kefalas (2005); Edin and Nelson (2013); Sassler and Miller (2017); Turney (2014); Wilson (1987).

4. Portes and Rumbaut (2006).

5. Donato, Durand, and Massey (1992); Kossoudji and Cobb-Clark (2002); Rytina (2002).

6. Capps, Fix, and Zong (2017); Gonzales, Terriquez, and Ruszczyk (2014); Patler and Laster Pirtle (2018).

7. For a discussion, see Abrego (2018).

8. Elder (1998).

9. Abrego (2006); Enriquez (2017a); Gonzales (2016).

10. Millán (2018).

11. For examples, see O'Brien (2013); Strasser (2018).

12. Hagan, Rodriguez, and Castro (2011); Licona and Maldonado (2014).

13. Flores and Schachter (2018); S. J. García (2017); LeBrón et al. (2018).

14. Novak, Geronimus, and Martinez-Cardoso (2017).

15. Lesser and Batalova (2017); Zong and Batalova (2018).

16. Clarke, Turner, and Guzman (2017).

17. Latino Decisions (2013).

18. Alba and Nee (2003); Kasinitz et al. (2008); Portes and Rumbaut (2001, 2006).

19. Alba et al. (2011); Telles and Ortiz (2008); Waldinger and Feliciano (2004).

20. Bean, Brown, and Bachmeier (2015, 7).

21. Passel and Cohn (2018).

22. Ramakrishnan and Shah (2017).

23. Cho (2017); Enriquez (2019); Enriquez, Vazquez Vera, and Ramakrishnan (2019).

24. Cebulko and Silver (2016).

25. NILC (2019).

26. CPD (2013).

27. Armacost (2016). For a list, see Griffith and Vaughn (2019).

28. Abrego and Schmalzbauer (2018).

29. Arizona's Senate Bill 1070 (2010) and Hazleton, Pennsylvania's Illegal Immigration Relief Act Ordinance (2007), are two examples of omnibus anti-immigrant legislation.

30. Gulasekaram and Ramakrishnan (2015).

31. For a discussion, see Ochoa (2004); Pastor (2018).

32. Colbern and Ramakrishnan (2018).

33. Abrego (2011); Armenta (2016); Cebulko (2018); Cho (2017); Dao (2017); Enriquez (2017a, 2019); Enriquez, Vazquez Vera, and Ramakrishnan (2019); Golash-Boza and Hondagneu-Sotelo (2013); Hagan (1998); Herrera (2016); Terriquez (2015b); Valdez and Golash-Boza (2018).

34. Brabeck et al. (2016).

35. Thrush (2018); Winfield Cunningham (2018).

36. Fremstad (2018).

37. Initial DACA applications were not to be accepted after September 5, 2017. DACA recipients whose protections expired between September 5, 2017, and March 5, 2018, were allowed to file for renewal before October 5, 2017. All DACA protections were expected to expire in the two years after March 5, 2018 (Duke 2017).

38. Gerstein (2017); Savage (2017); UCOP (2017).

39. Congress voted on the federal DREAM Act in December 2010; it passed in the House of Representatives but did not receive enough votes to overcome a filibuster in the Senate (Herszenhorn 2010). Activism for the DREAM Act reemerged in September 2017, in a response to DACA's rescission. In January 2018, Congress forced a three-day government shutdown by tying the act to a short-term spending bill (Gay Stolberg and Kaplan 2018).

40. Regents of Univ. of Cal. v. U.S. Dep't of Homeland Sec., 279 F. Supp. 3d 1011 (N.D. Cal. 2018); aff'd, 908 F.3d 476 (9th Cir. 2018).

41. Benner and Medina (2018); Jordan (2018).

42. Phillips (2018); Thompson (2018).

43. Baker (2019).

APPENDIX A. REFLECTIONS ON METHODS
AND POSITIONALITY

1. Wessler (2018).

APPENDIX B. DEMOGRAPHIC CHARACTERISTICS OF
STUDY PARTICIPANTS

1. Hayes and Hill (2017).

REFERENCES

Abrego, Leisy J. 2006. "'I Can't Go to College Because I Don't Have Papers': Incorporation Patterns of Latino Undocumented Youth." *Latino Studies* 4 (3): 212–31.

———. 2011. "Legal Consciousness of Undocumented Latinos: Fear and Stigma as Barriers to Claims-Making for First- and 1.5-Generation Immigrants." *Law & Society Review* 45 (2): 337–70.

———. 2014. *Sacrificing Families: Navigating Laws, Labor, and Love across Borders.* Stanford, CA: Stanford University Press.

———. 2018. "Renewed Optimism and Spatial Mobility: Legal Consciousness of Latino Deferred Action for Childhood Arrivals Recipients and Their Families in Los Angeles." *Ethnicities* 18 (2): 192–207.

Abrego, Leisy J., and Leah Schmalzbauer. 2018. "Illegality, Motherhood, and Place: Undocumented Latinas Making Meaning and Negotiating Daily Life." *Women's Studies International Forum* 67: 10–17.

ACOG (American College of Obstetricians and Gynecologists). 2016. "Practice Bulletin No. 175: Ultrasound in Pregnancy." *Obstetrics & Gynecology* 128 (6): e241–56.

Acosta, Katie L. 2013. *Amigas y Amantes: Sexually Nonconforming Latinas Negotiate Family.* New Brunswick, NJ: Rutgers University Press.

Alba, Richard, Dalia Abdel-Hady, Tariqul Islam, and Karen Marotz. 2011. "Downward Assimilation and Mexican Americans: An Examination of Intergenerational Advance and Stagnation in Educational Attainment." In *The Next Generation: Immigrant Youth in a Comparative Perspective,* edited by Richard Alba and Mary C. Waters, 95–109. New York: New York University Press.

Alba, Richard, and Victor Nee. 2003. *Remaking the American Mainstream: Assimilation and Contemporary Immigration.* Cambridge, MA: Harvard University Press.

Allen, Brian, Erica M. Cisneros, and Alexandra Tellez. 2013. "The Children Left Behind: The Impact of Parental Deportation on Mental Health." *Journal of Child and Family Studies* 24 (2): 386–92.

AIC (American Immigration Council). 2016. *How the United States Immigration System Works*. Washington, DC: AIC.

Amuedo-Dorantes, Catalina, and Francisca Antman. 2016. "Can Authorization Reduce Poverty among Undocumented Immigrants? Evidence from the Deferred Action for Childhood Arrivals Program." *Economics Letters* 147: 1–4.

Amuedo-Dorantes, Catalina, and Esther Arenas-Arroyo. 2017. "Immigrant Fertility in the Midst of Intensified Enforcement." GLO Discussion Paper, no. 1. Global Labor Organization, Essen, Germany. https://ideas.repec.org/p/zbw/glodps/1.html.

Aranda, Elizabeth M., Sallie Hughes, and Elena Sabogal. 2014. *Making a Life in Multiethnic Miami: Immigration and the Rise of a Global City*. Boulder, CO: Lynne Rienner.

Aranda, Elizabeth, and Elizabeth Vaquera. 2015. "Racism, the Immigration Enforcement Regime, and the Implications for Racial Inequality in the Lives of Undocumented Young Adults." *Sociology of Race and Ethnicity* 1 (1): 88–104.

Armacost, Barbara E. 2016. "'Sanctuary' Laws: The New Immigration Federalism." *Michigan State Law Review*, no. 5, 1197–265.

Armenta, Amada. 2016. "Racializing Crimmigration: Structural Racism, Colorblindness, and the Institutional Production of Immigrant Criminality." *Sociology of Race and Ethnicity* 3 (1): 82–95.

———. 2017. *Protect, Serve, and Deport: The Rise of Policing as Immigration Enforcement*. Berkeley, CA: University of California Press.

Arnett, Jeffrey J. 2000. "Emerging Adulthood: A Theory of Development from the Late Teens through the Twenties." *American Psychologist* 55 (5): 469–80.

Ayón, Cecilia, and David Becerra. 2013. "Mexican Immigrant Families Under Siege: The Impact of Anti-immigrant Policies, Discrimination, and the Economic Crisis." *Advances in Social Work* 14 (1): 206–28.

Baker, Peter. 2019. "Trump's National Address Escalates Border Wall Fight." *New York Times*, January 8. www.nytimes.com/2019/01/08/us/politics/donald-trump-speech.html.

Balderas, Carissa N., Edward A. Delgado-Romero, and Anneliese A. Singh. 2016. "Sin Papeles: Latino Parent-Child Conversations about Undocumented Legal Status." *Journal of Latina/o Psychology* 4 (3): 158–72.

Bank of America. 2018. *2018 Better Money Habits Millennial Report*. https://bettermoneyhabits.bankofamerica.com/content/dam/bmh/pdf/ar6vnln9-boa-bmh-millennial-report-winter-2018-final2.pdf.

Barton, Bernadette. 2012. *Pray the Gay Away: The Extraordinary Lives of Bible Belt Gays*. New York: New York University Press.

Bean, Frank D., Susan K. Brown, and James D. Bachmeier. 2015. *Parents without Papers: The Progress and Pitfalls of Mexican-American Integration*. New York: Russell Sage Foundation.

Benner, Katie, and Jennifer Medina. 2018. "Trump Administration Sues California over Immigration Laws." *New York Times*, March 6. www.nytimes.com/2018/03/06/us/politics/justice-department-california-sanctuary-cities.html.

Bernhardt, Annette, Michael W. Spiller, and Diana Polson. 2013. "All Work and No Pay: Violations of Employment and Labor Laws in Chicago, Los Angeles and New York City." *Social Forces* 91 (3): 725–46.

Bianchi, Suzanne M., and Melissa A. Milkie. 2010. "Work and Family Research in the First Decade of the 21st Century." *Journal of Marriage and Family* 72 (3): 705–25.

Boehm, Deborah A. 2016. *Returned: Going and Coming in an Age of Deportation.* Berkeley: University of California Press.

Brabeck, Kalina M., Erin Sibley, Patricia Taubin, and Angela Murcia. 2016. "The Influence of Immigrant Parent Legal Status on U.S.-Born Children's Academic Abilities: The Moderating Effects of Social Service Use." *Applied Developmental Science* 20 (4): 237–49.

Breiding, M. J., J. Chen, and M. C. Black. 2014. *Intimate Partner Violence in the United States—2010.* Atlanta, GA: National Center for Injury Prevention and Control, Centers for Disease Control and Prevention.

Bridges, Tristan, and Melody L. Boyd. 2016. "On the Marriageability of Men." *Sociology Compass* 10 (1): 48–64.

Broder, Tanya, Avideh Moussavian, and Jonathan Blazer. 2015. *Overview of Immigrant Eligibility for Federal Programs.* Los Angeles: National Immigration Law Center.

Brownell, Peter. 2005. *The Declining Enforcement of Employer Sanctions.* Washington, DC: Migration Policy Institute.

Burrows, James, dir. 1999a. "Guess Who's Not Coming to Dinner." *Will & Grace*, season 2, episode 1. Los Angeles: NBC.

———. 1999b. "Object of My Rejection." *Will & Grace*, season 1, episode 22. Los Angeles: NBC.

———. 1999c. "Whose Mom Is It Anyway?" *Will & Grace*, season 2, episode 4. Los Angeles: NBC.

———. 2000a. "Ben? Her? Part 1." *Will & Grace*, season 2, episode 23. Los Angeles: NBC.

———. 2000b. "Ben? Her? Part 2." *Will & Grace*, season 2, episode 24. Los Angeles: NBC.

———. 2006a. "The Definition of Marriage." *Will & Grace*, season 8, episode 15. Los Angeles: NBC.

———. 2006b. "I Love L. Gay." *Will & Grace*, season 8, episode 14. Los Angeles: NBC.

Cammarota, Julio. 2008. *Sueños Americanos: Barrio Youth Negotiating Social and Cultural Identities.* Tucson: University of Arizona Press.

Capps, Randy, Michael Fix, and Jie Zong. 2017. *The Education and Work Profiles of the DACA Population.* Washington, DC: Migration Policy Institute.

CBPP (Center on Budget and Policy Priorities). 2017. *Policy Basics: Special Supplemental Nutrition Program for Women, Infants, and Children.* Washington, DC: CBPP.

Ceballo, Rosario, Traci M. Kennedy, Allyson Bregman, and Quyen Epstein-Ngo. 2012. "Always Aware (Siempre Pendiente): Latina Mothers' Parenting in High-Risk Neighborhoods." *Journal of Family Psychology* 26 (5): 805–15.

Cebulko, Kara. 2016. "Marrying for Papers? From Economically Strategic to Normative and Relational Dimensions of the Transition to Adulthood for Unauthorized 1.5-Generation Brazilians." *Sociological Perspectives* 59 (4): 760–75.

———. 2018. "Privilege without Papers: Intersecting Inequalities among 1.5-Generation Brazilians in Massachusetts." *Ethnicities* 18 (2): 225–41.

Cebulko, Kara, and Alexis Silver. 2016. "Navigating DACA in Hospitable and Hostile States: State Responses and Access to Membership in the Wake of Deferred Action for Childhood Arrivals." *American Behavioral Scientist* 60 (13): 1553–74.

Chacón, Jennifer M. 2007. "Loving across Borders: Immigration Law and the Limits of Loving. *Wisconsin Law Review* 2007 (2): 345–78.

Chaudry, Ajay, Randy Capps, Juan Manuel Pedroza, Rosa Maria Casteñeda, Robert Santos, and Molly M. Scott. 2010. *Facing Our Future: Children in the Afermath of Immigration Enforcement.* Washington, DC: Urban Institute.

Chavez, Leo. 2008. *The Latino Threat: Constructing Immigrants, Citizens, and the Nation.* Stanford, CA: Stanford University Press.

Cherlin, Andrew J. 2014. *Labor's Love Lost: The Rise and Fall of the Working-Class Family in America.* New York: Russell Sage Foundation.

Cho, Esther Yoona. 2017. "Revisiting Ethnic Niches: A Comparative Analysis of the Labor Market Experiences of Asian and Latino Undocumented Young Adults." *RSF: The Russell Sage Foundation Journal of the Social Sciences* 3 (4): 97–115.

Choo, Hae Yeon, and Myra Marx Ferree. 2010. "Practicing Intersectionality in Sociological Research: A Critical Analysis of Inclusions, Interactions, and Institutions in the Study of Inequalities." *Sociological Theory* 28 (2): 129–49.

Christiansen, Shawn L., and Rob Palkovitz. 2001. "Why the 'Good Provider' Role Still Matters: Providing as a Form of Paternal Involvement." *Journal of Family Issues* 22 (1): 84–106.

Cianciarulo, Marisa S. 2015. "Seventeen Years since the Sunset: The Expiration of 245 (i) and Its Effect on U.S. Citizens Married to Undocumented Immigrants." *Chapman Law Review* 18 (2): 451–79.

Clarke, Wyatt, Kimberly Turner, and Lina Guzman. 2017. *One Quarter of Hispanic Children in the United States Have an Unauthorized Immigrant Parent.* Bethesda, MD: National Research Center on Hispanic Children and Families.

Colbern, Allan, and S. Karthick Ramakrishnan. 2018. "Citizens of California: How the Golden State Went from Worst to First on Immigrant Rights." *New Political Science* 40 (2): 353–67.

Collins, Patricia Hill. 2000. *Black Feminist Thought: Knowledge, Consciousness, and the Politics of Empowerment.* New York: Routledge.

Conger, R. D., L. E. Wallace, Y. Sun, R. L. Simons, V. C. McLoyd, and G. H. Brody. 2002. "Economic Pressure in African American Families: A Replication and Extension of the Family Stress Model." *Developmental Psychology* 38 (2): 179–93.

Cook, Philip W. 2009. *Abused Men: The Hidden Side of Domestic Violence.* Westport, CT: Praeger.

Coontz, Stephanie. 2005. *Marriage, a History: How Love Conquered Marriage.* New York: Penguin.

Cort, David A. 2011. "Reexamining the Ethnic Hierarchy of Locational Attainment: Evidence from Los Angeles." *Social Science Research* 40 (6): 1521–33.

Cort, David A., Ken-Hou Lin, and Gabriela Stevenson. 2014. "Residential Hierarchy in Los Angeles: An Examination of Ethnic and Documentation Status Differences." *Social Science Research* 45:170–83.

Coutin, Susan Bibler. 2007. *Nations of Emigrants: Shifting Boundaries of Citizenship in El Salvador and the United States.* Ithaca, NY: Cornell University Press.

CPD (Center for Popular Democracy). 2013. *Who We Are: Municipal ID Cards as a Local Strategy to Promote Belonging and Shared Community Identity.* Brooklyn, NY: CPD.

Crenshaw, Kimberlé. 1991. "Mapping the Margins: Intersectionality, Identity Politics, and Violence against Women of Color." *Stanford Law Review* 43 (6): 1241–99.

Cutrona, Carolyn E., Daniel W. Russell, W. Todd Abraham, Kelli A. Gardner, Janet N. Melby, Chalandra Bryant, and Rand D. Conger. 2003. "Neighborhood Context and Financial Strain as Predictors of Marital Interaction and Marital Quality in African American Couples." *Personal Relationships* 10 (3): 389–409.

Dao, Loan Thi. 2017. "Out and Asian: How Undocu/DACAmented Asian Americans and Pacific Islander Youth Navigate Dual Liminality in the Immigrant Rights Movement." *Societies* 7 (3): 17–31.

Deeb-Sossa, Natalia, and Jennifer Bickham Mendez. 2008. "Enforcing Borders in the Nuevo South: Gender and Migration in Williamsburg, Virginia, and the Research Triangle, North Carolina." *Gender & Society* 22 (5): 613–39.

De Genova, Nicholas P. 2002. "Migrant 'Illegality' and Deportability in Everyday Life." *Annual Review of Anthropology* 31: 419–47.

de Graauw, Els. 2014. "Municipal ID Cards for Undocumented Immigrants." *Politics & Society* 42 (3): 309–30.

DHCS (California Department of Health Care Services). n.d. "Criteria for Emergency and Pregnancy-Related Services for Persons Entitled to Restricted Benefits Only." Accessed December 10, 2019. www.dhcs.ca.gov/services/medi-cal/Documents/ManCriteria_06_EmergPreg.htm.

DIR (State of California Department of Industrial Relations). n.d. "History of California Minimum Wage." Accessed December 10, 2019. www.dir.ca.gov/iwc/minimumwagehistory.htm.

DMV (State of California Department of Motor Vehicles). 2013. "California DMV Statistics." http://apps.dmv.ca.gov/about/profile/ca_dmv_stats.pdf.

———. 2017. "AB 60 Driver License." www.dmv.ca.gov/portal/dmv/detail/ab60.

Donato, Katharine M. 2010. "U.S. Migration from Latin America: Gendered Patterns and Shifts." *Annals of the American Academy of Political and Social Science* 630 (1): 78–92.

Donato, Katharine M., Jorge Durand, and Douglas S. Massey. 1992. "Changing Conditions in the US Labor Market: Effects of the Immigration Reform and Control Act of 1986." *Population Research and Policy Review* 11 (2): 93–115.

Donato, Katharine M., and Donna Gabaccia. 2015. *Gender and International Migration: From the Slavery Era to the Global Age.* New York: Russell Sage Foundation.

Donato, Katharine M., and Blake Sisk. 2012. "Shifts in the Employment Outcomes among Mexican Migrants to the United States, 1976–2009." *Research in Social Stratification and Mobility* 30 (1): 63–77.

Donato, Katharine M., Brandon Wagner, and Evelyn Patterson. 2008. "The Cat and Mouse Game at the Mexico-U.S. Border: Gendered Patterns and Recent Shifts." *International Migration Review* 42 (2): 330–59.

Donato, Katharine M., Chizuko Wakabayashi, Shirin Hakimzadeh, and Amada Armenta. 2008. "Shifts in the Employment Conditions of Mexican Migrant Men and Women: The Effect of U.S. Immigration Policy." *Work and Occupations* 35 (4): 462–95.

Douglas, Emily M., and Denise A. Hines. 2011. "The Helpseeking Experiences of Men Who Sustain Intimate Partner Violence: An Overlooked Population and Implications for Practice." *Journal of Family Violence* 26 (6): 473–85.

Dreby, Joanna. 2010. *Divided by Borders: Mexican Migrants and Their Children.* Berkeley: University of California Press.

———. 2012. "The Burden of Deportation on Children in Mexican Immigrant Families." *Journal of Marriage and Family* 74 (4): 829–45.

———. 2015a. *Everyday Illegal: When Policies Undermine Immigrant Families.* Berkeley: University of California Press.

———. 2015b. "U.S. Immigration Policy and Family Separation: The Consequences for Children's Well-Being." *Social Science & Medicine* 132: 245–51.

Dreby, Joanna, and Leah Schmalzbauer. 2013. "The Relational Contexts of Migration: Mexican Women in New Destination Sites." *Sociological Forum* 28 (1): 1–26.

Duke, Elaine. 2017. "Memorandum on Rescission of Deferred Action for Childhood Arrivals (DACA)." www.dhs.gov/news/2017/09/05/memorandum-rescission-daca.

Eagly, Ingrid V. 2017. "Criminal Justice in an Era of Mass Deportation: Reforms from California." *New Criminal law Review* 20 (1): 12–38.

Eaton, Asia A., and Suzanna M. Rose. 2012. "Scripts for Actual First Date and Hanging-Out Encounters among Young Heterosexual Hispanic Adults." *Sex Roles* 67 (5): 285–99.

Edin, Katharyn, and Maria Kefalas. 2005. *Promises I Can Keep: Why Poor Women Put Motherhood before Marriage.* Berkeley: University of California Press.

Edin, Katharyn, and Timothy J. Nelson. 2013. *Doing the Best I Can: Fatherhood in the Inner City.* Berkeley: University of California Press.

Edwards, Benjamin P. 2013. "Welcoming a Post-DOMA World: Same-Sex Spousal Petitions and Other Post-Windsor Immigration Implications." *Family Law Quarterly* 47 (2): 173–89.

Elder, Glen H. 1998. "The Life Course as Developmental Theory." *Child Development* 69 (1): 1–12.

Enriquez, Laura E. 2015. "Multigenerational Punishment: Shared Experiences of Undocu-mented Immigration Status within Mixed-Status Families." *Journal of Marriage and Family* 77 (4): 939–53.

———. 2016. "'I Talk to Them but I Don't Know Them': Undocumented Young Adults Negotiating Belonging in the U.S. through Conversations with Mexico." In *Click and Kin: Transnational Identity and Quick Media,* edited by May Friedman and Silvia Schultermandl, 27–47. Toronto: University of Toronto Press.

———. 2017a. "A 'Master Status' or the 'Final Straw'? Assessing the Role of Immigration Status in Latino Undocumented Youths' Pathways out of School." *Journal of Ethnic and Migration Studies* 43 (9): 1526–43.

———. 2017b. "Gendering Illegality: Undocumented Young Adults' Negotiation of the Family Formation Process." *American Behavioral Scientist* 61 (10): 1153–71.

———. 2019. "Border-Hopping Mexicans, Law-Abiding Asians, and Racialized Illegality: Analyzing Undocumented College Students Experiences through a Relational Lens." In *Relational Formations of Race: Theory, Method and Practice,* edited by Natalia Molina, Daniel Martinez HoSang, and Ramón A. Gutiérrez, 257–77. Berkeley: University of California Press.

Enriquez, Laura E., and Daniel Millán. 2019. "Situational Triggers and Protective Loca-tions: Conceptualising the Salience of Deportability in Everyday Life." *Journal of Ethnic and Migration Studies,* doi: 10.1080/1369183X.2019.1694877.

Enriquez, Laura E., Daisy Vazquez Vera, and S. Karthick Ramakrishnan. 2019. "Driver's Licenses for All? Racialized Illegality and the Implementation of Progressive Immigration Policy in California." *Law & Policy* 41 (1): 34–58.

EOPUS (Executive Office of the President of the United States). 2014. *The Economic Effects of Administrative Action on Immigration.* https://obamawhitehouse.archives.gov/sites/default/files/docs/cea_2014_economic_effects_of_immigration_executive_action.pdf.

Ezer, Nicole Lawrence. 2006. "The Intersection of Immigration Law and Family Law." *Family Law Quarterly* 40 (3): 339–66.

Feldman, Amy F., and Jennifer L. Matjasko. 2005. "The Role of School-Based Extracurricular Activities in Adolescent Development: A Comprehensive Review and Future Directions." *Review of Educational Research* 75 (2): 159–210.

Feliciano, Cynthia, Rennie Lee, and Belinda Robnett. 2011. "Racial Boundaries among Latinos: Evidence from Internet Daters' Racial Preferences." *Social Problems* 58 (2): 189–212.

Ferguson, Jason L., and Douglas D. Ready. 2011. "Expanding Notions of Social Reproduction: Grandparents' Educational Attainment and Grandchildren's Cognitive Skills." *Early Childhood Research Quarterly* 26 (2): 216–26.

Ferrera, America, dir. 2017. "Mateo's Last Day." *Superstore*, season 2, episode 18. Los Angeles: NBC.

Fletcher, Anne, dir. 2009. *The Proposal.* Burbank, CA: Walt Disney Studios.

Flores, René D., and Ariela Schachter. 2018. "Who Are the 'Illegals'? The Social Construction of Illegality in the United States." *American Sociological Review* 83 (5): 839–68.

Fremstad, Shawn. 2018. *Trump's "Public Charge" Rule Would Radically Change Legal Immigration.* Washington, DC: Center for American Progress.

Fryman, Pamela, dir. 2009. "The Possimpible." *How I Met Your Mother*, season 4, episode 14. Los Angeles: CBS.

Gabrielson, Ryan. 2010. "Sobriety Checkpoints Catch Unlicensed Drivers." *New York Times*, February 13. www.nytimes.com/2010/02/14/us/14sfcheck.html?_r=0.

García, Angela S. 2019. *Legal Passing: Navigating Undocumented Life and Local Immigration Law.* Berkeley: University of California Press.

García, San Juanita. 2017. "Racializing 'Illegality': An Intersectional Approach to Understanding How Mexican-Origin Women Navigate an Anti-immigrant Climate." *Sociology of Race and Ethnicity* 3 (4): 474–90.

Gay Stolberg, Sheryl, and Thomas Kaplan. 2018. "Government Shutdown Ends after 3 Days of Recriminations." *New York Times*, January 22. www.nytimes.com/2018/01/22/us/politics/congress-votes-to-end-government-shutdown.html.

Gerson, Kathleen. 2010. *The Unfinished Revolution: Coming of Age in a New Era of Gender, Work, and Family.* New York: Oxford University Press.

Gerstein, Josh. 2017. "DACA Recipients File Suit over Trump's Move to End Program." *Politico*, September 18. www.politico.com/blogs/under-the-radar/2017/09/18/daca-lawsuit-trump-242838.

Gibson-Davis, Christina M., Kathryn Edin, and Sara McLanahan. 2005. "High Hopes but Even Higher Expectations: The Retreat from Marriage among Low-Income Couples." *Journal of Marriage and Family* 67 (5): 1301–12.

Gleeson, Shannon. 2010. "Labor Rights for All? The Role of Undocumented Immigrant Status for Worker Claims Making." *Law and Social Inquiry* 35 (3): 561–602.

———. 2016. *Precarious Claims: The Promise and Failure of Workplace Protections in the United States*. Berkeley: University of California Press.

Gleeson, Shannon, and Roberto G. Gonzales. 2012. "When Do Papers Matter? An Institutional Analysis of Undocumented Life in the United States." *International Migration* 50 (4): 1–19.

Golash-Boza, Tanya. 2015. *Deported: Immigrant Policing, Disposable Labor and Global Capitalism*. New York: New York University Press.

Golash-Boza, Tanya, and Pierrette Hondagneu-Sotelo. 2013. "Latino Immigrant Men and the Deportation Crisis: A Gendered Racial Removal Program." *Latino Studies* 11 (3): 271–92.

Golash-Boza, Tanya, and Zulema Valdez. 2018. "Nested Contexts of Reception: Undocumented Students at the University of California, Central." *Sociological Perspectives* 61 (4): 535–52.

Goldstein, Daniel M., and Carolina Alonso-Bejarano. 2017. "E-Terrify: Securitized Immigration and Biometric Surveillance in the Workplace." *Human Organization* 76 (1): 1–14.

Gomberg-Muñoz, Ruth. 2015. "The Punishment/El Castigo: Undocumented Latinos and US Immigration Processing." *Journal of Ethnic and Migration Studies* 41 (14): 2235–52.

———. 2016. "The Juárez Wives Club: Gendered Citizenship and US Immigration Law." *American Ethnologist* 43 (2): 339–52.

———. 2017. *Becoming Legal: Immigration Law and Mixed-Status Families*. Oxford: Oxford University Press.

Gonzales, Roberto G. 2011. "Learning to Be Illegal: Undocumented Youth and Shifting Legal Contexts in the Transition to Adulthood." *American Sociological Review* 76 (4): 602–19.

———. 2016. *Lives in Limbo: Undocumented and Coming of Age in America*. Berkeley: University of California Press.

Gonzales, Roberto G., and Edelina M. Burciaga. 2018. "Segmented Pathways of Illegality: Reconciling the Coexistence of Master and Auxiliary Statuses in the Experiences of 1.5-Generation Undocumented Young Adults." *Ethnicities* 18 (2): 178–91.

Gonzales, Roberto G., Veronica Terriquez, and Stephen P. Ruszczyk. 2014. "Becoming DACAmented: Assessing the Short-Term Benefits of Deferred Action for Childhood Arrivals (DACA)." *American Behavioral Scientist* 58 (14): 1852–72.

Gould, Elise, and Tanyell Cooke. 2015. *High Quality Child Care Is Out of Reach for Working Families*. Washington, DC: Economic Policy Institute.

Graber, Lena, and Jose Magaña-Salgado. 2016. "Practice Advisory: DACA, Advance Parole, and Family Petitions." San Francisco, CA: Immigrant Legal Resource Center.

Griffith, Bryan, and Jessica M. Vaughn. 2019. "Maps: Sanctuary Cities, Counties, and States." Center for Immigration Studies, April 16, 2019. https://cis.org/Map-Sanctuary-Cities-Counties-and-States.

Gulasekaram, Pratheepan, and S. Karthick Ramakrishnan. 2015. *The New Immigration Federalism*. New York: Cambridge University Press.

Ha, Yoonsook, Marci Ybarra, and Anna D. Johnson. 2017. "Variation in Early Cognitive Development by Maternal Immigrant Documentation Status." *Early Childhood Research Quarterly* 41: 184–95.

Hacker, Karen, Jocelyn Chu, Carolyn Leung, Robert Marra, Alex Pirie, Mohamed Brahimi, Margaret English, Joshua Beckmann, Dolores Acevedo-Garcia, and Robert P. Marlin. 2011. "The Impact of Immigration and Customs Enforcement on Immigrant Health: Perceptions of Immigrants in Everett, Massachusetts, USA." *Social Science & Medicine* 73 (4): 586–94.

Hagan, Jacqueline. 1998. "Social Networks, Gender, and Immigrant Incorporation: Resources and Constraints." *American Sociological Review* 63 (1): 55–67.

Hagan, Jacqueline, Nestor Rodriguez, and Brianna Castro. 2011. "Social Effects of Mass Deportations by the United States Government, 2000–10." *Ethnic and Racial Studies* 34 (8): 1374–91.

Hainmueller, Jens, Duncan Lawrence, Linna Martén, Bernard Black, Lucila Figueroa, Michael Hotard, Tomás R. Jiménez, Fernando Mendoza, Maria I. Rodriguez, Jonas J. Swartz, and David D. Laitin. 2017. "Protecting Unauthorized Immigrant Mothers Improves Their Children's Mental Health." *Science* 357 (6355): 1041–44.

Hall, Matthew, Emily Greenman, and George Farkas. 2010. "Legal Status and Wage Disparities for Mexican Immigrants." *Social Forces* 89 (2): 491–513.

Halpern-Meekin, Sarah, Katharyn Edin, Laura Tach, and Jennifer Sykes. 2015. *It's Not Like I'm Poor: How Working Families Make Ends Meet in a Post-welfare World*. Berkeley: University of California Press.

Hamilton, Erin R. 2015. "Gendered Disparities in Mexico-U.S. Migration: Differences across Class, Ethnic, and Geographic Groups." *Demographic Research* 32 (17): 533–42.

Hardcastle, Alex, dir. 2009. "Practice Date." *Parks and Recreation,* season 2, episode 4. Los Angeles: NBC.

Harrison, Jill Lindsey, and Sarah E. Lloyd. 2013. "Illegality at Work: Deportability and the Productive New Era of Immigration Enforcement." *Antipode* 44 (2): 365–85.

Hart, Betty, and Todd R. Risley. 2002. *Meaningful Differences in the Everyday Experience of Young American Children*. Baltimore: Brookes.

Hayes, Joseph, and Laura Hill. 2017. *Undocumented Immigrants in California*. San Francisco, CA: Public Policy Institute of California.

Hays, Sharon. 1996. *The Cultural Contraditions of Motherhood*. New Haven, CT: Yale University Press.

Herrera, Juan. 2016. "Racialized Illegality: The Regulation of Informal Labor, and Space." *Latino Studies* 14 (3): 320–43.

Herszenhorn, David M. 2010. "Senate Blocks Bill for Young Illegal Immigrants." *New York Times,* December 18. www.nytimes.com/2010/12/19/us/politics/19immig.html.

Heyman, Josiah M. 2013. "The Study of Illegality and Legality: Which Way Forward?" *PoLAR: Political and Legal Anthropology Review* 36 (2): 304–7.

Hochschild, Arlie Russell. 2003. *The Second Shift*. 2nd ed. New York: Penguin.

Hochschild, Jennifer L. 1995. *Facing Up to the American Dream: Race, Class, and the Soul of the Nation*. Princeton, NJ: Princeton University Press.

Holland, Dean, dir. 2009. "Greg Pikitis." *Parks and Recreation,* season 2, episode 7. Los Angeles: NBC.

———. 2010. "Sweetums." *Parks and Recreation,* season 2, episode 15. Los Angeles: NBC.

Hondagneu-Sotelo, Pierrette. 1994. *Gendered Transitions: Mexican Experiences of Immigration*. Berkeley: University of California Press.

Hsin, Amy, and Francesc Ortega. 2018. "The Effects of Deferred Action for Childhood Arrivals on the Educational Outcomes of Undocumented Students." *Demography* 55 (4): 1487–506.

Ingraham, Chrys. 1999. *White Weddings: Romancing Heterosexuality in Popular Culture.* New York: Routledge.

ILRC (Immigrant Legal Resource Center). 2017. "Family Preparedness Plan." Immigrant Legal Resource Center, March 1, 2017. www.ilrc.org/family-preparedness-plan.

Jaramillo-Sierra, Ana L., and Katherine R. Allen. 2012. "Who Pays after the First Date? Young Men's Discourses of the Male-Provider Role." *Psychology of Men & Masculinity* 14 (4): 389–99.

JCC (Judicial Council of California). 2013. *Uniform Bail and Penalty Schedules.* San Francisco, CA: JCC. www.courts.ca.gov/documents/2013-JC-BAIL.pdf.

Jefferies, Julián. 2014. "Fear of Deportation in High School: Implications for Breaking the Circle of Silence Surrounding Migration Status." *Journal of Latinos and Education* 13 (4): 278–95.

Jillson, Cal. 2004. *Pursuing the American Dream: Opportunity and Exclusion over Four Centuries.* Lawrence: University Press of Kansas.

Jordan, Miriam. 2018. "Is America a 'Nation of Immigrants'? Immigration Agency Says No." *New York Times,* February 22. www.nytimes.com/2018/02/22/us/uscis-nation-of-immigrants.html.

Kasinitz, Phillip, John H. Mollenkopf, Mary C. Waters, and Jennifer Holdaway. 2008. *Inheriting the City: The Children of Immigrants Come of Age.* Boston: Harvard University Press.

Katz-Wise, Sabra L., Heather A. Priess, and Janet S. Hyde. 2010. "Gender-Role Attitudes and Behavior across the Transition to Parenthood." *Developmental Psychology* 46 (1): 18–28.

Kim, Hyun Sik. 2011. "Consequences of Parental Divorce for Child Development." *American Sociological Review* 76 (3): 487–511.

Kossoudji, Sherrie A., and Deborah A. Cobb-Clark. 2002. "Coming out of the Shadows: Learning about Legal Status and Wages from the Legalized Population." *Journal of Labor Economics* 20 (3): 598–628.

Kowalski, Daniel M. 2015. "From AILA: USCIS Provides I-601 and I-601a Statistics for FY2010—FY2015." www.lexisnexis.com/legalnewsroom/immigration/b/insidenews/archive/2015/05/04/from-aila-uscis-provides-i-601-and-i-601a-statistics-for-fy2010-fy2015.aspx.

Lakhani, Nina. 2015. "U.S.-Born Students in Mexico Risk Becoming 'Lost Generation.'" *Los Angeles Times,* March 9. www.latimes.com/world/mexico-americas/la-fg-mexico-schools-americans-20150309-story.html.

Lamont, Ellen. 2014. "Negotiating Courtship: Reconciling Egalitarian Ideals with Traditional Gender Norms." *Gender & Society* 28 (2): 189–211.

Landry, Bart. 2000. *Black Working Wives: Pioneers of the American Family Revolution.* Berkeley: University of California Press.

Laner, Mary R., and Nicole A. Ventrone. 2000. "Dating Scripts Revisited." *Journal of Family Issues* 21 (4): 488–500.

Lareau, Annette. 2003. *Unequal Childhoods: Class, Race, and Family Life.* Berkeley: University of California Press.

Latino Decisions. 2013. "Latino Consortium/Latino Decisions CIR Poll Toplines—Released March 18, 2013." www.latinodecisions.com/files/1913/6357/1744/Latino_Consortium_Toplines_-_March_18_Release.pdf.

LeBrón, Alana M. W., William D. Lopez, Keta Cowan, Nicole L. Novak, Olivia Temrowski, Maria Ibarra-Frayre, and Jorge Delva. 2017. "Restrictive ID Policies: Implications for Health Equity." *Journal of Immigrant and Minority Health* 20 (2): 255–60.

LeBrón, Alana M. W., Amy J. Schulz, Cindy Gamboa, Angela Reyes, Edna A. Viruell-Fuentes, and Barbara A. Israel. 2018. "'They Are Clipping Our Wings': Health Implications of Restrictive Immigrant Policies for Mexican-Origin Women in a Northern Border Community." *Race and Social Problems* 10 (3): 174–92.

Lee, Catherine. 2013. *Fictive Kinship: Family Reunification and the Meaning of Race and Nation in American Immigration.* New York: Russell Sage Foundation.

Lee, Jongho, Louis Tornatzky, and Celina Torres. 2004. *El Sueño de su Casa: The Homeownership Potential of Mexican-Heritage Families.* Claremont, CA: Tomás Rivera Policy Institute.

Lesser, Gabriel, and Jeanne Batalova. 2017. *Central American Immigrants in the United States.* Washington, DC: Migration Policy Institute.

Lever, Janet, David A. Frederick, and Rosanna Hertz. 2015. "Who Pays for Dates? Following Versus Challenging Gender Norms." *SAGE Open* 5 (4): 1–14.

Licona, Adela C., and Marta Maria Maldonado. 2014. "The Social Production of Latin@ Visibilities and Invisibilities: Geographies of Power in Small Town America." *Antipode* 46 (2): 517–36.

López, Jane Lilly. 2015. "'Impossible Families': Mixed-Citizenship Status Couples and the Law." *Law & Policy* 37 (1–2): 93–118.

———. 2017. "Redefining American Families: The Disparate Effects of IIRIRA's Automatic Bars to Reentry and Sponsorship Requirements on Mixed-Citizenship Couples." *Journal on Migration and Human Security* 5 (2): 236–51.

Luibhéid, Eithne. 2008. "Sexuality, Migration, and the Shifting Line between Legal and Illegal Status." *GLQ: A Journal of Lesbian and Gay Studies* 14 (2–3): 289–315.

Lynskey, Eileen P. 1989. "Immigration Marriage Fraud Amendments of 1986: Till Congress Do Us Part?" *Immigration and Nationality Law Review* 41 (5): 1087–116.

Lytle Hernandez, Kelly. 2010. *Migra! A History of the U.S. Border Patrol.* Berkeley: University of California Press.

Magaña, Lisa, and Erik Lee, eds. 2013. *Latino Politics and Arizona's Immigration Law SB 1070.* New York: Springer.

Mancuso, Gail, dir. 1995. "The One with Phoebe's Husband." *Friends,* season 2, episode 4. Los Angeles: NBC.

Massey, Douglas S., Jorge Durand, and Karen A. Pren. 2016. "Why Border Enforcement Backfired." *American Journal of Sociology* 121 (5): 1557–600.

Matthews, Hannah. 2017. *Immigrant Eligibility for Federal Child Care and Early Education Programs.* Washington, DC: Center for Law and Social Policy.

McFarland, Joel, Bill Hussar, Xiaolei Wang, Jijun Zhang, Ke Wang, Amy Rathbun, Amy Barmer, Emily Forrest Cataldi, and Farrah Bullock Mann. 2018. *The Condition of Education 2018.* Washington, DC: National Center for Educationl Statistics.

McLanahan, Sara. 2009. "Fragile Families and the Reproduction of Poverty." *Annals of the American Academy of Political and Social Science* 621 (1): 111–31.

McLoyd, Vonnie. 1998. "Socioeconomic Disadvantage and Child Development." *American Psychologist* 53 (2): 185–204.

Menjívar, Cecilia. 2006. "Liminal Legality: Salvadoran and Guatemalan Immigrants' Lives in the United States." *American Journal of Sociology* 111 (4): 999–1037.

Menjívar, Cecilia, and Leisy J. Abrego. 2012. "Legal Violence: Immigration Law and the Lives of Central American Immigrants." *American Journal of Sociology* 117 (5): 1380–421.

Menjívar, Cecilia, and Daniel Kanstroom, eds. 2014a. *Constructing Immigrant "Illegality": Critiques, Experiences, and Responses.* New York: Cambridge University Press.

Menjívar, Cecilia, and Daniel Kanstroom. 2014b. "Introduction—Immigrant 'Illegality': Constructions and Critiques." In *Constructing Immigrant "Illegality": Critiques, Experiences, and Responses,* edited by Cecilia Menjívar and Daniel Kanstroom, 1–33. New York: Cambridge University Press.

Menjívar, Cecilia, and Sarah M. Lakhani. 2016. "Transformative Effects of Immigration Law: Migrants' Personal and Social Metamorphoses through Regularization." *American Journal of Sociology* 122 (6): 1818–55.

Menjívar, Cecilia, and Olivia Salcido. 2002. "Immigrant Women and Domestic Violence: Common Experiences in Different Countries." *Gender & Society* 16 (6): 898–920.

Millán, Daniel. 2018. *Undocumented and Distracted: How Immigration Laws Shape the Academic Experiences of Undocumented College Students.* San Diego, CA: California Immigration Research Initiative.

Miller, Troy, dir. 2009. "Tom's Divorce." *Parks and Recreation,* season 2, episode 11. Los Angeles: NBC.

Mistry, Rashmita S., Elizabeth A. Vandewater, Aletha C. Huston, and Vonnie C. McLoyd. 2002. "Economic Well-Being and Children's Social Adjustment: The Role of Family Process in an Ethnically Diverse Low-Income Sample." *Child Development* 73 (3): 935–51.

Montes, Veronica. 2013. "The Role of Emotions in the Construction of Masculinity: Guatemalan Migrant Men, Transnational Migration, and Family Relations." *Gender & Society* 27 (4): 469–90.

Nevins, Joseph. 2010. *Operation Gatekeeper and Beyond: The War on "Illegals" and the Remaking of the U.S.-Mexico Boundary.* New York: Routledge.

NILC (National Immigration Law Center). 2015. "Access to Driver's Licenses for Immigrant Youth Granted DACA." NILC, last updated May 31, 2015. www.nilc.org/issues/drivers-licenses/daca-and-drivers-licenses/.

———. 2019. "State Laws Providing Access to Driver's Licenses or Cards, Regardless of Immigration Status." National Immigration Law Center, last updated August 2019. www.nilc.org/wp-content/uploads/2015/11/drivers-license-access-table.pdf.

Nixon, Ron. 2017. "U.S. to Collect Social Media Data on All Immigrants Entering Country." *New York Times,* September 28. www.nytimes.com/2017/09/28/us/politics/immigrants-social-media-trump.html.

Noah, Aggie J., and Nancy S. Landale. 2017. "Behavioral Functioning among Mexican-Origin Children: The Roles of Parental Legal Status and the Neighborhood Context." In *Health and Health Care Concerns among Women and Racial and Ethnic Minorities,* edited by Jennie Jacobs Kronenfeld, 231–48. Bingley, UK: Emerald.

Novak, Nicole, Arline T. Geronimus, and Aresha Martinez-Cardoso. 2017. "Change in Birth Outcomes among Infants Born to Latina Mothers after a Major Immigration Raid." *International Journal of Epidemiology* 46 (3): 839–49.

O'Brien, Chris. 2013. "Minecraft Offers a Virtual Way to Be with Their Deported Friend." *Los Angeles Times,* September 2. www.latimes.com/local/la-fi-c1-rodrigos-world-20130902-dto-htmlstory.html.

Obama, Barack. 2012. "Remarks by the President on Immigration." www.whitehouse.gov/the-press-office/2012/06/15/remarks-president-immigration.

Ocampo, Anthony C. 2014. "The Gay Second Generation: Sexual Identity and Family Relations of Filipino and Latino Gay Men." *Journal of Ethnic and Migration Studies* 40 (1): 155–73.

Ochoa, Gilda L. 2004. *Becoming Neighbors in a Mexican American Community: Power, Conflict, and Solidarity.* Austin: University of Texas Press.

Olivos, Edward M., and Marcela Mendoza. 2010. "Immigration and Educational Inequality: Examining Latino Immigrant Parents' Engagement in U.S. Public Schools." *Journal of Immigrant & Refugee Studies* 8 (3): 339–57.

OMNYC (Office of the Mayor, New York City). 2014. "Mayor Bill De Blasio Signs into Law Bills to Dramatically Reduce New York City's Cooperation with U.S. Immigration and Customs Enforcement Deportations." November 14, 2014. www1.nyc.gov/office-of-the-mayor/news/520–14/mayor-bill-de-blasio-signs-law-bills-dramatically-reduce-new-york-city-s-cooperation-with#/0.

Orrenius, Pia M., and Madeline Zavodny. 2015a. "The Impact of E-Verify Mandates on Labor Market Outcomes." *Southern Economic Journal* 81 (4): 947–59.

———. 2015b. "The Impact of Temporary Protected Status on Immigrants' Labor Market Outcomes." *American Economic Review* 105 (5): 576–80.

Osborne, Cynthia, and Sara McLanahan. 2007. "Partnership Instability and Child Well-Being." *Journal of Marriage and Family* 69 (4): 1065–83.

Otnes, Cele C., and Elizabeth Pleck. 2003. *Cinderella Dreams: The Allure of the Lavish Wedding.* Berkeley: University of California Press.

Parrado, Emilio A., and Chenoa A. Flippen. 2005. "Migration and Gender among Mexican Women." *American Sociological Review* 70 (4): 606–32.

Passel, Jeffrey S., and D'Vera Cohn. 2015. *Share of Unauthorized Immigrant Workers in Production, Construction Jobs Falls since 2007.* Washington, DC: Pew Research Center.

———. 2018. *U.S. Unauthorized Immigrant Total Dips to Lowest Level in a Decade.* Washington, DC: Pew Research Center.

Pastor, Manuel. 2018. *State of Resistance: What California's Dizzying Descent and Remarkable Resurgence Mean for America's Future.* New York: New Press.

Patler, Caitlin, and Whitney Laster Pirtle. 2018. "From Undocumented to Lawfully Present: Do Changes to Legal Status Impact Psychological Wellbeing among Latino Immigrant Young Adults?" *Social Science & Medicine* 199 (1): 39–48.

Phillips, Kristine. 2018. "How a Photographer Captured the Image of a Migrant Mother and Her Children Fleeing Tear Gas." *Washington Post,* November 27. www.washingtonpost.com/world/2018/11/26/how-photographer-captured-image-migrant-mother-her-children-fleeing-tear-gas/?noredirect=on&utm_term=.9668acdbddda.

Pila, Daniela. 2016. "'I'm Not Good Enough for Anyone': Legal Status and the Dating Lives of Undocumented Young Adults." *Sociological Forum* 31 (1): 138–58.

Portes, Alejandro, and Rubén G. Rumbaut. 2001. *Legacies: The Story of the Immigrant Second Generation*. Berkeley: University of California Press.

———. 2006. *Immigrant America: A Portrait*. Berkeley: University of California Press.

Rackin, Heather M., and Christina M. Gibson-Davis. 2017. "Low-Income Childless Young Adults' Marriage and Fertility Frameworks." *Journal of Marriage and Family* 79 (4): 1096–110.

Ramakrishnan, S. Karthick, and Sono Shah. 2017. "One out of Every 7 Asian Immigrants Is Undocumented." *Data Bits* (blog), AAPI Data, updated September 8, 2017. http://aapidata.com/blog/asian-undoc-1in7/.

Rendón, María G. 2019. *Stagnant Dreamers: How the Inner City Shapes the Integration of Second Generation Latinos*. New York: Russell Sage Foundation.

Ridgeway, Cecilia L. 2011. *Framed by Gender: How Gender Inequality Persists in the Modern World*. New York: Oxford University Press.

Ridgeway, Cecilia L., and Shelley J. Correll. 2004. "Unpacking the Gender System: A Theoretical Perspective on Gender Beliefs and Social Relations." *Gender & Society* 18 (4): 510–31.

Roberts, Dorothy. 2002. *Shattered Bonds: The Color of Child Welfare*. New York: Basic Books.

Rodriguez, Naomi Glenn-Levin. 2017. *Fragile Families: Foster Care, Immiration, and Citizenship*. Philadelphia: University of Pennsylvania Press.

Romagnoli, Amy, and Glenda Wall. 2012. "'I Know I'm a Good Mom': Young, Low-Income Mothers' Experiences with Risk Perception, Intensive Parenting Ideology and Parenting Education Programmes." *Health, Risk & Society* 14 (3): 273–89.

Román González, Betsabé, Eduardo Carrillo Cantú, and Rubén Hernández-León. 2016. "Moving to the 'Homeland': Children's Narratives of Migration from the United States to Mexico." *Mexican Studies/Estudios Mexicanos* 32 (2): 252–75.

Rosenblum, Marc R., and Lang Hoyt. 2011. *The Basics of E-Verify, the U.S. Employer Verification System*. Washington, DC: Migration Policy Institute.

Rubin, Lilian B. 1994. *Families on the Fault Line: America's Working Class Speaks about the Family, the Economy, Race, and Ethnicity*. New York: Harper Collins.

Rytina, Nancy. 2002. *IRCA Legalization Effects: Lawful Permanent Residence and Naturalization through 2001*. Washington, DC: U.S. Immigration and Naturalization Service.

Salcido, Olivia, and Madelaine Adelman. 2004. "'He Has Me Tied with the Blessed and Damned Papers': Undocumented-Immigrant Battered Women in Phoenix, Arizona." *Human Organization* 63 (2): 162–72.

Salcido, Olivia, and Cecilia Menjívar. 2012. "Gendered Paths to Legal Citizenship: The Case of Latin-American Immigrants in Phoenix, Arizona." *Law & Society Review* 46 (2): 335–68.

Sánchez García, Juan, and Edmund T. Hamann. 2016. "Educator Responses to Migrant Children in Mexican Schools." *Mexican Studies/Estudios Mexicanos* 32 (2): 199–225.

Sassler, Sharon, and Amanda J. Miller. 2017. *Cohabitation Nation: Gender, Class, and the Remaking of Relationships*. Berkeley: University of California Press.

Savage, David. 2017. "15 States, D.C. File Lawsuit Challenging Trump's DACA Shutdown." *Los Angeles Times,* September 6. www.latimes.com/politics/la-dreamers-decision-live-updates-washington-state-says-it-will-join-with-1504720942-htmlstory.html.

Schiller, Rob, dir. 2012a. "From Russia with Love." *Melissa & Joey,* season 2, episode 14. Los Angeles: ABC Family.

———. 2012b. "Mel Marries Joe." *Melissa & Joey,* season 2, episode 15. Los Angeles: ABC Family.

Schmalzbauer, Leah. 2009. "Gender on a New Frontier: Mexican Migration in the Rural Mountain West." *Gender & Society* 23 (6): 747–67.

———. 2014. *The Last Best Place: Gender, Family, and Migration in the New West.* Stanford, CA: Stanford University Press.

Schneider, Daniel, and Orestes P. Hastings. 2015. "Socioeconomic Variation in the Effect of Economic Conditions on Marriage and Nonmarital Fertility in the United States: Evidence from the Great Recession." *Demography* 52 (6): 1893–915.

Schwartz, Christine R., and Robert D. Mare. 2005. "Trends in Educational Assortative Marriage from 1940 to 2003." *Demography* 42 (4): 621–46.

Selena. 1992. "La Carcacha." *Entre a mi mundo.* EMI Latin.

Settersten, Richard A., Jr., Frank F. Furstenberg, and Rubén G. Rumbaut. 2005. *On the Frontier of Adulthood: Theory, Research, and Public Policy.* Chicago: University of Chicago Press.

Shirani, Fiona, Karen Henwood, and Carrie Coltart. 2012. "Meeting the Challenges of Intensive Parenting Culture: Gender, Risk Management and the Moral Parent." *Sociology* 46 (1): 25–40.

Shumway, David. 2003. *Modern Love: Romance, Intimacy, and the Marriage Crisis.* New York: New York University Press.

Smith, Robert Courtney. 2006. *Mexican New York: Transnational Lives of New Immigrants.* Berkeley: University of California Press.

Smock, Pamela J., Wendy D. Manning, and Meredith Porter. 2005. "'Everything's There Except Money': How Money Shapes Decisions to Marry among Cohabitors." *Journal of Marriage and Family* 67 (3): 680–96.

Strasser, Franz. 2018. "The Missing—Consequences of Trump's Immigration Crackdown." BBC News, January 15. www.bbc.com/news/av/world-us-canada-42667659/the-missing-consequences-of-trump-s-immigration-crackdown.

Stuesse, Angela, and Mathew Coleman. 2014. "Automobility, Immobility, Altermobility: Surviving and Resisting the Intensification of Immigrant Policing." *City & Society* 26 (1): 51–72.

Suárez-Orozco, Carola, and Marcelo Suárez-Orozco. 1995. *Transformations: Immigration, Family Life, and Achievement Motivation among Latino Adolescents.* Stanford, CA: Stanford University Press.

Telles, Edward E., and Vilma Ortiz. 2008. *Generations of Exclusion: Mexican Americans, Assimilation, and Race.* New York: Russell Sage Foundation.

Terriquez, Veronica. 2015a. "Dreams Delayed: Barriers to Degree Completion among Undocumented Community College Students." *Journal of Ethnic and Migration Studies* 41 (8): 1302–23.

———. 2015b. "Intersectional Mobilization, Social Movement Spillover, and Queer Youth Leadership in the Immigrant Rights Movement." *Social Problems* 62 (3): 343–62.

Terriquez, Veronica, Tizoc Brenes, and Abdiel Lopez. 2018. "Intersectionality as a Multi-purpose Collective Action Frame: The Case of the Undocumented Youth Movement." *Ethnicities* 18 (2): 260–76.

Thompson, Ginger. 2018. "Listen to Children Who've Just Been Separated from Their Parents at the Border." *ProPublica*, June 18. www.propublica.org/article/children-separated-from-parents-border-patrol-cbp-trump-immigration-policy.

Thrush, Glenn. 2018. "Trump's 'Harvest Box' Isn't Viable in SNAP Overhaul, Officials Say." *New York Times*, February 13. www.nytimes.com/2018/02/13/us/harvest-box-snap-food-stamps.html.

Townsend, Nicholas. 2002. *The Package Deal: Marriage, Work, and Fatherhood in Men's Lives*. Philadelphia, PA: Temple University Press.

Trail, Thomas E., and Benjamin R. Karney. 2012. "What's (Not) Wrong with Low-Income Marriages." *Journal of Marriage and Family* 74 (3): 413–27.

Turney, Kristin. 2014. "Stress Proliferation across Generations? Examining the Relationship between Parental Incarceration and Childhood Health." *Journal of Health and Social Behavior* 55 (3): 302–19.

———. 2015. "Liminal Men: Incarceration and Relationship Dissolution." *Social Problems* 62 (4): 499–528.

———. 2017. "The Unequal Consequences of Mass Incarceration for Children." *Demography* 54 (1): 361–89.

UCOP (University of California Office of the President). 2017. "University of California Sues Trump Administration on Unlawful Repeal of DACA Program." www.universityofcalifornia.edu/press-room/university-california-sues-trump-administration-unlawful-repeal-daca-program.

USCIS (U.S. Citizenship and Immigration Services). 2009. "Chapter 40.9 Section 212 (a) (9) of the Act—Aliens Unlawfully Present after Previous Immigration Violations in Adjudicator's Field Manual—Redacted Public Version." www.uscis.gov/ilink/docView/AFM/HTML/AFM/0-0-0-1/0-0-0-17138/0-0-0-18383.html.

———. 2011. "Green Card through the Life Act (245 (i) Adjustment)." www.uscis.gov/green-card/other-ways-get-green-card/green-card-through-legal-immigration-family-equity-life-act.

———. 2012. "Form I-797c, Notice of Action. Request for Applicant to Appear for Initial Interview."

———. 2015a. "Number of I-821d,Consideration of Deferred Action for Childhood Arrivals by Fiscal Year, Quarter, Intake, Biometrics and Case Status: 2012–2015 (December 31)." www.uscis.gov/sites/default/files/USCIS/Resources/ReportsandStudies/ImmigrationFormsData/AllFormTypes/DACA/I821d_performancedata_fy2015_qtr1.pdf.

———.2015b. "2014 Executive Actions on Immigration." www.uscis.gov/archive/2014-executive-actions-immigration.

———. 2015c. "Visa Availability and Priority Dates." www.uscis.gov/green-card/green-card-processes-and-procedures/visa-availability-and-priority-dates.

———. 2016. "Number of I-821d, Consideration of Deferred Action for Childhood Arrivals by Fiscal Year, Quarter, Intake, Biometrics and Case Status 2012–2016

(September 30)." www.uscis.gov/sites/default/files/USCIS/Resources/ReportsandStudies/ ImmigrationFormsData/AllFormTypes/DACA/daca_performancedata_fy2016_qtr4.pdf.

———. 2018a. "Child Status Protection Act (CSPA)." www.uscis.gov/greencard/child-status-protection-act.

———. 2018b. "DACA Frequently Asked Questions." www.uscis.gov/archive/frequently-asked-questions.

———. 2018c. "Form G-1055, Fee Schedule." www.uscis.gov/g-1055.

———. 2018d. "Provisional Unlawful Presence Waivers." www.uscis.gov/provisionalwaiver.

———. 2018e. "Remove Conditions on Permanent Residence Based on Marriage." www. uscis.gov/green-card/after-green-card-granted/conditional-permanent-residence/ remove-conditions-permanent-residence-based-marriage.

———. 2018f. "Victims of Criminal Activity: U Nonimmigrant Status." www.uscis.gov/ humanitarian/victims-human-trafficking-other-crimes/victims-criminal-activity-u-nonimmigrant-status/victims-criminal-activity-u-nonimmigrant-status.

———. 2019a. "Affidavit of Support." www.uscis.gov/greencard/affidavit-support.

———. 2019b. "Historical National Average Processing Time for All USCIS Offices." https: //egov.uscis.gov/processing-times/historic-pt.

———. 2019c. "Naturalization for Spouses of U.S. Citizens." www.uscis.gov/us-citizenship/ citizenship-through-naturalization/naturalization-spouses-us-citizens.

———. 2019d. "Policy Manual/Volume 9-Waivers/Part B—Extreme Hardship." www.uscis. gov/policy-manual/volume-9-part-b-chapter-2.

———. n.d. "Adjudicator's Field Manual—Redacted Public Version \ Chapter 21 Family-Based Petitions and Applications \ 21.3 Petition for a Spouse." www.uscis.gov/ilink/ docView/AFM/HTML/AFM/0-0-0-1/0-0-0-3481/0-0-0-4484.html.

USDS (U.S. Department of State). 2012. "Visa Bulletin for May 2012." https:// travel.state.gov/content/visas/en/law-and-policy/bulletin/2012/visa-bulletin-for-may-2012.html.

———. 2014. "Visa Bulletin for May 2014." https://travel.state.gov/content/travel/en/legal/ visa-law0/visa-bulletin/2014/visa-bulletin-for-may-2014.html.

Valdez, Carmen R., Brian Padilla, and Jessa Lewis Valentine. 2013. "Consequences of Arizona's Immigration Policy on Social Capital among Mexican Mothers with Unauthorized Immigration Status." *Hispanic Journal of Behavioral Sciences* 35 (3): 303–22.

Valdez, Zulema, and Tanya Golash-Boza. 2018. "Master Status or Intersectional Identity? Undocumented Students' Sense of Belonging on a College Campus." *Identities,* doi: 10.1080/1070289X.2018.1534452.

Varsanyi, Monica W. 2006. "Interrogating 'Urban Citizenship' Vis-à-Vis Undocumented Migration." *Citizenship Studies* 10 (2): 229–49.

Vasquez-Tokos, Jessica. 2017. *Marriage Vows and Racial Choices.* New York: Russell Sage Foundation.

Venkataramani, Atheendar S., Sachin J. Shah, Rourke O'Brien, Ichiro Kawachi, and Alexander C. Tsai. 2017. "Health Consequences of the US Deferred Action for Childhood Arrivals (DACA) Immigration Programme: A Quasi-experimental Study." *Lancet Public Health* 2 (4): e175–81.

Vespa, Jonathan. 2009. "Gender Ideology Construction: A Life Course and Intersectional Approach." *Gender & Society* 23 (3): 363–87.

Villalón, Roberta. 2010. *Violence against Latina Immigrants: Citizenship, Inequality, and Community.* New York: New York University Press.

Waldinger, Roger, and Cynthia Feliciano. 2004. "Will the New Second Generation Experience 'Downward Assimilation'? Segmented Assimilation Re-assessed." *Ethnic and Racial Studies* 27 (3): 376–402.

Warren, Robert, and Donald Kerwin. 2017. "The 2,000 Mile Wall in Search of a Purpose: Since 2007 Visa Overstays Have Outnumbered Undocumented Border Crossers by a Half Million." *Journal on Migration and Human Security* 5 (1): 124–36.

Waters, Mary C., and Marisa Gerstein Pineau, eds. 2015. *The Integration of Immigrants into American Society.* Washington, DC: National Academies Press.

Weir, Peter, dir. 1990. *Green Card.* New York: Buena Vista Pictures.

Wessler, Seth Freed. 2018. "Is Denaturalization the Next Front in the Trump Administration's War on Immigration?" *New York Times,* December 19. www.nytimes.com/2018/12/19/magazine/naturalized-citizenship-immigration-trump.html.

Western, Bruce. 2006. *Punishment and Inequality in America.* New York: Russell Sage Foundation.

Wilson, William Julius. 1987. *The Truly Disadvantaged: The Inner City, the Underclass, and Public Policy.* Chicago: University of Chicago Press.

Winfield Cunningham, Paige. 2018. "The Health 202: CHIP Won in the Government Shutdown. But Community Health Centers Did Not." *Washington Post,* January 23. www.washingtonpost.com/news/powerpost/paloma/the-health-202/2018/01/23/the-health-202-chip-won-in-the-government-shutdown-but-community-health-centers-did-not/5a66316730fb0469e88402e7/?utm_term=.0ced10f5d985.

Winstok, Zeev, and Murray A. Straus. 2016. "Bridging the Two Sides of a 30-Year Controversy over Gender Differences in Perpetration of Physical Partner Violence." *Journal of Family Violence* 31 (8): 933–5.

Wong, Tom K., and Carolina Valdivia. 2014. "In Their Own Words: A Nationwide Survey of Undocumented Millennials." Working paper 191. Center for Comparative Immigration Studies, University of California, San Diego.

Ybarra, Megan, and Isaura L. Peña. 2016. "'We Don't Need Money, We Need to Be Together': Forced Transnationality in Deportation's Afterlives." *Geopolitics* 22 (1): 34–50.

Yoo, Hana, Suzanne Bartle-Haring, Randal D. Day, and Rashmi Gangamma. 2014. "Couple Communication, Emotional and Sexual Intimacy, and Relationship Satisfaction." *Journal of Sex & Marital Therapy* 40 (4): 275–93.

Yoshikawa, Hirokazu. 2012. *Immigrants Raising Citizens: Undocumented Parents and Their Young Children.* New York: Russell Sage Foundation.

Yoshikawa, Hirokazu, Carola Suárez-Orozco, and Roberto G. Gonzales. 2016. "Unauthorized Status and Youth Development in the United States: Consensus Statement on the Society for Research on Adolescence." *Journal of Research on Adolescence* 27 (1): 4–19.

Zayas, Luis H. 2015. *Forgotten Citizens: Deportation, Children, and the Making of American Exiles and Orphans.* New York: Oxford University Press.

Zayas, Luis H., Sergio Aguilar-Gaxiola, Hyunwoo Yoon, and Guillermina Natera Rey. 2015. "The Distress of Citizen-Children with Detained and Deported Parents." *Journal of Child and Family Studies* 24 (11): 3213–23.

Zhang, Hong, and Elizabeth Fussell. 2017. "Strategic Gender Egalitarianism in Rural China: The Impacts of Husbands' Migration on Gender Relations." *American Behavioral Scientist* 61 (10): 1192–213.

Zong, Jie, and Jeanne Batalova. 2018. *Mexican Immigrants in the United States.* Washington, DC: Migration Policy Institute.

INDEX

Founded in 1893,
UNIVERSITY OF CALIFORNIA PRESS
publishes bold, progressive books and journals
on topics in the arts, humanities, social sciences,
and natural sciences—with a focus on social
justice issues—that inspire thought and action
among readers worldwide.

The UC PRESS FOUNDATION
raises funds to uphold the press's vital role
as an independent, nonprofit publisher, and
receives philanthropic support from a wide
range of individuals and institutions—and from
committed readers like you. To learn more, visit
ucpress.edu/supportus.